GALVIN

a Cookbook de Luxe

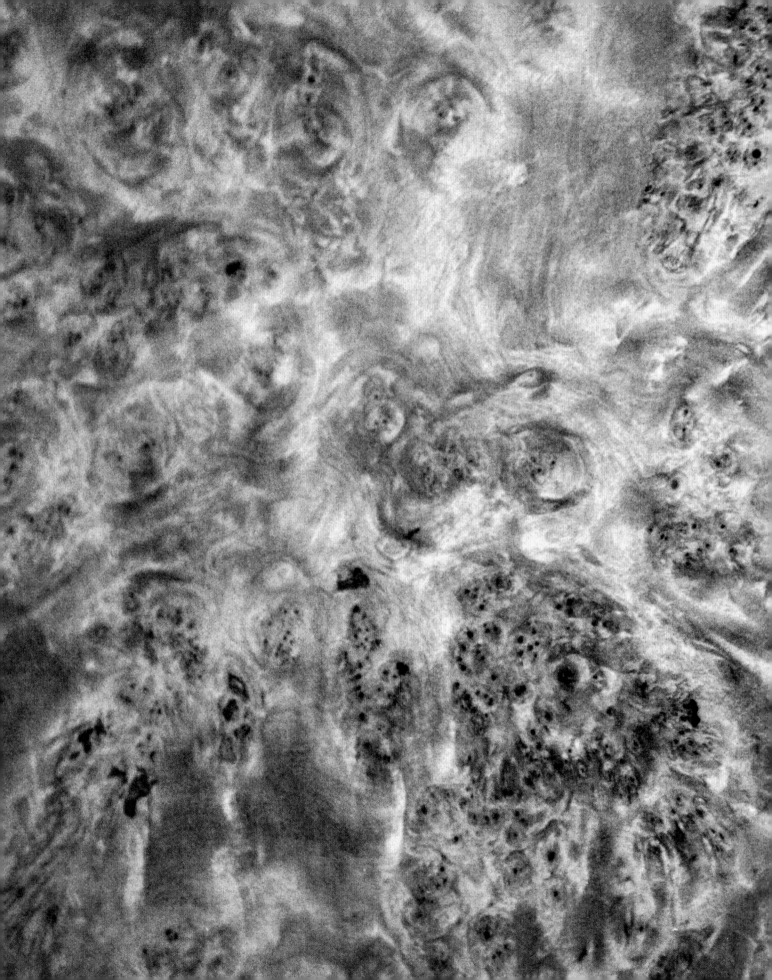

GALVIN

a Cookbook de Luxe

CHRIS GALVIN • JEFF GALVIN

First published in Great Britain
in 2011 by
Absolute Press
Scarborough House
29 James Street West
Bath BA1 2BT
Phone 44 (0) 1225 316013
Fax 44 (0) 1225 445836
E-mail info@absolutepress.co.uk
Website www.absolutepress.co.uk

Text © Chris and Jeff Galvin
Photography © Lara Holmes

Publisher Jon Croft
Commissioning Editor Meg Avent
Art Direction & Design Matt Inwood
Design Assistant Claire Siggery

Editor Jane Middleton
Copy-editor Anne Sheasby
Photographer Lara Holmes
Food Stylists Chris and Jeff Galvin,
André Garrett

ISBN 9781906650568

A catalogue record of this book is
available from the British Library.

Printed and bound in Italy by Jeming.

A note about the text
This book is set in three serif typefaces.
Two of them form part of the large
family of fonts revived or inspired by the
18th-century typeface designs of William
Caslon. Caslon 3 was designed by
American Type Founders in 1905.
A much more distant relation, Caslon
Open Face was a decorative headline
font designed by Barnhart Brothers and
Spindler in 1915. The third serif used is
Sabon, which was designed by Jan
Tschichold in 1964. The roman Sabon
design is based on type by Claude
Garamond, whereas the italic Sabon
design is based on types by Robert
Granjon. The script font used is
Linoscript, designed in 1905 by Morris
Fuller Benton. The decorative elements at
the foot of the pages are part of the
Rococo Ornaments font family, designed
by Ascender Corp.

*The cover image of the walnut burl
veneer, or loupe de noyer, was taken at
Les Halles in Lyons. The walnut adorns
the doors beneath the butcher's block
where Colette 'Coco' Sibilia, the
'Queen of Charcuterie', works.*

CONTENTS

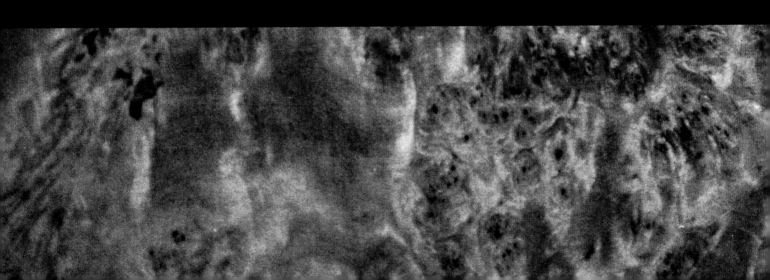

DEDICATION

Jeff: To my gorgeous wife, Georgette, and our beautiful boys, Daniel and William. And to my precious mother, Kathy.

Chris: For my wife, Sara, and my children, Emile, Jessica, George and Joey, and of course, my Mum.

FOREWORD BY RAYMOND BLANC

Eating at the Galvin restaurants is always a treat for me.
I admire their style, their skills and, above all, their commitment
to both the quality and the ethical sourcing of their ingredients.
Their dishes are almost always located in the heart of a
tradition, frequently French, but equally often British.
They give the lie to anyone who thinks British food is in any
way dull. Who can fault their Ballotine of Mackerel and Tartare
with Soft-boiled Quail's Eggs and Bone Marrow and Parsley
Custard, for example? Here the techniques of the French
kitchen are applied to wonderful English ingredients such as
absolutely fresh mackerel and rich marrow, which have the
virtue of being both humble and luxurious at the same time.

This dish is typical of the good taste and thoughtfulness of
the Galvin brothers, and shows their dedication to the good
things that surround us here in the UK. But they also feature
plenty of classic French dishes, from Tarte Tatin to Tête de Veau
with Sauce Ravigote.

What they look for first and foremost is quality – and they
do not mind (indeed they probably rejoice) if the search for
the best ingredients takes them to France. That's why this
book features Burgundy snails, lamb from the Pyrenees and
Noirmoutier potatoes. But the recipes also call for the
(superior) English grey-leg partridge, Dorset crab, Loch Duart
salmon and Denham Estate venison. Moreover, Chris and Jeff
are confident enough in their own culinary traditions to borrow
from others when it's appropriate, as in the case of the
pomegranate and maple dressing for their partridge salad, or
the mozzarella, blood oranges and speck that go into an endive
salad. This is where taste comes in, as much as it does in the
spaces the brothers have created for their de luxe dining rooms.

I love eating the Galvin brothers' dishes. Use this book and
you will too!

SEPTEMBER 2011

CHRIS'S STORY

I was born in Romford, Essex, and brought up in Brentwood, in a house surrounded by woods. As children, we were free to roam and some of our favourite pastimes were fishing and scrumping. The former needs no explanation, but the latter expression is hardly ever used today. Scrumping was the art of taking fruit from an allotment or an overhanging tree in someone's garden. I became a connoisseur of pear, apple and cherry varieties, and because I was the oldest I had to look after my brothers wherever we went. Many was the time I had to pick Jeff up and run when we were chased by an angry gardener.

My grandmother, Gertrude Grover, was probably the instigator here. She had the most amazing fruit and vegetable garden imaginable and always encouraged us to try something, but only if she said so. Nicking gooseberries too early would result in a fair old chase, with Nan wielding the slipper. Now I realise she was probably only thinking about our stomachs, which would inevitably pay the price a few hours later!

Nan was a remarkable woman. She would often have as many as twenty people descend on her house every Saturday. I know deep down she loved it, but it must have been hard keeping everyone fed with the stew that seemed always to be ticking away on the stove – or, as the French say, *mijoter* (I love that word!). I remember her famous apple pies, fruit cakes, jams and, best of all, her tub of dripping that, once you were tall enough to reach on tiptoe, you could dip her homemade bread into. If you dug deep enough, you would be rewarded with the jelly at the bottom.

When I was seven, my Dad won a Yankee, or accumulator, on the horses, bought a Vauxhall Viva and drove us across France and into Spain. I will never forget seeing grapes growing next to the road, which brought a whole new meaning to scrumping when we stopped for a break. There were apricots and peaches sold at the roadside, which we bought to quench our thirst. I can still smell those fruits now. Mum and Dad worked out that the cheapest food was sold at the roadside cafés with the red and blue signs – I was hooked. Now I realise they were pretty brave to stop at Les Routiers and try to order food in deepest France with their limited command of the language.

Our life took a turn for the worse when our father disappeared. We had never had much money anyway and I detested always being so hard up. But when he left, things were just awful. I was wearing second-hand clothes, charities gave us toys for my brothers' Christmas presents and Mum was working herself into the ground. As the eldest, I knew I had to make it.

One day, on my way home from school, I went into Ye Olde Logge restaurant in Brentwood and asked if they had any work. A young sous chef called Antony Worrall Thompson told me there was a job in the plate wash, so there I was, getting pans and silver salvers sent spinning like frisbees into the sink from the most flamboyant, swashbuckling person I had ever met. Poor Antony became my surrogate dad. The head chef was from the Savoy Hotel and had a very classical approach to cooking. Antony, on the other hand, was fascinated by the growing energy of *nouvelle cuisine*. He was one of the most talented and inventive chefs I have ever worked with, and would often try out new dishes on the head chef's night off. This was 1975, when waiters would take out the food on a silver salver and use a spoon and fork to arrange it on the customer's plate. With *nouvelle cuisine*, it left the kitchen already plated, and at the Olde Logge on a Saturday, with the chef out of the way, it was no different. I loved every minute of it: I was warm, well fed, working in a family atmosphere and enjoyed being allowed to plate the starters and the vegetables. If the truth be known, I would have paid to do it, but instead I was getting £3 a session. Every service was so electric I couldn't sleep for hours afterwards. Cue entry for my brothers, David and Jeff. I dare not tell you how young Jeff was when he started, for fear of getting anyone into trouble. We always dreamt of going back and buying the Olde Logge one day but tragically it was razed to the ground in a terrible fire.

A chance visit in 1977 to the new Habitat store in Romford market was a revelation to me. I still remember the smell as I walked in: sandalwood, cedar, raffia matting and cinnamon. It was heady stuff. The other astonishing thing was that you could pick up the goods and handle them without attracting the notice of the store detectives or constantly being badgered by staff. It was here that I first set eyes on the book that was to

change me completely – *La Cuisine Gourmande* by Michel Guérard, translated by Caroline Conran. The hairs on my arms still stand up when I pick it up to read. Then I got a copy of *Great Chefs of France* and was hooked. I have always been a terrible dreamer and I became lost in the world of *grande cuisine*, fantasising about one day having my own Michelin star.

A chance came up to work as a commis chef at a dinner in honour of the hotel group, Relais et Châteaux Grande Bretagne, where Michel and Albert Roux headed up a team of member chefs from around the UK. I was assigned to work with Nick Gill, brother of the food writer, A. A. Gill. He was extremely warm and encouraging and I was spellbound by the food and the energy on the night. Nick arranged a stage for me at Hambleton Hall, where he was at the time the youngest British chef to earn a Michelin star. I loved every moment of working with him. He had immense talent and possessed the hallmark that I have come to expect from great chefs: making sublime dishes seem effortlessly simple. Typical of Nick's generosity was the fact that he set me up not only with a stage at the Waterside Inn with Michel Roux but also with an interview at the Ritz.

Working at the Waterside Inn made me even more determined to succeed. The ingredients coming into the kitchen were the most amazing I had ever seen and they were handled and prepared with a speed and accuracy I could barely believe possible. Michel Roux was everywhere. What impressed me most was that once when the tasting menu was not selling, he picked up a waiter's pad and worked the room himself. The next ten orders to arrive on the pass were… yes, you guessed it, *menu exceptionnelle*! 'C'marche, deux menus, c'marche, quatre menus, c'marche, deux menus…' The chef was calling the orders out like a machine gun. Note to self: talk to customers!

Michel very kindly spent an hour with me, a twenty-one-year-old nobody from nowhere, and made me feel like the most important person in his life. When he asked what I wanted to do, I told him I wanted my own restaurant and he replied, 'Good, never take a room with less than seventy seats, otherwise you work for nothing.'

Then came the surprising question: are you stubborn? Crikey, I thought, is this a trick question? I decided that since I was

sitting in front of a legend I had better be honest, so I replied, 'Yes, chef, I am.'

'How stubborn?' he asked.

Oh no, I thought, he can see me on the inside. 'Stubborn as a mule, chef, it's the Irish in me.'

'Good,' he said, 'you will make it.' And with that he went off to meet Barbara Cartland, who had dined at the Waterside and was waiting patiently for the great man to finish with a nobody.

Armed with Michel Roux's encouragement, I went to work at the Ritz, which was another turning point in my career. Arriving at the Ritz, you walk through the side door, the tradesman's entrance, into the bowels of the building. I was terrified already, but to put the fear of God in you further, just before walking into the kitchen you were met by a huge sign saying, 'You are now entering the kitchens of the Ritz', complete with the blue and gold Ritz crest. It reminded me of the sign hung above the players' tunnel at Liverpool FC, 'This is Anfield'. Apparently it makes the opposition wobble and at that moment I could understand why.

Working at the Ritz was inspirational and I met some remarkable chefs. I was fortunate to be there at a time when it was more prestigious to eat in the chef's office than in the restaurant itself. It was a beautiful room, and Michael Quinn, the head chef, could survey the whole kitchen through lace curtains. While we were working hard in the kitchen, it was not uncommon to see Bruce Forsyth, Debbie Harry or even Margaret and Denis Thatcher there, plus a host of sports stars. I also saw my future wife, Sara, there for the first time. She was working upstairs for the management as an assistant, and didn't go unnoticed in her short skirts and high heels. One day the head chef chased her round the fridges after enticing her in there!

The food was outstanding and I was part of an inspired group of young chefs. I still have my team photo and am proud to see so many of today's stellar chefs in it. We also had Jack Dee, the comedian, working in the larder, and he was very funny even then.

The most important thing I learned at the Ritz was respect for the quality of ingredients. I often visited Billingsgate in the early hours of the morning and, although I was just a commis chef, many of the suppliers made time to show me around the market. I was fascinated by what I saw. Sadly the fish markets are now a shadow of what they once were. One of the chef's golden rules was that when we prepared the meat or fish we had to lay it out as if it was being presented in a butcher's shop or a fishmonger's, and woe betide anyone not doing so. This gave us added respect for our work and allowed the chef to tour round with surprise visitors and view his fridges filled with gleaming produce.

One of my jobs in the larder was to prepare two huge cheeseboards, one French and one British, which had to mirror each other in content and quality. I hadn't realised that we produced such wonderful cheeses in the British Isles, and it was a real treat to work with them.

The Ritz was the first professional kitchen that Jeff visited. He was only fifteen and, as he waited for me to finish one day, Michael Quinn spotted him at the end of the kitchen corridor. Typically, he left Denis Thatcher waiting in his office while he showed Jeff around!

My next job was with Paul Gayler at Inigo Jones, a restaurant in Covent Garden that is now sadly closed. In the 1980s it was a hotbed of ideas and invention. Paul Gayler is one of the most talented chefs I have ever had the good fortune to work with. He is also the most creative. I spent all my time at Inigo Jones working on the fish section, often not knowing what we were going to cook until the van arrived from the port. When the chef went out to decide what to buy, I used to pray that he wouldn't go too mad. Often he would spot something amazing, like sea urchins, and buy the whole tray. He would come back into the kitchen and say, 'Right, I've got it, a nice urchin soufflé!' My heart would drop – this was going to be a swine of a day – but I remember saying to myself, you have come to work for the best, so just keep your mouth shut and learn. Learn I did. Paul Gayler was like a magician with his menu writing. He was a simply brilliant chef who could cook anything he wanted better than anyone else, and if we ever had an issue with preparing or cooking something he would always stand next to us and show us how to do it. A true master.

After leaving Inigo Jones, I taught City and Guilds at Southend Technical College. I loved teaching but it was fairly shortlived, as the government decided to dispense with City and Guilds and bring in the NVQ system. I went on a residential to see how we would deliver the course and was horrified at the vagueness of the new system. I knew my days were numbered, as I have never been good at hiding my feelings when dealing with second-rate ideas.

In 1986 I had a chance meeting with Antony Worrall Thompson in the stands at Chelsea football club, where he told me how well he was doing with his new restaurant, Ménage à Trois. I had heard of it of course, as it was famously ahead of its time, giving people what they wanted with small plates of delicious tapas – or starters and puds, as Antony liked to put it. He was having problems settling a chef in his restaurant in Manhattan and asked if I fancied going to America. He came up with a plan for me to open a restaurant there, then return to London, where he would invest in me to open a restaurant that would push for a Michelin star. It was music to my ears, and so I spent a couple of weeks in his Beauchamp Place restaurant before setting off for New York. The Big Apple was fascinating but also lonely and very tough. The chefs' hours were monitored by the unions, which seemed ridiculous to me, as I had come from kitchens where an eighty-hour week was not unusual into one that was barely doing thirty-eight hours. After a conversation with the team along the lines of 'are you with me or without me?' we lost only three chefs and the rest, to their credit, got stuck in and cooked extremely well. I was exhausted but proud of my efforts, 3,000 miles from home and not knowing a soul.

The quality of the produce in New York blew my mind. There was a beautiful fish market in East Fulton Street near Brooklyn Bridge, which made me feel at home and helped keep homesickness at bay for a while. The fish, many of which I didn't recognise, were in sparkling condition, laid out on the cobbled streets. The tuna were so big that the guys cutting the loins had to walk along their length when making the incisions, using machete-type knives. Sadly, due to overfishing, we will probably never see this again.

Until I went to the States, I had always looked to Paris, and increasingly London, as great food cities, but New York completely changed that. I was very isolated, but dining out on one's own there is a real pleasure. It was where I gained my love of eating at a bar: you have instant company, get a drink quicker than those dining at the tables, and in New York the barmen have a great bedside manner, holding you in conversation for as long as you need it.

There was also a culinary freedom amongst the chefs and restaurateurs in New York that I hadn't experienced in London, where we were so heavily influenced by the French. The Americans were also embracing Italian, Asian and, of course, Mexican food in a very authentic way. I visited shops such as Balducci's and Dean & Deluca just to look at the beautiful produce on show. I had always been led to believe that good food didn't exist in the States. How wrong I was, and now I go there for inspiration whenever I can.

Eventually, visa issues arose and I had to return to England, where I went to work in Streatley-on-Thames. By a stroke of luck, this village was home to the most famous cheese shop in England, run by Major Patrick Rance and his son, Hugh. I have mentioned how I loved preparing the cheeseboards at the Ritz, but to work with the acknowledged champion of British cheese was a true blessing. Both father and son always had time for me, and I would visit the store two or three times a week to look at new arrivals from both sides of the Channel. There was always a story to accompany each visit. The smell of the shop pervaded your clothes and made you hungry even if you had just eaten. Once I was there when a minibus filled with WI members came for a cheese sampling. The moment they were all in, they opened their handbags and produced knives from nowhere – it was carnage, but the Rance family didn't bat an eyelid. They were always really happy for people to share in their finds.

My next job was in Ludlow, Shropshire, at Dinham Hall. It was 1988, when restaurants were booming, and one of the fashions at the time was for 'restaurants with rooms'. They are probably called boutique hotels today. It was a double joy for me, as Shropshire is a beautiful county and my brother was old enough to come and join me for the first time. We had two very happy years there, working with the land and seasons like never before. We bought a small van and got up at 3am twice a week to drive to Birmingham central market, where we bought our base vegetables and any fish that were especially fresh. The rest of the ingredients were grown locally and farmed within a very short radius. Jeff and I fondly remember a pensioner coming to the back door with a basket of huge courgettes for sale. They were almost as big as marrows, but hidden at the bottom were a couple of finger-length courgettes with flowers – perfect! We offered 20 pence for every one he could collect and he was away like a dog out of the traps at Romford, then back with an even bigger basket full of courgette flowers. We served them as starters, main-course garnishes and even as a cheese course, filled with goat's cheese and drizzled with honey.

Unfortunately, the recession spelled the end of this special time. We went from a full hotel and restaurant to looking out for the occasional solitary diner. It was heartbreaking to watch business after business fold. We were not immune and the hotel went into administration. I can't say it was a shock because a month or so earlier I had been looking at a trade magazine and came across a full-page picture of the business in the property section. I immediately called the owner, who denied it and said he would sue them!

Sitting at a table opposite the receivers will always rate as one of the worst experiences in my career. When you have worked your fingers to the bone and breathed life into a business, it feels like the end of the world. The problem with working in the country is that when your place of employment goes, you need to move. We lost a fortune on our house, getting only a third of the price we paid for it, but I made a promise to myself that I would move back to London so that if this ever happened again I could roll my knives up and move 200 yards down the road to find another job, without putting my family through the trauma of leaving their home.

I was lucky enough to end up working with Martin Lam at Nick Lander's restaurant, L'Escargot, in Soho. It turned out to be one of my most enjoyable jobs ever. Jeff, who had left Shropshire earlier than me to gain experience at the Savoy

Hotel, joined me there and helped fill the ranks with some of his colleagues from the Savoy. I had always dreamt of working with Martin, who was known for his robust cooking and his regard for seasonality and provenance. He was years ahead of other chefs at the time in this respect. He also took a great interest in my welfare and education as a chef, plus he always made sure we all ate properly. I felt the luckiest person ever because every day I got to eat with Martin and Elena Salvoni, one of the country's greatest restaurant maître d's. We would sit down just as lunch was finishing and discuss the ebbs and flows of service. They would talk about what customers liked and disliked, who had been in and where they were seated. Elena really inspired my interest in the room. I had never had any contact with it before but now suddenly it was very real to me and I was getting feedback thick and fast: 'Why were we slow today?', 'Why weren't there more fish dishes?', 'Today was sensational, great', 'They loved the venison daube', and so on.

I always looked forward to our daily rendezvous with great anticipation. Elena delivered her advice in a kindly manner and I would hang on her every word. Martin is a very intelligent chef and would quickly solve any issues concerning speed or ease of service. But most of all, the reason I enjoyed our lunches was that I loved their warmth and experience.

Unfortunately the recession wasn't finished with me. After Nick Lander sold the restaurant, the business foundered. Our suppliers weren't getting paid and by 1990 I could see all the warning signs that it was time to move. Out of the blue I got a call to join Paul Gayler at the Lanesborough Hotel as executive sous chef. It was an astonishing project to be involved in, converting St George's Hospital on Hyde Park Corner into one of London's most glamorous five-star hotels. Part of our mission statement was to 'exceed the customers' expectations'. The training was simply the best, and many of the lessons I learned there we employ today. My wife, Sara, was also part of the opening team. We often came into contact, as she would come to the chef's office to discuss the menus. I remember the chef was always tough but she gave as good as she got!

I was now working side by side with Paul Gayler and was in awe of his strength and prowess as a chef. He pushed me over the edge on many occasions but it only made me stronger, as I wanted to be part of delivering something special at the Lanesborough. I was extremely proud to work at the hotel and even more so to be one of the opening team. Typical of the family spirit we had, I still feel as if I work there and believe I always will.

Nevertheless, after five years I realised it was time to try to get my first head chef's position. Sir Terence Conran was busy changing the face of restaurants in London. I loved what he had done at Le Pont de la Tour and Quaglino's, and it was rumoured that he was going to open a Bibendum in north London. 'That's got my name written all over it,' I thought, but how? When a job came up opening another Conran establishment, Mezzo, an aircraft hanger of a restaurant in Soho, I really didn't fancy doing something so huge, but thought it might be a way in. Then I met John Torode, who was going to be the executive chef there. He's almost impossible to describe – a ball of fun, anger, love, fire, soft, mad, bad, crazy, intelligent. I could go on… but really, underneath everything, John was an amazingly good chef, who had a remarkable knowledge of not only French ingredients but also Asian. A strong leader, he was only in his twenties when he opened Mezzo, which at its height was doing 2,000 covers per day. I was head chef downstairs and I had a huge brigade of around thirty-eight chefs, with ten of them from Michelin-starred restaurants. We made everything by hand, including a beautiful egg yolk ravioli that was poached and served on top of some fat asparagus: when you cut the ravioli open, the yolk spilled on to the asparagus, forming a sauce with the juices and butter.

I lasted eighteen months at Mezzo, but when I began calling checks out in my sleep, I knew it was time to move on. The new restaurant in north London was now becoming a reality and John Torode very unselfishly put me forward for it. To get the job, I had to impress not only Sir Terence but also the managing director, Joel Kissin. Joel was the best restaurateur I had ever come across. He gave me a difficult time convincing him I was right for the position, but to his credit he made me earn it. The site was to be called Orrery. Most people couldn't say it and still can't, but it was Sir Terence's choice, as it was the name of his very first restaurant.

An orrery is a mechanical model of the solar system, and there is an example in the lobby of the restaurant. The general manager, Patrick Fischnaller, and I worked like clockwork together – it was just one of those situations where you are in the right place at the right time. As a bonus, Jeff joined me there from Chez Nico, where he had really earned his spurs as part of the team that helped Nico Ladenis win his much-deserved third Michelin star.

Cooking at Orrery was a magical time for me and everything came together. However, someone claiming to have been let in on a secret told me that Michelin would never award a star to any restaurant owned by Terence Conran. I knew there wasn't necessarily any love lost between them, but this news was a blow. I had just turned forty and was starting to get more aches and pains. I had always wondered where all the old chefs went to – it was as if there was an elephants' graveyard for chefs somewhere. So I enrolled on a BSc in Gastronomy, which also included learning about human resources, marketing and financial control. My family had always had to put up with my absence and now all my spare time was spent either at Thames Valley University or at the library. But the Michelin myth was bust when we were awarded a star in the 2000 guide. I was overcome with pride and Patrick treated me to lunch at Le Gavroche, where Michel Roux Jr and Silvano Giraldin, the restaurant director, treated us like kings. It was the most memorable meal of my life.

A few months after receiving the star, I gained my Bachelor of Science. Over the previous twenty-five years I had regularly written to the best kitchens in France asking to work as a *stagier* – a position where you work for free for a period of a few days to a year, depending on your circumstances. To be fair to Sara and our growing family of Emile, Jessica, George and Joey, I decided to hang my apprentice's apron up and stop working my days off and holidays. I had been really fortunate over the years and had got to work at L'Oustau de Baumanière, Maison Troisgros and Jean Bardet in the Loire Valley, plus a host of small, one-star restaurants. Orrery was going from strength to strength and I was cooking some of the best food

of my life. Jeff had left to work with Marco Pierre White, who suggested that we open a restaurant called Galvins. At Conran, meanwhile, I had a great time with Sir Terence and Patrick opening another restaurant, the Almeida, opposite the theatre of the same name in Islington. I was very fortunate to be working so closely with someone who was at the forefront of redefining British restaurants. During the nine years I worked for Conran Restaurants, I helped open a number of them, from Bluebird in Chelsea to Senso in Paris. We were always given great autonomy and I was exposed to everything, from designing kitchens and restaurants, marketing, and standard operating procedures to the balance and feel of the tabletop equipment and, most importantly, how to stay in business. I will forever owe Sir Terence my gratitude for guiding me and encouraging me to be as good as I could be. I would have happily worked for him forever but I still had an ambition to see what I could really achieve. At this point, my life took another fortuitous turn when I got the opportunity to work with two truly great restaurateurs, Jeremy King and Chris Corbin.

Jeremy and Chris had created three of London's most popular restaurants, the Ivy, Sheekey's and La Caprice, before selling them at the height of their success. They planned to open another, and when I looked at the site of what would become the Wolseley, in Piccadilly, I was very impressed. They took me to cities such as Vienna, Milan and Paris to experience café culture, then we set about breaking the biggest taboo in restaurants and aiming to become all things to all people – supplying breakfast, elevenses, lunch, afternoon tea, *plats du jour* and dinner, followed by supper. Phew!

With attention to detail like I had never seen before, the restaurant slowly came to life. Although it was hard work, I learned an incredible amount from Chris and Jeremy. No leaf was ever left unturned and everything had to bear scrutiny. We would spend more time than you would ever imagine possible checking, questioning and debating in microscopic detail any product that might be used in the restaurant or that a customer might come into contact with. It used to make me smile to see countless other restaurateurs coming in to learn the secret of doing 1,300 covers per day with style. I would look at them and think, if only you knew the pain and ecstasy we've gone through to get near our goal. I consider the Wolseley to be the SAS of my education as a restaurateur and I think I earned my stripes. I had a wonderful young chef working next to me at the time, called Ed Wilson. He is a bright future talent and certainly added a sparkle to the Wolseley.

By 2005, Jeff and I were meeting most afternoons for mint tea and a chat at Momo's. Deciding it was probably now or never when it came to opening our own restaurant, we took advice from an old friend and customer, Ken Sanker, who became our business partner. There was a site available in Baker Street that had repeatedly failed to work for other people but Ken and Nick Lander believed we could make a go of it. Max Renzland, the restaurateur, took us to Royal China ten doors down to show us how they did 200 covers on a wet Tuesday night and told us, 'You will do 200 covers a day here, boys. Be ready.'

During the early 1990s I had been inspired by the *bistrot moderne* movement in Paris – namely where Christian Constant, chef at the Hotel Crillon, advised his sous chefs to take to the bistrots of Paris during the recession. There they cooked simple, classic dishes that, in the hands of young magicians like Yves de Camdeborde, became extremely special. I had visited as many as I could and wanted to work in a similar vein. Jeff and I had achieved a certain degree of fame as the first British brothers to hold a Michelin star each, so expectations were going to be high, but we wanted to take a different route: we planned to buy cheap cuts of meat or offal, go to the markets as frequently as possible and pass the saving on to our customers. The plan was a bistrot with a little luxury, so we called it Galvin Bistrot de Luxe

It opened on a Monday evening, 5th September 2005, with my wife, Sara, on reception and the kids cleaning the restaurant. We were busy from the off, with wonderful customers. Ken was a tower of strength and put up with our business naivety without ever letting on. Jeff's partner, Georgette, kept us out of trouble by being our HR at the end of the phone, and we were learning at a rate of knots each day.

The London critics were pouring through the doors but we had no time to stop and so were doubly lucky with our reviews. It feels as if Giles Coren's write-up changed our lives forever. Neither of us had a day off for nearly two months, and we regularly topped and tailed on the banquette seating to get a bit of sleep. It was like a dream come true, and the most magical point was when our mum, Kathy, stood across the road and looked up at the sign above the door. Priceless…

We went on to open Galvin at Windows with our new partners, Hilton, installing André Garrett as chef and Fred Sirieix as restaurant general manager. Again, we worked ferociously hard, and between us created a special restaurant twenty-eight floors up on Park Lane It is a restaurant that has simply got better with age and we are all really proud of our achievements there.

In 2009 we opened the beautiful La Chapelle and Café à Vin in Spitalfields, where all our hard-earned experience came together. Sara came to join us in a permanent role and our brother, David, took over the market run, as Jeff and I were by this time very definitely flat out! My son, Emile, is now with us, so we are a proper family-run business. Ken is part of the family and neither Jeff nor I could ever imagine working without him. He is an incredibly special person who would probably have been a brilliant restaurateur had he so wished, but that's another story…

JEFF'S STORY

When I was eight, my mother started working lunchtimes at a local restaurant, Ye Olde Logge – a job she chose because she was determined to take me to school and pick me up each day. She also used to assist the owners, who lived above the premises with their two small children. This meant she occasionally had to take me along with her in school holidays. I was fascinated by the amount of freedom the chefs seemed to have: they started work early if they had a lot on, but otherwise would arrive at eleven. This seemed very cool to me and as soon as I was old enough I got a Saturday job there doing the pots. By the time I was fourteen, I was a commis chef. The head chef at the time was a big guy called Richard – a great joke teller, who loved horse racing, drinking and womanising. He was also very talented, but even at an early age I could see that a kitchen was a pretty brutal place: highly pressurised, and hot beyond belief in the summer. Most of the staff were poorly paid and permanently tired, and Richard's role was often to lift morale with a funny story. There were only three full-time chefs and by the time I was fifteen I was working the entire weekend plus one night during the week and full time every school holiday. My wages amounted to a £5 note per service, for which I had to wait till the end of each session.

When I was fifteen, we had a careers day at school. I already knew that I wanted to work in the restaurant or hotel business, with either food or wine, but when I told the careers adviser she simply handed me over to a fire officer, who was there looking for recruits. I thought this very odd, but it was typical of the attitude at the time – catering was seen as a no-hope industry. Luckily my brother, Chris, was working at the Ritz by this point and he suggested that I go up to meet the head cellarman, who looked after the wines. I duly travelled up to London and was given a tour around before being taken to the kitchens to meet up with Chris. Left outside the head chef's office to wait for him, I couldn't resist having a peek inside. It was a massive room and there was Michael Quinn, the head chef, having lunch with about ten guests. Just as I realised that the guests included Denis Thatcher, whose wife was Prime Minister at the time, and various members of the cabinet, Michael caught me looking. To my horror, he stood up and made his way to the door – at which point I thought I had surely lost my brother his job.

In fact, Michael simply asked in his broad Yorkshire accent whether I was Chris's brother, then put his arm around me and proceeded to show me round the kitchen and its pristine fridges. When Chris returned, Michael shook my hand and said that it was a pleasure to meet me, then rejoined his guests. It was a bizarre episode and I couldn't believe how gracious he had been, but it was the point at which my wine career ended and my cooking career began.

When I left school in 1986 I enrolled at Thurrock Technical College to study cooking and restaurant service. Chris was teaching the same course in Southend-on-Sea but we decided it wouldn't be a good idea if he became one of my tutors. I really loved college, as it felt a world away from school and I had a head start on everyone else since I was already familiar with kitchen life. I was very fortunate to have an amazing set of tutors there, one of whom, Patrick Mayo, still helps us in the restaurants today with young recruits from college.

After I left, my first job was with my brother at Dinham Hall, a new country house hotel in Ludlow, Shropshire. It was a stunning place to live and a great foundation for my career. The hotel was small, with just eight bedrooms and a restaurant that seated thirty-five people. I spent two and a half years there, before moving to the Savoy Hotel in London, where I was astonished at the number of chefs. I loved the hierarchy and discipline at the Savoy, although sometimes it could get very aggressive, I remember borrowing a small ladle without asking the sauce cook and you would think I had insulted his mother; he wanted to kill me. Nevertheless, some of the chefs I met there are still good friends twenty years on.

Chris moved back down to London shortly afterwards to work with Martin Lam at L'Escargot in Soho, and after a year at the Savoy I decided to join him as a chef de partie. It was a great restaurant, with a real family feel about it, but after a year there I was hungry to see other things. I was sharing a house near Wembley with four other cooks and every night when I arrived home I would hear different stories from each of them. One of the guys worked at The Capital Hotel in Knightsbridge,

and when he told me there was a vacancy there for a chef de partie, I arranged to go for a trial day. I was mesmerised by head chef Philip Britten's technical ability. The Capital was a small hotel by London standards, privately owned by Margaret and David Levin, whose attention to detail was second to none. I stayed for two and a half years but it was very intense, and quite nerve jangling much of the time. I thought maybe that was how it was in Michelin restaurants – so it was odd that my next move was to Chez Nico at Ninety Park Lane, which held two Michelin stars. Nico Ladenis was considered to be one of the toughest chefs in the country but from the day I started working there I loved every moment – particularly the family aspect, with Nico's wife, Dinah-Jane, and their two daughters all working together. During my five amazing years as sous chef there, we attained three Michelin stars.

Nevertheless, in May 1997, when Chris told me he was going to open a restaurant for Sir Terence Conran, I felt it was time to move on. I relished the whole process of conceiving a restaurant from scratch, and particularly the chance to design a kitchen. Orrery was at the top of Marylebone High Street and had originally been a stable block for horses used for hunting in Regent's Park. I was lucky to receive a reference from Nico – a very unusual thing to have, as he was renowned for firing people when they said they were leaving. I think he understood that I was going to work with my brother so that was okay. However, he didn't like the idea of my working for Sir Terence. Nico was a guest columnist for *The Sunday Times* when Jonathan Meades was on holiday and was kind enough to mention our new project in his review. The picture accompanying his piece showed a giant hand pulling at a chef – a clear reference to Sir Terence stealing his staff.

Orrery was really tough at the beginning, and after six months I got a call from Marco Pierre White. I had met him on a number of occasions, and Chris and I had come close to working for him before. Marco wanted me to go and work at his three-Michelin-starred Oak Room restaurant in Knightsbridge before taking up residence in a new site. It was a very exciting time. I started at the Oak Room under head chef Robert Reid, who was very kind to me considering I had spent so much time with Nico Ladenis, Marco's rival. Marco was a perfectionist and a remarkable craftsman, and could be extremely funny as well as tough. After three months he called me to his office to tell me the devastating news that the restaurant had fallen through. I thought long and hard about rejoining Chris but working with Marco was incredible and Chris's advice was to stay where I was if I was enjoying it. That's the lovely thing about family advice; it's always unconditional. I remained at the Oak Room until Marco offered me the job of head chef at L'Escargot, which he now owned. He told me I could run it on my own and he would only come by if there was trouble. Obviously I knew L'Escargot from my stint there ten years previously. It had a small restaurant on the first floor serving forty covers, a brasserie on the ground floor serving up to 180 covers, plus two large private dining rooms – quite a big undertaking but I relished the challenge and was extremely happy there. It was like starting from scratch – learning about food costs, labour costs, budgeting, marketing, hiring, firing – and it brought home to me that cooking was only one part of the jigsaw. I have to thank Marco for his trust in me, as he was true to his word and left me to it.

Although Chris and I had never really spoken about it, I guess we assumed that one day we would go it alone. Then an opportunity came up through a chap called Ken Sanker, who Chris had met many years previously as a regular at Orrery. We looked at a site on Baker Street that had been an Italian restaurant called Anda, run by the well-respected Alan Yau. Anda had traded for only nine months then gone bust and the site had been empty for a year. I wasn't keen initially – probably because Alan is very successful indeed, which made me suspect that if he had failed there, the location might be a bit dodgy. First impressions were not good. We walked into the restaurant and the entire floor space was three inches deep in rainwater. 'Let's get out of here,' I thought, but the agent quickly said, 'Let me show you the kitchen.' That was it for Chris and me. It was stunning and hardly used. We quickly set about working out a deal with our prospective partner, Ken, which was very easy. We would split it three ways, with Chris and I putting our homes up as equity – not advisable but we were so confident it would work I never thought about our families becoming homeless.

Everyone probably expected us to create a fine-dining establishment. But we loved the *bistrots modernes* of Paris and I loved the simplicity of the brasserie at L'Escargot. So a bistrot was what we decided on – in spirit and price points at least. However, we were determined to over deliver and when Chris came up with the name Galvin Bistrot de Luxe, it seemed to sum it up perfectly. A couple of months later we were ready to open. I brought a sous chef and pastry chef with me who had worked with both Chris and me before, while Chris brought two young cooks from the Wolseley. On front of house we had the ex-manager from Chez Nico, Jean Luc Giquel.

The levels of business were amazing from day one and the reviews in the press were just as startling. Chris and I were feeling the pressure a bit by the end of the first two months. Neither of us had had a day off and we spent many nights sleeping at the restaurant. It's a good job there were two of us. All through the opening and to this day we haven't had a cross word, so it's fair to say we get on very well. I brought a small van so I could visit New Covent Garden market each morning to buy produce. There are a lot of French food importers there selling poultry, foie gras and meat, and besides fruit and vegetables we used to get all our flowers there too, so the menu was genuinely market led. Any money we saved by going to the market helped us keep our prices down. There is something magical about the Bistrot. I think it's the atmosphere that sets it apart from other places. Our proudest moment came when our Mum came up for Sunday lunch. She stood on the other side of the road and just stared at the name above the door.

Shortly after we opened, we were contacted by Donald Morrison from the Hilton Corporation, who asked us if we would be interested in running the restaurant and bar on the twenty-eighth floor of the Park Lane Hilton. The only problem was that it had to be trading in seventeen weeks' time. It was already becoming clear at the Bistrot that Chris and I would one day have to do something else, as essentially we had the same role. The Hilton site was stunning. Moreover, by chance

André Garrett, who had worked with Chris at Orrery and then taken over as head chef when he left, had been to see us two weeks earlier saying he was looking to move on. With André on board, it was a no brainer and in May 2006 we opened Galvin at Windows. My son Daniel was born around the time of the opening and Chris insisted I take a week off to spend with the new arrival. Because of this we decided that I would remain at the Bistrot and Chris would look after Windows. It was a great success, winning a Michelin star in 2010.

For the next four years, we consolidated and improved the Bistrot, which now employed nearly fifty members of staff – quite a difference from the dozen we had opened with. But then we learned of a restaurant site just off Bishopsgate – St Botolph's Hall, the assembly hall of the Central Foundation School for Girls. Friends and regular customers were always suggesting we open in the city, and when I first saw St Botolph's I was speechless. I couldn't believe such a beautiful, historic building could exist amongst the modern buildings that dwarf it, let alone be available as a restaurant space. The presentation process was long and nerve-racking, as London's entire who's who of restaurateurs were after it. Eventually we got the great news that it was ours. We decided to name it Galvin La Chapelle, after the famous Hermitage wine produced in the northern Rhône (see pages 38–39), when Chris and I were on one of the many vineyard trips we go on each year with the producer, Paul Jaboulet. At the top of the Hermitage hill is a small chapel that resembles our building. We have a relationship with Paul Jaboulet whereby we have one of the largest lists of different vintages of La Chapelle wines direct from their cellar. In the new part of the building, we have created a separate restaurant, Café à Vin, which serves simpler dishes and champions natural wines.

This page:
André Garrett, our brilliant head chef at Galvin at Windows
Opposite page:
top left: Fred Sirieix, our charismatic general manager at Galvin at Windows
top right: Sara Galvin, Chris's wife and our indispensable link to the outside world
bottom left: Emile Galvin, Chris's son – as adept with a ratchet in his hand as he is with a saucepan
bottom right: David Galvin, our brother and market buyer, who provides us with so much of our great produce

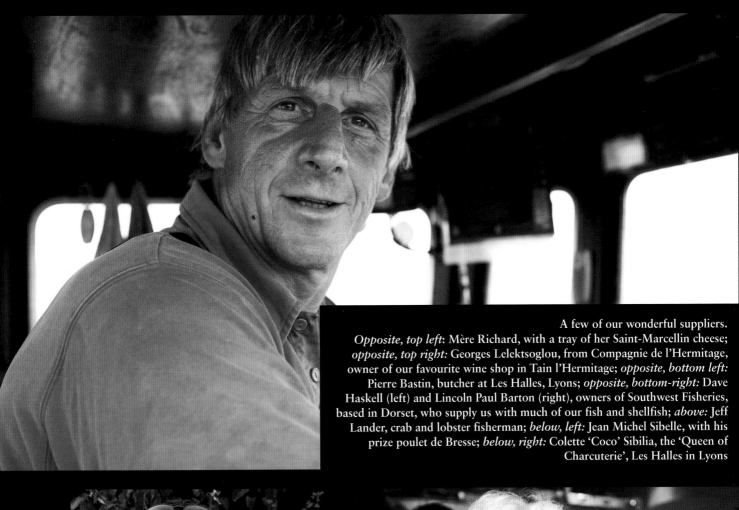

A few of our wonderful suppliers.
Opposite, top left: Mère Richard, with a tray of her Saint-Marcellin cheese; *opposite, top right:* Georges Lelektsoglou, from Compagnie de l'Hermitage, owner of our favourite wine shop in Tain l'Hermitage; *opposite, bottom left:* Pierre Bastin, butcher at Les Halles, Lyons; *opposite, bottom-right:* Dave Haskell (left) and Lincoln Paul Barton (right), owners of Southwest Fisheries, based in Dorset, who supply us with much of our fish and shellfish; *above:* Jeff Lander, crab and lobster fisherman; *below, left:* Jean Michel Sibelle, with his prize poulet de Bresse; *below, right:* Colette 'Coco' Sibilia, the 'Queen of Charcuterie', Les Halles in Lyons

OUR THOUGHTS ON FOOD

We both agree that the way we cook is almost instinctive. When we visit markets or go fishing together, we always break into conversation about how we would like to cook things. When we are working side by side, though, we rarely talk, and things happen without discussion. It can be quite unnerving for new chefs who don't know us.

We love harmony at work and probably have some of the quietest kitchens in London. In our view, if the shouting starts it's generally because we didn't explain something properly to the brigade, or the equipment isn't right, or we are simply asking too much of someone. We grew up in some very tough kitchens with plenty of aggression and testosterone in them, but we always wondered how on earth this was supposed to sit side by side with warmth, generosity, courtesy and genuine hospitality.

We are both classically trained and, of course, classical cooking means French cooking. A brief history lesson is important here. French cuisine dominated Britain from the early nineteenth century, when the Prince Regent, later George IV, employed 'the king of chefs and the chef of kings', Marie-Antoine Carême. Then Georges-Auguste Escoffier arrived in London with César Ritz to open the Savoy Hotel in 1889, followed by The Carlton in 1899 and the Ritz in 1906. Escoffier is credited with creating the kitchen brigade and *partie* system. At the head of this hierarchy was the chef de cuisine, supported by the sous chefs, who in turn watched over the various *parties*: sauce, larder, fish, vegetable and pastry, plus many no longer used, such as *potager*, *hors d'oeuvrier* and *rôtisseur*. These all had a head of section known as a chef de partie. They were supported by a first, second and third commis, then the lowly *apprentis*, whose job was often to load the stove with charcoal or coal and keep it stoked. This system is very much alive in our kitchens today, though the coal has gone, thank heavens.

In 1975, when Chris first entered the kitchen, the only ones worth working in were French. Unfortunately this meant that young British chefs were at a great disadvantage, because the chefs' bibles, *Le Répertoire de la Cuisine* by Louis Saulnier and Escoffier's *Le Guide Culinaire*, were available only in French. We had to learn French terminology at college, learn to run a service in French, learn the names of every ingredient in French

– it was the language of the kitchen. The menus were written in French (often with awful English translations underneath), and any kitchen worth its salt had a French chef de cuisine and a sprinkling of French sous chefs and chefs de parties. However, when Michael Quinn became the first British chef de cuisine at the Ritz in 1981, his first question was, why French? And so it was all change. We could speak in English, write the menus in English and have English ingredients taking centre stage with French ones. It is important to understand that this wasn't an anti-French move, simply a long-overdue opportunity to celebrate the best of British. Others besides Michael had been making similar reforms, and unfortunately we don't have space to name them all here, but these special people should be celebrated for bringing this about.

The consequence was that the new generation of chefs have had their wings freed and can now really fly when it comes to creative cooking, as there are no longer the strict rules in place that we once had to observe. I have to admit, cooking from the two bibles was a bit like being in a straitjacket. What must never be forgotten, though, is the debt we owe to the French for teaching us so much, especially the importance of seasonality and quality of ingredients, an array of techniques and, most importantly, the intrinsic link between food, wine and *joie de vivre*.

Our particular French heroes are Raymond Blanc, the Roux family, Michel Bourdin and Pierre Koffmann. They have all invested a lifetime's work in teaching and encouraging young British chefs to achieve their best; we are nationally indebted to them.

At our restaurants we are happily married to French cuisine as a result of our formative training and experiences and our love of the discipline French cooking involves. Our favourite restaurants are French, as are many of our favourite ingredients. Plus, we always have a great excuse to disappear to France looking for inspiration!

When we opened the Bistrot de Luxe in 2005, we had the opportunity to work 'our way'. We slowly set about putting our philosophy into practice, visiting the market daily, sharing ideas with each other, and indeed inviting customers to come to the market or work alongside us. We constantly talk to our valued suppliers – farmers, fishermen, winemakers, game suppliers and cheese makers – some of whom we have known and worked with for over twenty years. We always share recipes and like to get feedback from the room, even if it is something we would rather not hear. Each day at staff briefing, we serve a dish from the menu so the front-of-house team can try it before explaining it to our customers – not forgetting that they need to taste the wine that we will be recommending with the dish.

Seasonality is of huge importance to us. We love the fact that in late spring the asparagus season is so short, starting with the French and leading to the English. Then in summer, we work with the abundant young, tender vegetables, beautiful salads and wonderful Dorset crabs. In autumn the emergence of the game season neatly encompasses figs and ceps, which are followed by the root vegetables and brassicas of winter, with all the deep, slow cooking we love so much. Then it starts all over again, waiting for the first Yorkshire rhubarb, blood oranges and black truffles.

We have gone to the markets ever since I can remember and love the sights, smells and banter. When we were taking pictures for this book in the Rungis fish market, just outside Paris, we explained to one stallholder that we would like a shot of his fish for the book. First the Frenchman feigned shock, then disbelief that the English would attempt such a thing. To make matters worse, he called all his friends over, who had a good laugh at our expense. But the joy of walking around the market feels almost primordial and we would miss it terribly if it were taken away from us – though that said, we can no longer make it each day and so David, our brother, continues to travel to Covent Garden market every night, choosing the very best for the next day in our restaurants.

Whether you are cooking at home or in a professional kitchen, equipment is very important. You don't need a huge *batterie de cuisine* but having a few good-quality pots and a good frying pan is vital. Thick-bottomed pans help distribute the heat and give even cooking. A good chopping board large enough to work on and thick enough to chop large ingredients on is a necessity. Next you will need sharp knives. We can see from a distance the chefs that work with blunt knives because of the blurred edges of the

meat or fish that they have prepared, and any herbs get bruised rather than chopped cleanly. The best knife in our kit is the 25cm cook's knife. It can do almost any job in the kitchen and buying the best quality will repay you ten times over. It should last you a lifetime, but buy a good sharpener – there are lots on the market. Remember that knives only need a stroke on the sharpener now and then. Too much sharpening is as bad as not enough.

Next is your oven. All the recipes in this book are cooked in the kitchens of our restaurants and there is a world of difference between a professional chef's oven and a domestic one. The most important distinction is the intensity of the heat and the oven's ability to keep the heat stable, even when it is being constantly opened for basting and being filled with pans as the orders come thick and fast. The reason for the difference between professional and domestic ovens is twofold: one is the gas pressure and the gauge of pipe coming into a professional kitchen, which is much larger than in a domestic home. The second is the thickness of the cast-iron plates used to line professional ovens – they are up to ten times thicker and, once hot, resonate heat for a long time. This is to give a very constant heat even when full and, as mentioned, when the door is being constantly opened and shut. At home, our partners often comment that we cook on high temperatures, but this is because we need to compensate for heat loss. Jeff is better at checking things, and often uses a small portable thermometer, which he places in the ovens at work to check their accuracy. It is a good idea to use one at home; they are relatively inexpensive and worth investing in.

The beauty of being a chef is that no two days are the same, and no two ingredients either for that matter, so every day in the kitchen is a new day. We are always sad to hear people say they can't cook. Of course they can, they just don't know it yet! First you need to decide what you are going to cook. Look at what's in season and decide how much you want to spend. Read a little about the dishes you are going to cook, and plan carefully. Next there is the shopping to be done – allow time for this and don't be surprised if it takes the best part of a morning. If what you find isn't quite right, don't use it. A golden restaurant rule is either find something else or abort the dish and use an ingredient that is in spanking-good nick.

Make sure your chosen menu doesn't involve too much last-minute finishing – so, for example, if you need to put a lot of work into the main course, ensure the first course is simple and preferably served cold. Always remember that your guests don't want to see you stressed, as they have come to spend time with you. Find dishes that you can master before progressing; it may seem boring but your guests will appreciate it. One of our top tips is to read your recipe and cook the dish from start to finish in your head: visualisation. You will quickly think about things you might need to get, such as whisks, mixing bowls etc, and it also gives you the opportunity to consider where you might put things whilst cooking, where to rest your meat and so on. It really works. Put very simply, what you put in you get out, and so by planning ahead, buying the best seasonal produce and caring for it simply and confidently, you will cook beautifully!

Something that will enhance your cookery skills beyond measure is very simply to taste what you are cooking. We always encourage the chefs in our kitchens to have tasting spoons to hand so that they can try a dish during each part of its preparation to check sweetness, acidity and so on. We also encourage the seasoning of an ingredient. Using too much salt is definitely not a good thing for us but, as with all cooking, balance is the key, and an underseasoned dish is almost tasteless. It is a shame to go to all the effort of preparing and cooking something just to serve it up bland. Salt enlarges our taste buds and receptors, which in turn detect the different flavour notes a dish has to offer, while a twist of pepper will add subliminal warmth. So put a teaspoon in your apron pocket next time you cook, season and taste as you go, then get ready for the compliments!

In today's whirlwind pace of life, try to stop and enjoy planning, preparation and cooking a meal, and allow proper time for the care needed to produce good food. When we are at home, we spend a long time preparing dishes ourselves. There are not many shortcuts to doing something well – why do we always have to rush?

Staff training and feeding are big on our agendas and, like an army, restaurants march on their stomach. You would be horrified if you knew how many kitchens feed their staff rubbish or don't feed them at all – staff that within an hour or so are going to cook and serve some of the greatest dishes in the country. Training is never ending, and we are always looking at different ways to encourage and teach. As with many creative occupations, you can never know everything. We have spent over fifty years simply scraping the surface of regional French cuisine. There is always something different to learn. We draw our inspiration from food markets, the seasons, the media, books and many other influences. Our job is to ensure consistency once we have created a dish. This means assigning someone to show each new chef de partie how to prepare and cook the dish, training someone to work on the sauce, fish, garnish and larder and, nowadays, also the pastry, as we do not see as many pâtissiers as we once did.

We encourage our staff to travel to other chefs' kitchens to learn, and to go to other restaurants to eat, which we then discuss and evaluate. We also visit vineyards, taking staff with us when we can, in order to understand the expression of a certain winemaker – a tough life but someone has to do it!

Last, though by no means least, we have a huge amount of respect for the front-of-house team. Again, we were brought up in the days of the kitchen versus the front-of-house – who on earth decided this was a good idea? For chefs, it is without doubt challenging to have the waiters asking how long something will be, or sending multiple orders in at once, but we have to work this one out. We see the front-of-house as our partners, explaining the dishes, serving them skilfully, effortlessly and in a timely fashion. We really admire *l'art de la table*.

There is, thank goodness, a much more relaxed style of service throughout restaurants today. This does not mean it is any less disciplined or skilful, but it is certainly warmer and more informal. A great friend and patron of ours, David Morgan Hewitt, managing director of the Goring Hotel, once said to us, 'Boys, one of life's greatest pleasures is to be waited upon.' What David brought home to us was that good service means caring enough to have another's comfort and wellbeing at heart. This is truly something magical, and something we should all appreciate and hold dear.

OUR THOUGHTS ON WINE

CHRIS GALVIN

When we decided to open our first restaurant, Galvin Bistrot de Luxe, we spent long days there, working physically hard with the builders and also preparing the restaurant from A to Z. This included one area in which we realised we were not as confident as we would have wished: the wine list.

Most of our career had been spent working around some award-winning lists, but if you ask chefs about wine many of them will tell you that it is the area in which they are least strong. The fact is that drinking wine can be expensive and chefs working through the ranks earn very little indeed, so buying good wine comes a long way down their list of priorities. Some young chefs are lucky enough to work for a proprietor, manager or head chef who understands the importance of pairing food with wine and is willing to invest in regular tastings.

Every chef that we involve in our tastings is, without fail, amazed at his or her ability to detect the various characters of a given wine. They suddenly realise it is fun and that wine is a living, breathing thing that deserves their attention, especially when served with food.

So where to start? Jeff had been at a college where students were encouraged to study wine and he almost made his career in front-of-house, especially on wine service, but compiling a restaurant wine list take a lot of knowledge and needs to be considered carefully.

When the wine list was put together at the Wolseley, the owners, Chris Corbin and Jeremy King, scoured wine merchants' lists in their desire to get the best. One man, Eric Narioo, owner of Les Caves de Pyrène, was to turn our ideas on wine upside down. I will never forget his tasting. It was held at Jeremy's house and Eric turned up with bottles under one arm and a duffel bag under the other containing a hunk of Comté cheese, a piece of Bayonne ham, a ballotine of foie gras and a beautiful country loaf. He said simply that we had to taste his wines with food. He made more sense about the marriage of food and wine than anyone I had met before and the wines were simply delicious, in perfect harmony with the food.

So when the Bistrot list was first discussed, Eric was the only person we consulted. He had a strong connection with the people growing and producing his wines and a genuine understanding of simple French country cooking – something we planned to offer at the Bistrot. The list was put together in his inimitable style, including some challenging, taboo-breaking wines, and it encouraged our customers to drink some delicious and affordable bottles.

After a year of trading, Eric suggested we introduce some other suppliers and we now have ten providing wines for our restaurants. We have regular tastings and Jeff and I often visit the vineyards with our sommeliers and other staff to meet the growers. Sometimes we are lucky enough to eat with them, and more than once we have borrowed recipes that have found their way on to our menus – the Marinated Scallops with Noirmoutier Potatoes, Jerusalem Artichokes and Mâche on page 84 is one example.

A chance meeting with an old friend in Lyons was famously to change the path of one of our restaurants forever. Christophe Brunet is one of the liveliest and most charming men we know. At the time, he was working with Paul Jaboulet wines in Tain l'Hermitage, and we decided to meet at the famous La Mère Brazier restaurant in Lyons. He insisted on buying the wine, and selected a beautiful St Péray 'les Figures', made by the famous winemaker, Bernard Grippa. This was sensational and we still spoil ourselves with a glass now and again. For the main course, he chose a bottle of La Chapelle, the legendary wine from the hill of Hermitage. It was utterly sublime and we wanted to learn more, so we visited La Chapelle.

On arrival at Tain l'Hermitage, we were struck by its beauty, then we went up the hill to visit La Chapelle itself. I don't like to think about heaven too much but this is our idea of it, looking down on the beautifully arranged vines whilst the River Rhône winds its way towards the south. You can see for miles and miles, with some of the great Rhône vineyards stretching before you. On top of the hill stands a chapel, and legend recounts that it was built by a knight returning from the crusades full of remorse, who became a hermit there. The chapel, which is made of terracotta, reminded Jeff and me of our new site in Spitalfields – and so a name for our new restaurant was born. La Chapelle 1961 was one of the twelve greatest wines produced last century and we really wanted to have it on our list, which we now have. We almost hope we never sell it. Hermitage wines have been known to last a very long time indeed, so who knows?

The more we discovered, the more we fell in love with the Rhône. It seemed to have a great deal of resonance with our cooking, especially its depth and minerality. Our passion for the area only intensified when Eric introduced us to Domaine Gramenon, run by an amazing woman called Michelle Aubery-Laurent from her vineyard in southern Rhône.

Jeff and I had arranged to meet Eric at the vineyard but found ourselves there early, so we went in and met Michelle. She didn't worry that Eric wasn't with us and that our French is at best schoolboy level. She proceeded to march us across her vineyards, showing us the youngest vines to the oldest, with some of them around a hundred years old. When we returned, Eric and his assistant had arrived and we went down to the cellar and had the tasting of a lifetime, followed by a great evening, full of laughter, in a local restaurant near Carpentras, which is famous for its truffle market. I remember we had a truffle omelette with lots of wine, the only problem being that we had all forgotten to bring any money. Silly, I know, but this just made us laugh even more. The owner very kindly let Eric pay the bill the next day.

So our wine rules are fairly straightforward. The wines must be food friendly, which means good acidity; they must taste juicy and be representative of the grape, the grower, the terroir and the vintage; and we must know about the wines we sell. And herein lie a couple of the most important things about wine: to have good knowledge you must taste often and you need a good memory. Nowadays, a great aide-mémoire is to use your phone to photograph the label of a wine you like the taste of. This way you can remember it much more easily.

Wine is very subjective and it is up to you and you alone to decide what works for you. Sure, there are certain marriages made in heaven and there is certainly lots of information available from books, tasting notes and the backs of labels. But by learning and listening to people who are experienced with wine, you can eventually make your own mind up. It's the finding out that's fun.

Finally, remember that it is vital to serve wines at the correct temperature. Put very simply, most of us drink our white wines too cold and our reds too warm. We learned from Eric and other friends in the wine world how important temperature was simply by trying wines at the right and wrong temperature. Getting it right meant a lot of investment at the restaurants – something we had not allowed for initially – but, as with everything else, once you know how it should be done, you cannot go back.

The general advice is to drink reds at room temperature. Well, that was fine thirty or forty years ago, before central heating, but nowadays most central heating is set at about 18–20°C. Red wine should be served at around 14–16°C, which is a big difference. Served too warm, it becomes flat and flabby, with a monotonous taste, if any. At this cooler temperature, you are hit with a symphony of flavourful smells, notes and tastes. With white wines, it is almost the opposite. Too cool and they become closed, offering us no sense of the fruits and minerals they might contain. This is because the taste buds on our tongues shrink with the cold and offer fewer pointers to a wine's flavour.

As a general rule, we aim to serve Champagne at around 10°C, white wines at 10–12°C, and great white wines at 12–14°C. We like to serve light reds at 12–14°C and the bigger wines at 14–18°C. Try to work towards this and you will be rewarded. Most importantly, taste as you go. It is easy to cool wine and then watch it open up as it slowly changes temperature. Wine is truly a living thing and deserves a little time and care.

BASICS

CHICKEN STOCK

Makes about 4 litres

2kg chicken wings
5 litres water
1 onion, roughly chopped
2 sticks celery, roughly chopped
2 leeks, white part only, roughly chopped
4 garlic cloves, peeled and left whole
1 small sprig of thyme
5–6 parsley stalks

Place the chicken wings in a large saucepan and cover with the water. Bring to the boil over a high heat, then reduce the heat to a simmer and skim off any froth or scum from the surface.

Add all of the remaining ingredients, increase the heat and bring back to the boil. Skim again, then reduce the heat to a low simmer and simmer for 2 hours, skimming when necessary.

Remove from the heat and leave to stand for 30 minutes. Pass the mixture through a fine sieve, leave to cool and then chill. Store in an airtight container in the fridge for up to 2 days or freeze in batches for up to 3 months.

BROWN CHICKEN STOCK

This recipe uses chicken necks to give the stock a good colour. If you can't get them, use 2kg chicken wings instead and roast them in a little oil at 180°C/Gas Mark 4 until golden, before transferring them to the stove top, adding the water and vegetables and continuing as below.

Makes about 3 litres

2kg chicken necks
5 litres water
1 onion, roughly chopped
2 sticks celery, roughly chopped
10 large carrots, roughly chopped
1 leek (remove and discard very dark
   green part), roughly chopped
1 garlic clove, peeled and left whole
1 sprig of thyme
5–6 parsley stalks
500ml white wine
200ml brandy
200ml tomato juice

Place the chicken necks in a large saucepan and cover with the water. Bring to the boil over a high heat, then reduce the heat to a simmer and skim off any froth or scum from the surface.

Add all of the vegetables together with the garlic and herbs. Increase the heat and bring back to the boil. Skim again, then reduce the heat to a low simmer. Add the white wine, brandy and tomato juice, bring back to the boil, then simmer gently for 6 hours, skimming when necessary.

Pass the mixture through a fine sieve, leave to cool and then chill. Store in an airtight container in the fridge for up to 2 days or freeze in batches for up to 3 months.

VENISON STOCK

Makes 1.5 litres

750g venison bones, chopped
3 tablespoons vegetable oil
1 small carrot, roughly chopped
½ leek, roughly chopped
1 celery stick, roughly chopped
3 garlic cloves, peeled but left whole
1 sprig of thyme
2 litres water

Roast the bones in an oven preheated to 180°C/Gas Mark 4 for 40 minutes, until golden brown. Heat a frying pan until very hot, add the oil, then add the vegetables and fry until golden. Transfer to a saucepan, add the bones and thyme, then cover with the water. Bring quickly to the boil, then turn down to a gentle simmer. Cook for 3 hours, skimming regularly, then pass through a fine sieve.

Leave to cool and then chill. Store in an airtight container in the fridge for up to 2 days or freeze in batches for up to 3 months.

BROWN CHICKEN JUS

It's a good idea to freeze this in ice cube trays, or in the little tubs you get for baby food – then you can just take out a few cubes at a time to use as you need them.

Makes about 600ml

Take one batch of Brown Chicken Stock (see opposite page) and pour it into a large saucepan. Bring to the boil and then reduce the heat to a steady simmer, skimming off any fat or scum that rises to the surface of the stock.

Keep simmering the stock until it has reduced to a sauce consistency that will coat the back of a spoon – this will take about 1 hour.

Leave to cool, then store in an airtight container in the fridge for 4–5 days or freeze in batches for up to 3 months.

FISH STOCK

Makes about 1.7 litres

1kg white fish bones (such as sole, turbot or brill)
30g unsalted butter
1 onion, finely chopped
1 leek, white part only, finely chopped
2 sticks celery, finely chopped
100ml dry white wine
100ml Noilly Prat vermouth
2 litres water
5 white peppercorns, crushed
1 bay leaf
1 sprig of thyme
1 small sprig of curly parsley

Remove and discard any gills and eyes from the fish bones, then roughly chop them. Place in a container, cover with cold water and leave for 3–4 hours. Drain well.

Melt the butter in a large saucepan, add the chopped vegetables and cook for 4–5 minutes or until soft but not coloured. Add the drained fish bones and sweat for 3 minutes. Add the alcohol, increase the heat and bring to the boil. Boil until the liquid is reduced by half.

Add the water and bring to the boil over a high heat, then reduce the heat to a simmer, skimming off any scum from the surface. Add the peppercorns and herbs and simmer for 20 minutes.

Pass the mixture through a muslin-lined sieve, leave to cool and then chill. Store in an airtight container in the fridge for up to 2 days or freeze in batches for up to 3 months.

COURT BOUILLON

Makes about 2 litres

2 onions
1 stick celery
2 leeks, white part only
2 carrots
1.5 litres water
1 bottle of white wine
3 tablespoons white wine vinegar
4 black peppercorns
$\frac{1}{2}$ star anise
2 tablespoons sea salt
1 sprig of thyme
5–6 parsley stalks

Finely slice all of the vegetables into 2–3mm pieces – this is to aid quick cooking. Place the chopped vegetables and all the rest of the ingredients in a saucepan and bring to the boil over a high heat, then reduce the heat and simmer for 15 minutes.

Pass the mixture through a fine sieve, leave to cool and then chill. Store in an airtight container in the fridge for up to 3 days.

RED WINE JUS

Makes about 150ml

1 tablespoon olive oil
4 shallots, finely sliced
1/2 garlic clove, finely sliced
1 sprig of thyme
50ml red wine
25ml port
150ml Brown Chicken Jus (see page 45)
5g chilled unsalted butter

Heat the olive oil in a heavy-based saucepan over a medium heat, add the shallots and garlic and cook slowly until golden brown and caramelised – this should take 7–8 minutes.

Add the thyme, red wine and port and bring to the boil, then boil until the mixture is reduced to three-quarters of its original volume. Add the brown chicken jus and bring gently to the boil, then simmer for 10 minutes.

Pass the mixture through a muslin-lined sieve into a small saucepan. Return to the heat and bring to the boil, then whisk in the cold butter.

Leave to cool, then store in an airtight container in the fridge for 2–3 days.

MADEIRA JUS

Makes about 150ml

1 tablespoon olive oil
4 shallots, finely sliced
1/2 garlic clove, finely sliced
1 sprig of thyme
75ml Madeira
150ml Brown Chicken Jus (see page 45)
5g chilled unsalted butter

Heat the olive oil in a heavy-based saucepan over a medium heat, add the shallots and garlic and cook slowly until golden brown and caramelised – this should take 7–8 minutes.

Add the thyme and Madeira and bring to the boil, then boil until the mixture has reduced to three-quarters of its original volume. Add the brown chicken jus and bring gently to the boil, then simmer for 10 minutes.

Pass the mixture through a muslin-lined sieve into a small saucepan. Return to the heat and bring to the boil, then whisk in the cold butter.

Leave to cool, then store in an airtight container in the fridge for 2–3 days.

CLASSIC VINAIGRETTE

Makes about 350ml

5g white peppercorns, crushed
a large pinch of sea salt
1 small shallot, finely chopped
70ml white wine vinegar
5 teaspoons Dijon mustard
1 teaspoon English mustard
300ml vegetable oil

Combine the crushed peppercorns, salt, shallot and vinegar in a small bowl and leave to marinate in the fridge for 24 hours.

Place the marinated mixture in a blender or food processor with the mustards and blend for 1 minute. With the motor running, slowly add the vegetable oil, as if making mayonnaise, until the mixture becomes emulsified and thick.

Pass the mixture through a fine sieve. Store in a sealed plastic bottle or in an airtight container in the fridge for up to 2 weeks. The dressing will need a shake each time it is used.

SIMPLE VINAIGRETTE

Makes about 200ml

2 tablespoons white wine vinegar
$\frac{1}{2}$ teaspoon Dijon mustard
4 tablespoons groundnut oil
100ml extra virgin olive oil
fine sea salt and freshly ground white
  pepper

Place the vinegar and mustard in a small mixing bowl, add a small pinch of salt and some pepper and whisk together.

Gradually whisk in the groundnut and olive oils until amalgamated. Taste and adjust the seasoning, if necessary.

Store in a sealed plastic bottle or in an airtight container in the fridge for up to 2 weeks. The dressing will need a shake each time it is used.

RAVIGOTE DRESSING

2 hard-boiled free-range eggs, finely
  chopped
1 small onion, finely chopped
1 tablespoon Dijon mustard
1 tablespoon capers, chopped
4 small cornichons, chopped
2 tablespoons walnut oil
2 tablespoons chopped chives
4 tablespoons chopped parsley
sea salt and freshly ground white pepper

Mix all of the ingredients together just before serving.

MAYONNAISE

Makes about 350ml

2 free-range egg yolks
2 tablespoons white wine vinegar
$^1/_2$ teaspoon fine sea salt
$1^1/_2$ teaspoons Dijon mustard
300ml groundnut oil
$1^1/_2$ teaspoons hot water
a squeeze of lemon juice
a small pinch of cayenne pepper

Place the egg yolks, vinegar, salt and mustard in a food processor and whiz until fully combined. With the motor running, slowly trickle in the groundnut oil in a steady stream, until the mayonnaise is thick, then add the hot water. Add lemon juice and cayenne pepper to taste.

Store in an airtight container in the fridge for up to 2 days.

CLARIFIED BUTTER

Place the required amount of unsalted butter (you will lose about 15 per cent during the clarification process) into a pan and melt over a medium heat. Reduce the heat to the lowest possible setting and leave the butter over this heat for 1 hour. After this period of time, the milky sediments should have separated and sunk to the bottom of the pan, while the butter on top should resemble a clear, deep yellow oil.

Remove from the heat and carefully pour off the clear butter through a fine sieve into a clean container, being careful not to get any sediment in it. Discard the sediment.

Store in an airtight container in the fridge for up to 1 week.

PASTA DOUGH

Makes about 500g

280g strong plain white flour
a pinch of sea salt
2 free-range eggs
3 free-range egg yolks
1 tablespoon olive oil

Sift the flour and salt into a food processor, then add the eggs, egg yolks and olive oil. Blitz for a couple of minutes until the mixture forms pea-sized lumps.

Turn the mixture out on to a lightly floured work surface and knead together for a few minutes until the dough is very smooth and fairly springy.

Wrap the dough tightly in cling film and chill for at least 1 hour before rolling out. The pasta dough will keep in the fridge for up to 1 day.

PARMESAN GNOCCHI

Makes 20

1 large Desiree potato, weighing about 400g
100g fine sea salt
1 small free-range egg
35g Parmesan cheese, finely grated
50g Italian '00' flour
8g sea salt
freshly ground white pepper

Wash the potato well and prick it with a fork. Place the fine salt on a small baking tray, put the potato on top and place in an oven preheated to 190°C/Gas Mark 5. Bake for about $1^{1}/_{2}$ hours, until tender. Remove from the oven, cut the potato in half and use a spoon to scoop out the flesh. Pass it through a fine sieve into a bowl; you should have about 200g sieved potato.

Lightly beat the egg with the Parmesan, them work this mixture into the potato with a spatula or wooden spoon. Make sure the mixture is well combined but be careful not to overwork it. Add the flour, salt and a few twists of pepper and mix together to make a dough. Turn the dough out on to a work surface and shape into a long sausage, about 1.5cm thick. Cut it into 20 pieces.

Add the gnocchi to a large pan of boiling salted water. They will sink to the bottom initially but when they rise to the top, they are cooked. Remove from the pan with a slotted spoon, refresh in iced water and then drain well.

HERB GNOCCHI

Follow the recipe for Parmesan Gnocchi, above, adding 1 tablespoon of chopped mixed herbs (chervil, parsley and tarragon) with the flour and salt.

PIZZA DOUGH

We use mineral water quite a lot in our cooking, and particularly in bread dough, because the chlorine and other additives in tap water can inhibit the action of the yeast.

Makes about 400g

5g fresh yeast
170ml still mineral water, warmed
250g strong white flour
5g fine sea salt
a pinch of caster sugar
$1/4$ teaspoon olive oil

In a large bowl, whisk together the yeast and warm water until the yeast has dissolved, then mix in 125g of the flour. Clean down the sides of the bowl and cover with cling film. Leave in a warm place for $1^{1}/_{2}$–2 hours. By this stage the mixture should have risen by two-thirds and be clearly active, with lots of bubbles on top.

Place the remaining flour in the bowl of an electric stand mixer fitted with a dough hook attachment, then add the risen dough, the salt, sugar and olive oil. Mix on the slowest setting for about 8 minutes. The dough should be firm but slightly sticky at this stage. If necessary, add a little more water, but only a little at a time, then beat on the fastest speed for 1 minute. The dough should now be elastic and springy to the touch.

Transfer the dough to a bowl that is large enough for it to treble in size, cover with cling film and put in a fairly cool place to prove for $1^{1}/_{2}$–2 hours. Once the dough has trebled in size, tip it out of the bowl on to a lightly floured surface and knead for 2–3 minutes. The dough is now ready to use.

PUFF PASTRY

Makes about 1.1kg

450g strong white flour
a pinch of sea salt
10g unsalted butter, melted
2 teaspoons white wine vinegar
180ml still mineral water
440g chilled unsalted butter

Sift the flour on to a clean work surface and make a well in the centre. Place the salt, melted butter, vinegar and water in the well and then, using your fingertips, gradually work the flour into the liquid to form a dough. Knead for a couple of minutes until it is smooth. Form the dough into a ball, then cut a cross in it halfway down through its depth. Wrap in cling film and refrigerate for 2 hours.

With a rolling pin, bash the chilled butter until it becomes pliable, then shape it into a 20cm square.

Place the dough on a lightly floured surface and pull out the 4 corners created by the cross cut earlier so they form a star shape. Roll each of these out to 3mm thick. Roll the thicker centre part of the dough to the same size as the butter. Place the butter in the centre and make sure the 4 flaps of dough are just large enough to enclose it completely when folded over. Fold each corner flap of dough over the butter, making sure any excess flour is brushed off.

Roll out, without turning the dough, into a 50cm x 20cm rectangle. Fold the top third down, then fold the bottom third up over it (like folding a letter), keeping the edges straight. Give the dough a quarter turn clockwise and roll out again to the same size, then fold again as before. Chill in the fridge for 40 minutes and then repeat the rolling and folding twice more (so a total of 4 rolls/folds and 3 rests), always turning the dough clockwise. Rest the pastry in the fridge, wrapped in cling film, for at least 1 hour before using.

It will keep in the fridge for up to 3 days or can be frozen for up to 3 months.

Rioja Jus

Chick.

Mad

Pigeon Gourmande

SWEET SHORTCRUST PASTRY

Makes about 440g

200g plain flour
a small pinch of sea salt
75g icing sugar
100g unsalted butter, at room
  temperature
1/2 vanilla pod, split in half lengthwise
  and seeds scraped out
1 free-range egg, beaten

Sift the flour and salt into a bowl and set aside. Using an electric stand mixer fitted with a paddle attachment, beat the icing sugar, butter and vanilla seeds together on a medium speed until pale in colour.

Gradually mix in half the beaten egg, then half the flour, then add the remainder of the beaten egg and finally the last of the flour. Turn out and knead lightly until you have a smooth dough but do not over work it.

Gather the dough into a ball, wrap in cling film and refrigerate for 2 hours before use.

POMMES PURÉES

Serves 4

600g Desiree potatoes, or similar floury
  potatoes, peeled and cut into large pieces
a good pinch of sea salt
150g chilled unsalted butter, diced
50ml double cream
50ml full-fat milk
sea salt

Place the potatoes in a large saucepan and cover with cold water. Add a good pinch of salt and bring quickly to the boil, then turn down to a slow simmer and cook until tender. Drain well in a colander, then return to the pan and place briefly over a low heat to drive off any remaining moisture.

Pass the potatoes through a fine sieve or a potato ricer into a clean saucepan. Using a whisk, beat in the butter, then the cream and milk. If at any time the purée splits, just add an extra 100ml of milk and whisk until it comes back together. Reheat gently, if necessary, adjust the seasoning and serve.

OVEN-DRIED TOMATOES

Makes 20

10 ripe tomatoes, skinned, halved and
  deseeded
olive oil, for drizzling
a few sprigs of thyme
sea salt and freshly ground white pepper

Arrange the tomato halves, cut-side up, on a baking sheet. Drizzle with olive oil, season with salt and pepper and then scatter over the leaves from the thyme sprigs.

Bake in an oven preheated to 140°C/ Gas Mark 1 for about 3 hours, until the tomatoes are wrinkled and semi-dried. Remove from the oven and leave to cool. Store in an airtight container in the fridge for up to 3 days.

HOW TO PREPARE BABY ARTICHOKES

Take each baby artichoke by the stalk and break off and discard the tough green outer leaves, stopping when you get down to the tender, pale green-yellow ones.

With a small, sharp knife, trim off the green, stringy outside of the stalk, trim around the choke itself, then finally slice off the pointed tops of the remaining leaves, leaving the choke intact.

Rub the cut edges of the artichokes with a lemon half as you go to prevent them turning black.

PRESERVED LEMONS

This recipe comes from the Troisgros brothers' famous restaurant in Rouanne.

1 organic or unwaxed lemon
1 tablespoon sea salt
200g caster sugar
$1/2$ vanilla pod
$1/2$ star anise

Cut the lemon lengthwise into 8 wedges. Put 400ml of water in a small saucepan with the salt and bring to the boil. Add the lemon wedges, bring back to the boil, then remove the pan from the heat. Leave at room temperature for 24 hours, then drain.

Put the sugar in a pan with 200ml water and bring to the boil, then add the lemon wedges, vanilla and star anise. Cover with a cartouche (a circle of greaseproof paper), reduce the heat right down and cook slowly for about 2 hours, until the lemon becomes slightly translucent. Don't let the syrup caramelise; add a little more water if necessary.

Remove from the heat and leave to cool. Store the lemons in their syrup in an airtight container in the fridge for up to 2 weeks.

LEMON OIL

Makes 100ml

100ml extra virgin olive oil
finely grated zest of 1 unwaxed lemon

Heat the olive oil in a pan until it is just warm to the touch, then remove from the heat and stir in the lemon zest. Cover with cling film and leave to infuse at room temperature for 24 hours.

Pass the mixture through a fine sieve and store in a sealed plastic bottle or an airtight container in the fridge for up to 3 weeks.

PAIN D'ÉPICES

This is really easy to make and keeps well.

125ml milk
250g honey
125g rye flour
125g plain flour
50g demerara sugar
20g baking powder
50g unsalted butter
3 free-range eggs
finely grated zest of ½ orange
finely grated zest of ½ lemon
30g mixed candied lemon and orange peel, finely chopped

1 teaspoon ground cinnamon
1 teaspoon ground ginger
a pinch of freshly grated nutmeg
a pinch of crushed aniseed
a pinch of ground cloves

Warm the milk and honey together in a saucepan until the honey has dissolved, then remove from the heat and leave to cool.

Put the flours, sugar, baking powder and butter in the bowl of an electric stand mixer and mix together on a low speed for a few minutes, until the mixture resembles breadcrumbs. Add the milk/honey mixture and beat together to form a smooth paste. Add all the remaining ingredients and mix together well.

Transfer the mixture to a greased 18cm x 7cm x 7cm loaf tin and bake in an oven preheated to 160°C/Gas Mark 3 for 40 minutes or until springy to the touch. Turn out on to a wire rack and leave to cool completely. Wrap tightly in cling film to store.

QUATRE-ÉPICES

This is a simple French spice blend that can be bought in shops in France but can also easily be made at home.

125g ground white pepper
4 teaspoons ground cloves
30g ground ginger
35g freshly grated nutmeg

Mix all the ingredients together in a bowl, then transfer to an airtight container and store in a cool, dry place for up to 1 month.

VANILLA ICE CREAM

Serves 6

25g liquid glucose
250ml double cream
250ml full-fat milk
2 vanilla pods, split in half lengthwise and seeds scraped out
7 free-range egg yolks
75g caster sugar

Put the liquid glucose, cream and milk in a pan with the vanilla pods and seeds and bring to the boil, then remove the vanilla pods and discard.

Whisk the egg yolks and sugar together in a bowl until pale. Gradually pour in the hot milk mixture, whisking constantly. Return to a clean pan and cook gently, stirring constantly with a wooden spoon, until the sauce is thick enough to coat the back of the spoon; it should register 82°C on a thermometer.

Remove from the heat, pour the mixture through a fine sieve and leave to cool. Transfer it to an ice cream maker and freeze according to the manufacturer's instructions.

STARTERS

POTAGE OF MUSSELS WITH CURRY SPICES

Serves 4

This is a version of mouclade, a mussel soup with a hint of curry from the west coast of France. In France they use the tip of a knife to put the curry powder in, so as not to overdo it.

1kg fresh mussels
40g potato, cut into 1cm dice
50g unsalted butter
1 onion, finely chopped
1 stick celery, finely chopped
1 leek, white part only, finely chopped
1/2 teaspoon curry powder
a small pinch of saffron strands
a pinch of cayenne pepper
a small sprig of thyme
1 bay leaf
600ml white wine
300ml Fish Stock (see page 46)
450ml double cream
2 tablespoons finely chopped chives
sea salt and freshly ground white pepper

Wash the mussels under cold running water, removing any barnacles and discarding any open mussels that don't close when tapped lightly on a work surface. Pull off any beards and wash again carefully, then set aside.

Put the diced potato in a pan of cold salted water, bring to the boil and simmer until tender. Drain and keep warm.

Melt the butter in a large pan, add the onion, celery and leek and sweat for 5 minutes, until softened but not coloured. Stir in the curry powder, saffron, cayenne pepper, thyme and bay leaf. Add the mussels, cover and cook gently for 1 minute. Add the wine and fish stock, increase the heat and cook, covered, for a few minutes longer, shaking the pan occasionally, until the mussels open. Strain the mussels through a fine sieve or muslin cloth set over a bowl, discarding any that have failed to open.

Pour the mussel cooking liquor into a pan and boil until reduced by half. Add the cream and boil until it reduces further and thickens to a coating consistency. Season to taste.

To serve, remove the mussels from their shells and divide between 4 soup bowls, adding the diced warm potato. Pour the hot soup over the mussels and sprinkle with the chopped chives.

VELOUTÉ OF CAULIFLOWER WITH POACHED SCALLOPS AND TRUFFLE

It's worth waiting for the French winter truffles to make this dish – expensive but worth it for a special occasion. If you can get hold of cauliflowers from Brittany, they are the best to use. They have tight, white curds and pack a lot of flavour.

4 scallops, preferably diver caught and in the shell
250g cauliflower florets
125g unsalted butter
$1/4$ onion, finely diced
500ml Chicken Stock (see page 44) or vegetable stock
65ml full-fat milk
$1/2$ lemon
1 small black truffle
sea salt and freshly ground white pepper

Carefully open the scallops (you could ask your fishmonger to do this), clean them and place on a cloth. Remove the orange roe – you won't need it in this recipe – and cut each scallop horizontally into 3 discs. Place in the fridge.

Take about 20 very small cauliflower florets and blanch for 2 minutes in boiling salted water. Drain and refresh in iced water, then set aside for garnish.

Melt the butter in a saucepan, add the onion and cook gently for 5 minutes until softened but not coloured. In a separate pan, bring 330ml of the stock to the boil. Add the cauliflower to the onion with some salt and pepper, then pour on the boiling stock. Bring back to the boil and simmer for 4 minutes or until the cauliflower is just tender. It is really important not to cook the soup for too long at this stage or it will taste of overcooked cauliflower. Remove the pan from the heat, then add the milk. Purée the soup in a blender or food processor and then pass through a fine sieve into a clean pan. Reheat gently and adjust the seasoning.

Bring the remainder of the stock to the boil in a small saucepan. Remove from the heat, add the sliced scallops and the small cauliflower florets and leave until the scallops are warm – just 30–60 seconds. Drain on kitchen paper, then season with a pinch of salt and a squeeze of lemon.

To serve, arrange the scallop slices in a rosette pattern in 4 soup plates and put the cauliflower florets on top. Pour on the hot soup, then shave the black truffle over it.

VICHYSSOISE OF ASPARAGUS AND LANGOUSTINES

Serves 6

In our restaurants we use live langoustines for this dish – it's always a good indication of their provenance and freshness. Once they're cooked, it's difficult to tell. A good fishmonger should be able to get hold of some for you.

36 medium langoustines, live or cooked
200g asparagus spears
320ml Chicken Stock (see page 44) or
   vegetable stock
80ml still mineral water
4 tablespoons extra virgin olive oil, plus
   extra to serve
80g unsalted butter
1 onion, finely diced
4 tablespoons crème fraîche
1 lemon, cut in half
2 tablespoons finely chopped chives
sea salt and freshly ground white pepper

If you are using live langoustines, place a large pan of salted water on to boil. Twist the head of each langoustine to remove it, then pull the centre section of the tail – the entrails will come out. Blanch the langoustines in the boiling water for 2 minutes, then drain and refresh in iced water. Leave to cool, then peel and set aside in the fridge.

Trim the asparagus by snapping off the woody base of the stem and then peel the spears, reserving the peelings. Blanch the asparagus and the peelings in a large pan of boiling salted water for 3 minutes, then refresh in iced water. Drain, then cut 2cm tips from the top of each asparagus spear and reserve for garnish. Keep the remaining stems, and the peelings, with excess liquid squeezed out, for making the soup.

Bring the stock and mineral water to the boil in a small pan. In a large saucepan, heat the olive oil and butter, add the onion and cook for 3–4 minutes, until tender but not coloured. Remove from the heat, then pour in the stock and add a good pinch of salt. Whisk in the crème fraîche. Put the mixture in a blender or food processor with the cooked asparagus (but not the tips) and blend until smooth, then pass through a fine sieve into a bowl. Chill over a bowl of ice. Adjust the seasoning to taste.

To serve, roll the langoustines and asparagus tips in a little olive oil, then season with a squeeze of lemon and some salt. Arrange these neatly in chilled soup bowls, garnish with the chives and then pour the chilled soup over at the table.

SPLIT PEA AND HAM SOUP WITH CRISPY PIG'S EARS

Serves 6-8

This is a lovely winter soup to share with friends, and the pig's ear adds a delicious textural contrast. If you're nice to your butcher, you might get it for free. Serve with warm crusty bread.

For the pig's ear
1 pig's ear
1/2 quantity of Court Bouillon (see page 46)
125ml milk
150g plain flour, seasoned with salt and pepper
vegetable oil, for deep-frying

For the soup
1 ham hock, weighing about 500g, soaked in cold water for 4 hours, then drained
2 litres Chicken Stock (see page 44)
125g unsalted butter
1/4 onion, finely chopped
350g dried split peas
sea salt and freshly ground white pepper
chopped parsley, to garnish

Leave the pig's ear under cold running water for 20 minutes, then place in a bowl, cover with cold water and leave to soak overnight. The next day, drain and place in a large pan. Cover with cold water, bring to the boil, then skim off any scum from the surface and drain again. Place in a clean pan, cover with the court bouillon and simmer for 3 hours, until tender – you should be able to push your finger through the flesh. Remove from the heat and leave to cool in the liquid.

Put the ham hock in a saucepan, cover with the chicken stock and bring to the boil. Simmer for 3 hours or until tender, then leave to cool in the stock. Remove the ham hock, reserving the stock, and shred the meat, discarding any fat or gristle.

Melt the butter in a saucepan, add the onion and cook gently for 5 minutes, until soft but not coloured. Add the peas and reserved stock, bring to the boil, then reduce to a simmer. Cook for $1^{1}/_{2}$ hours or until the peas are tender. Transfer to a blender, in batches, and blitz until smooth. Pass through a fine sieve into a clean pan, reheat gently and check the seasoning and consistency.

To cook the pig's ear, put the milk in a shallow dish and the seasoned flour in another. Slice the pig's ear into thin strips. Drop them into the milk, then remove, letting the excess milk drain off. Drop them into the flour and then remove and shake off the excess flour.

Heat the vegetable oil to 180°C in a deep-fat fryer and deep-fry the strips of pig's ear a few at a time, removing them when they rise to the surface and are crisp. Drain on kitchen paper and season.

To serve, divide the meat from the ham hock between 6–8 soup bowls and pour in the soup. Sprinkle with chopped parsley and serve with the hot pig's ear strips on the side.

MEDITERRANEAN FISH SOUP WITH ROUILLE AND CROÛTONS

Serves 8

This soup contains all our favourite Mediterranean flavours and we rarely take it off the Bistrot menu. This is simply the classic version and the best.

1.1kg mixed Mediterranean fish, such as red mullet, gurnard and rascasse, cleaned
a pinch of saffron strands
a pinch of cayenne pepper
4 tablespoons olive oil
90g carrot, chopped
20g celery, chopped
80g onion, chopped
20g fennel, chopped
1/2 garlic clove, lightly crushed
25g leek, chopped
40ml Pernod
20ml Armagnac
100g plum tomatoes, halved and deseeded
60g tomato purée
1 small waxy potato, about 60g, diced
2 litres Chicken Stock (see page 44)
lemon juice
salt

For the rouille
1 free-range egg yolk
1 garlic clove, finely chopped
1/2 teaspoon harissa paste
a pinch of saffron strands
85ml pomace oil (or vegetable oil)
50g cooked mashed potato
85ml vegetable oil

For the croûtons
1/4 baguette
1 tablespoon olive oil

Drain the fish in a colander, then mix with the saffron, cayenne pepper and 2 tablespoons of the olive oil. Leave to marinate in the fridge overnight.

The next day, place a colander over a bowl and pour the marinated fish in to drain, keeping the liquid that drains through. Heat a large frying pan, add a tablespoon of the remaining olive oil and fry the fish until golden on both sides.

Take a large, heavy-based saucepan and get it very hot on the hob. Add the remaining tablespoon of olive oil and fry the carrot, celery, onion, fennel, garlic and leek until golden brown. Add the Pernod and Armagnac and set them alight with a match, making sure your face is well away from the pan. Next, add the tomatoes and tomato purée and cook over a medium heat for 5 minutes. Lastly add the fried fish, juice from the marinade, the potato and the stock. Bring to the boil, then reduce to a simmer and cook for 1 1/2 hours.

Blend the soup in a blender or food processor until smooth and then pass it through a fine sieve into a clean pan. Season with lemon juice and salt.

For the rouille, blend the egg yolk, garlic, harissa and saffron with a pinch of salt in a mini food processor or using a pestle and mortar. Slowly add the pomace oil, as if making mayonnaise. Add the mashed potato and blend until smooth, then gradually mix in the vegetable oil. The rouille should be quite thick but if it becomes too thick to blend, thin it down slightly with a little warm water. Adjust the seasoning with salt and a little lemon juice.

For the croûtons, cut the baguette into 2mm-thick slices with a serrated knife. Place on a baking tray, drizzle with the olive oil and bake in an oven preheated to 180°C/Gas Mark 4 for 7 minutes or until golden.

Reheat the soup, if necessary, and serve in bowls, accompanied by the rouille and croûtons.

POTAGE OF BROAD BEANS WITH SMOKED DUCK AND PEA SHOOTS

Serves 6

This heralds the arrival of spring, celebrating the new broad beans and pea shoots. The addition of duck egg helps to enrich the soup.

2 free-range duck eggs
400g broad beans (shelled weight)
70g smoked duck breast (this should consist of about 25g skin and 45g meat)
700ml Chicken Stock (see page 44)
70g unsalted butter
1/4 Spanish onion, finely diced
200ml milk
1 punnet of pea shoots
1 tablespoon extra virgin olive oil
sea salt and freshly ground white pepper

Boil the duck eggs for 9 minutes, then cool under cold running water. Peel off the shells and cut the eggs into 1cm pieces. Cook the broad beans in a large pan of boiling salted water for 3 minutes, then drain and set aside.

Remove the fatty duck skin from the breast meat. Roughly dice it for cooking and finely shred the meat for garnish.

Put the chicken stock on to boil. In a large saucepan, melt the butter with the duck fat, then add the onion and cook gently for about 5 minutes, until soft but not coloured. Add the warm broad beans and then pour in the boiling stock. Simmer for 3–4 minutes.

Remove from the heat, add the milk, then purée the soup in a blender or food processor and pass it through a fine sieve. Adjust the seasoning, if necessary; you shouldn't need to add any salt as the duck skin normally provides enough.

Arrange the duck eggs, smoked duck and pea shoots in 6 soup bowls, drizzle with the olive oil, then pour on the soup at the table.

OUR FIRST CHRISTMAS AT BISTROT DE LUXE

After the Bistrot opened in September 2005, Christmas was the light at the end of the tunnel as far as days off were concerned. Chris and I had been at the restaurant day and night, taking breaks from the kitchen only to organise other aspects of the business. We decided to close after lunch on Christmas Eve until 27th December, giving staff – and us – two and a half days to spend with families and loved ones. On the morning of the 24th we planned to cook all the staff a festive champagne meal that they could enjoy in the restaurant, albeit at 10.30 in the morning, to thank them for such a big effort over the previous four months. Spirits were high on the 23rd as we, on top of our normal mise-en-place, prepared roast goose with all the trimmings for the following day.

On Christmas Eve I arrived at Baker Street at 7.45am. As soon as I set eyes on my brother, I could see that something was wrong. 'We've been robbed,' he told me. He was holding a scrap of paper in his hand that had been left on the hotplate – a 'Dear John' note from the head waiter, who had locked up the previous night. It read: 'My young brother back home in France is desperately ill and needs an urgent operation to save his life. I have taken all the cash from the safe and gone to France, but I will return it in full on Boxing Day.'

At first Chris thought there might be a grain of truth in this story, until the other waiters told him that the chap had regularly borrowed money from staff and moved himself into their house without paying any rent for three months. He had returned to the house that morning and, as far as they were aware, was still in bed.

Chris immediately rang the head waiter's ex-girlfriend, who we knew from his previous job. She revealed that he was a habitual gambler, who had previously 'borrowed' money to take to the casino, then returned it in the early hours of the morning without anyone being any the wiser. Obviously on this occasion he had lost everything.

When the manager arrived, he confirmed that there had been £7,500 in the safe. It was sickening to think that the fruit of all our endeavours had disappeared in a flash. By now Chris was on his way to Bethnal Green to try to catch our friend, and I was determined to put a brave face on for the staff so we could all enjoy our Christmas meal – something that proved very difficult for me as I was rather worried about what Chris might do if he caught him.

Long after the meal had finished, Chris returned. He had found the individual in bed nursing a hangover. His ex had been spot on – he admitted everything and, after establishing that the money was definitely not there, Chris took his house keys and waited outside for the police to arrive. We never received a penny back but the episode taught us a great lesson for the future: never put temptation in front of the staff. Keeping this amount of cash on the premises was asking for trouble.

Since this painful experience, I am happy to say we have been blessed with the most honest and loyal staff imaginable.

SOUPE À L'OIGNON GRATINÉE

Serves 6

The secret of this great classic soup is to caramelise the onions slowly and build up a good depth of colour. You also need to use a full-bodied stock – it's really worth making your own for this recipe.

50g unsalted butter
4 large onions, finely sliced
1 tablespoon thyme leaves
1 bay leaf
2 garlic cloves, sliced
80ml white wine
3 litres Brown Chicken Stock (see page 44)
120ml white port
sea salt and freshly ground white pepper

For the croûtons
¼ baguette
olive oil, for drizzling
120g Gruyère cheese, grated

Melt the butter in a heavy-based saucepan, add the onions and cook over a medium heat for 45 minutes or until soft and golden, stirring occasionally. Add the herbs and garlic and cook for 10 minutes, then add the wine and boil until reduced by half. Pour in the stock, bring to the boil and simmer gently for 1 hour. Stir in the port, bring back to the boil and then season to taste.

To make the croûtons, cut the baguette into 2mm-thick slices, place on a baking tray and then drizzle with olive oil. Bake in an oven preheated to 180°C/Gas Mark 4 for 7 minutes or until golden.

Ladle the soup into 6 bowls and cover the top of each portion with 6 or 7 croûtons. Scatter over the grated cheese and place under a hot grill until the cheese colours and bubbles. Leave the soup to cool for a couple of minutes before serving.

VELOUTÉ OF ROSCOFF ONIONS AND CIDER

Serves 6

Roscoff onions are small, white onions with a sweet intensity and good acidity. They have a natural affinity with cider – not surprisingly when you consider they are produced alongside each other in Brittany. However, you could use other white onions here, if necessary.

75g unsalted butter
1kg onions, finely sliced
2 garlic cloves, sliced
a small bunch of thyme
1 bay leaf
500ml French cider
1.5 litres Chicken Stock (see page 44)
125ml crème fraîche
4 tablespoons chopped chives
sea salt and freshly ground white pepper

Melt the butter in a heavy-based saucepan, add the onions and garlic and sweat until softened but not coloured. Add the thyme and bay leaf. Turn the heat up, pour in the cider and boil until reduced by half. Add the chicken stock and bring to the boil. Skim off any impurities from the surface, reduce to a simmer and cook for 45 minutes.

Remove the pan from the heat, take out the thyme and bay and discard them. Purée half the soup in a blender or food processor and then pour it through a fine sieve back into the pan, giving a rustic finish to the soup. Add the crème fraîche and bring back to the boil. Adjust the seasoning and check the consistency, which should be the thickness of single cream.

Pour the soup into bowls and sprinkle the chopped chives on top. We serve this with hot baguette and lots of Normandy butter.

VELOUTÉ OF POTIMARRON PUMPKIN
WITH ROAST CHESTNUTS AND CEPS

Serves 6

Potimarron pumpkins are much smaller than regular ones and you get an intense flavour from them without needing to cook off the water, as the flesh is quite dry. They are starting to become more readily available in the UK now. If you can't find one, look out for Ironbark instead.

400g Potimarron pumpkin, peeled, deseeded and roughly cut into 3cm pieces
100ml olive oil, plus 1 teaspoon olive oil
70g unsalted butter
¼ Spanish onion, finely diced
700ml Chicken Stock (see page 44)
200ml milk
2 large fresh ceps
12 chestnuts, roasted and peeled
1 tablespoon chopped curly parsley
2 teaspoons pumpkin seed oil
sea salt and freshly ground white pepper

Put the pumpkin flesh on a baking tray and roll it in the 100ml of olive oil. Place in an oven preheated to 160°C/Gas Mark 3 and bake for 1 hour, until tender.

Melt the butter in a saucepan, add the onion and sweat gently for 5 minutes, until softened but not coloured. Add the roasted pumpkin to the pan along with the chicken stock, bring to the boil and simmer for 5 minutes. Remove from the heat and add the milk. Purée the soup, in batches, in a blender or food processor and then pass it through a fine sieve into a clean pan. Reheat gently and season with salt and pepper.

Clean any loose dirt from the ceps with a pastry brush, give them a quick rinse in cold water and then pat dry. Trim 1cm off the stalks, then cut the ceps into 5mm-thick slices. Cut the chestnuts into quarters.

Heat the remaining teaspoon of olive oil in a frying pan, add the ceps and sauté over a high heat until golden on each side. Season with salt and pepper. Add the chestnuts to the pan to warm through, then finally add the chopped parsley.

To serve, pour the soup into soup bowls, spoon the ceps and chestnuts on top and finish with a drizzle of pumpkin seed oil.

JERUSALEM ARTICHOKE VELOUTÉ WITH TRUFFLE BUTTER AND MUSHROOM BRIOCHE

Serves 4

This is a signature dish from André Garrett, head chef at Windows. Jerusalem artichokes are one of our favourite vegetables and, together with truffle, this is a fantastically successful marriage of two tubers.

1kg Jerusalem artichokes
juice of 1 lemon
1 tablespoon olive oil
150g unsalted butter
½ onion, sliced
350ml milk
250ml whipping cream
12 slices from a small block of good aged Parmesan cheese
12 slices of black winter truffle, around 20g in total
sea salt and freshly ground white pepper

For the brioches
250g strong white flour
5g fine sea salt
20g caster sugar
15g fresh yeast
3 free-range eggs, lightly beaten
150g soft unsalted butter
1 tablespoon olive oil
1 shallot, finely sliced
½ garlic clove, finely chopped
200g mixed wild mushrooms, finely chopped
10g dried cep powder
1 free-range egg yolk, beaten with 1 tablespoon milk and a pinch of salt, to glaze

For the truffle butter
150g softened good-quality unsalted butter
1–2 teaspoons sea salt
3 teaspoons black truffle oil
3 grinds of black pepper
25–30g fresh winter black truffle, finely chopped

First make the brioches. Place the flour, salt, sugar and yeast in the bowl of an electric stand mixer fitted with a dough hook attachment and mix on a low speed just to amalgamate. Gradually beat in the eggs and beat on a fairly high speed until the mixture starts to come away from the sides of the bowl. Add the softened butter a little at time and beat for 4–5 minutes to develop a smooth, elastic dough. Cover with a damp cloth and leave until doubled in size.

Meanwhile, heat the olive oil in a saucepan over a medium heat, add the shallot and garlic and sweat for 3–4 minutes, until soft. Add the wild mushrooms, increase the heat and cook for 6–8 minutes, until the liquid that the mushrooms give off has evaporated. Season with salt and pepper, then set aside to cool.

Knock back the risen dough and roll it out on a lightly floured surface to a rectangle about 3mm thick. Dust with the cep powder and spread with the cooled mushroom mixture. Roll up like a Swiss roll and cut into 24 pieces, each about 3cm thick. Drop them into 2 buttered and floured 12-cup muffin tins, cover with a damp cloth and leave until doubled in size.

Brush each brioche with a good coating of the egg glaze and then place the tins in an oven preheated to 180°C/Gas Mark 4. Bake for 12–15 minutes, until the brioches are golden and sound hollow when turned out and tapped on the base. Leave to cool on a wire rack.

Peel the artichokes and slice quite thinly to ensure quick cooking. While preparing, drop the pieces into a bowl of cold water containing the lemon juice to prevent discoloration.

Place the olive oil and half the butter in a large, heavy-based pan set over a medium heat. When hot, add the onion, cover and sweat until soft but not coloured. Add the artichokes and continue to sweat for 3 minutes, then pour in the milk and bring to a simmer. Cook until the artichokes are soft and starting to break down. Add the cream, then remove the pan from the heat. Dice the remaining butter. Purée the soup, in small batches, in a blender or food processor until smooth, adding the diced butter a few pieces at a time to enrich while blending; it should have a light, creamy consistency. Pass the soup through a fine sieve and season with salt and pepper

To make the truffle butter, put all the ingredients in a bowl and beat with an electric mixer on medium speed for 4 minutes. Turn up to high speed and beat for another 30 seconds. You could serve the butter shaped into quenelles (ovals), made using 2 tablespoons dipped in hot water – do this in advance and keep in a cool place – or put it in a dish for everyone to help themselves at the table.

To serve, gently reheat the soup and adjust the seasoning. Pour into soup bowls, garnish with 3 slices each of Parmesan and truffle and accompany with the brioches and truffle butter.

WARM OCTOPUS WITH FLAT-LEAF PARSLEY, FRENCH BEANS, RATTE POTATOES AND TOMATO TAPENADE

Serves 4

Containing paprika, olives, tomatoes and octopus, this dish is a nod to the Basque region of France. You could even serve it as a tapas dish. It's fine to use frozen octopus. In fact, freezing tenderises it and a lot of chefs freeze fresh octopus specifically to improve the texture and flavour.

1kg octopus, cleaned
500ml Court Bouillon (see page 46)
100g waxy new potatoes, preferably Ratte
100g French beans, cut in half on the bias
80ml olive oil
smoked paprika, to taste
a knob of unsalted butter
a handful of flat-leaf parsley, chopped
¹⁄₂ lime
sea salt and freshly ground white pepper

For the tapenade
4 anchovy fillets
1 garlic clove, peeled and left whole
50g stoned green olives
50g stoned black olives
50g Oven-dried Tomatoes (see page 56)
1 tablespoon rose harissa
1 tablespoon extra virgin olive oil

To make the tapenade, place all the ingredients except the olive oil in a food processor and process until almost smooth. Stop the machine, add the oil, then whiz for 30 seconds. Transfer the mixture to a bowl and set aside.

Put the octopus in a pan, add the court bouillon and bring to a simmer. Reduce to the lowest possible heat, cover the pan and poach for 45 minutes, then remove from the heat and leave the octopus to cool in the liquid. Peel off the skin and then return the octopus to the court bouillon to keep it moist.

Cook the potatoes and French beans in separate pans of boiling salted water until tender, then drain. Slice the potatoes when they are cool enough to handle.

Take a heavy-based, shallow ovenproof dish and sprinkle with half the olive oil. Arrange the sliced potatoes over the base and season. Slice the octopus into 3–4cm pieces, arrange them on top and drizzle with a tablespoon of the court bouillon. Sprinkle with a little smoked paprika and the remaining olive oil. Place in an oven preheated to 180°C/Gas Mark 4 to heat through for 4–5 minutes.

Heat the butter in a pan and very briefly toss the beans and flat-leaf parsley together in it. Remove the octopus from the oven, squeeze a few drops of lime juice over it, then spoon the beans and parsley over the octopus. Finally, drizzle the tapenade over the top. Serve straight from the dish.

LASAGNE OF CRAB
WITH BEURRE NANTAISE

Serves 10

This is our signature dish at the Bistrot and it accounts for about 40 per cent of starter sales at every service. We once had a diner who ordered it as a starter and followed it with a double portion as a main course. The secret of its success is the lightness of the mousse and the freshness of the crab – be sure either to buy a large, live cock crab and cook it yourself or to use good fresh crab meat, not pasteurised.

1 quantity of Pasta Dough (see page 52)

For the mousse
400g fresh scallops (white part only)
480ml double cream
a pinch each of sea salt and cayenne
    pepper
650g fresh white crab meat

For the sauce
1 shallot, finely diced
200g unsalted butter, chilled and diced
50ml white wine
25ml white wine vinegar
50ml water
100ml Chicken Stock (see page 44)
25ml double cream
1 tablespoon finely chopped chives
sea salt and freshly ground white pepper

Roll the pasta out on a lightly floured surface until it is thin enough to go through the thickest setting on a pasta machine. Feed the dough through the machine, reducing the setting by one notch each time, until it is thin enough for you to see your fingers through it – this may well take 8–10 rolls through the machine.

Cut the pasta sheets into manageable lengths, about 30cm. Blanch them separately in a large pan of boiling salted water for 1 minute, then plunge into iced water and leave for 1 minute. Drain in a colander and lay out on a work surface. Using a metal ring 6cm in diameter, cut out 30 rounds. Lay out on a baking tray covered with cling film and store in the fridge.

For the mousse, place the bowl of a food processor in the freezer for 1 hour so it is thoroughly chilled, then blitz the scallop flesh in it for 3–4 minutes, scraping down the sides with a plastic spatula 3 or 4 times, until thoroughly puréed. With the machine running, slowly add half the double cream. Season with salt and cayenne pepper, then add the remainder of the cream a little faster. Transfer the mixture to a bowl and fold in the white crab meat. Taste and adjust the seasoning.

To assemble the lasagnes, place 1 disc of pasta in the bottom of each of ten 6cm metal rings, 4.5cm deep. Half fill each ring with some of the scallop and crab mixture, then add another pasta disc. Spoon some of the remaining scallop and crab mixture into each ring and then top with a final disc of pasta. Refrigerate the lasagnes while you make the sauce.

To make the sauce, cook the shallot in a little of the butter in a small pan until soft but not coloured. Add the white wine, vinegar and water and simmer until reduced to a thick, syrupy consistency. Add the chicken stock and boil until reduced by half, then add the double cream and boil for 1 minute. Whisk in the cold butter a little at a time, maintaining the heat in the sauce as you go. Adjust the seasoning and keep warm.

Put the lasagnes in a steamer and cook for 12 minutes, then transfer each one to a serving bowl. Run a small knife around the inside of each metal ring and remove it.

Add the chives to the sauce, spoon it over the lasagnes and serve.

MARINATED SCALLOPS WITH NOIRMOUTIER POTATOES, JERUSALEM ARTICHOKES AND MÂCHE

Serves 4

Noirmoutier potatoes are grown in sandy soil near the sea, rather like Jersey Royal potatoes. Chris had this dish cooked for him by a vigneronne, or vineyard owner's wife, near Bordeaux and enjoyed it so much he brought the recipe back with him.

6 extra-large scallops, preferably diver-caught
4 Jerusalem artichokes
8 Noirmoutier potatoes
2 tablespoons Simple Vinaigrette (see page 50)
150g mâche (lamb's lettuce)
sea salt
1 tablespoon finely chopped chives, to garnish

For the marinade
100ml extra virgin olive oil, plus extra for drizzling
40ml lemon juice
25g shallots, finely diced
20g distilled malt vinegar
finely grated zest of $1/2$ lemon
65g caster sugar

Slice each scallop horizontally into 3, giving a total of 18 round discs about 3–4mm thick. Place on a tray covered with cling film and chill in the fridge.

Peel the Jerusalem artichokes and potatoes and then cut them into discs the same size as the scallops. Steam the potatoes and artichokes separately until completely tender, with no bite at all. Leave to cool, then roll them in a little of the vinaigrette and season with a little salt.

Whisk all the ingredients for the marinade together in a small bowl and season with a pinch of salt.

Immediately before serving, paint the scallops with the marinade, using a pastry brush. Once marinated, they should be served within 2 or 3 minutes.

Lightly toss the mâche in the remaining vinaigrette and arrange in a rosette shape in the centre of each serving plate. Place the scallops, potatoes and artichokes around alternately and finish with a slice of scallop in the middle. Sprinkle a little sea salt and the chives over the scallops and then drizzle a little olive oil around the edge of each plate.

SCOTTISH SCALLOPS JUSTE TIÈDE WITH VANILLA, LIME AND CAVIAR

Serves 4

This is a lovely light dish. It's important that the scallops are served just warm. Try to get hold of Scottish scallops – they are simply the best in the world.

8 large, diver-caught scallops in the shell (ask your fishmonger to open them for you)
2 limes
2 teaspoons extra virgin olive oil
1 small tin (about 30g) of farmed caviar, preferably Italian Baeri or French Aquitaine

For the sauce
1 tablespoon olive oil
1 large shallot, finely diced
2 sprigs of thyme
1 sprig of tarragon
100ml dry white wine
1 vanilla pod
finely grated zest and juice of 1 lime
100ml whipping cream
200g unsalted butter, diced
sea salt and freshly ground black pepper

For the sauce, heat the olive oil in a pan, add the shallot and sweat until soft but not coloured. Add the thyme, tarragon and wine and simmer until the wine has reduced to a syrup. Slit open the vanilla pod and scrape out the seeds. Add them to the pan with the pod and then add the lime juice. Simmer until reduced by half, then pour in the cream and return to the boil. Whisk the butter into the sauce a few pieces at a time, being careful not to let the sauce boil or it will separate. Remove the vanilla pod and discard. Add the lime zest to the sauce and season with salt and pepper. You should have a creamy sauce, thick enough to coat the back of a spoon, with the flavour given a lift by the lime and vanilla.

Clean away the frill and sac from around the scallops, wash them in plenty of iced water containing a pinch of salt and then drain on kitchen paper. Slice each scallop horizontally into 3 and lay on a clean tray. Finely grate the lime zest straight on to the scallops, season with sea salt and drizzle with the olive oil. Leave to marinate for a few minutes before serving.

Lay the scallops on 4 plates and place under a very low grill to warm but not cook fully. Warm the sauce through, if necessary, and whisk to lighten it. Drizzle the sauce over each scallop, then spoon a small scoop of caviar on to each one. Serve immediately.

Fishing for crab and lobster in Dorset.

GRAVADLAX OF SALMON WITH SALAD OF QUAIL'S EGGS AND HERBS

Serves 4

This is a great dish to prepare at home and also makes a fine addition to a picnic. It's very straightforward and the salmon has to be done in advance, so there is very little last-minute preparation to worry about.

400g piece of salmon fillet, cut from the centre of the fish, skin on
100g fine sea salt
50g caster sugar
finely grated zest of 2 lemons
50g bunch of dill, leaves finely chopped, stalks chopped separately
1/2 teaspoon Dijon mustard

For the quail's egg and herb salad
10 quail's eggs
10g each of chervil, dill, tarragon, flat-leaf parsley and chives
1 punnet of shiso cress
30g frisée lettuce, white part only
1 tablespoon Classic Vinaigrette (see page 50)
sea salt and freshly ground black pepper

Remove any pin bones from the salmon with a pair of tweezers, then use a very sharp knife to score the skin 6 times, cutting 1mm deep. Mix the salt, sugar, lemon zest and chopped dill stalks together.

On a work surface, lay out a piece of cling film that is 4 times the size of the salmon. Lay another piece of cling film on top and flatten with a clean, dry cloth to expel any air. Pour half of the salt mixture on to the cling film and spread it out so it is exactly the same size as the salmon.

Place the raw salmon on top of this and then pour the remainder of the salt mixture on top. Carefully bring up the cling film around the edges and wrap the salmon up like a parcel, so it is quite tight. Leave to marinate in the fridge for 6 hours.

Unwrap the salmon, discard the salt mixture and gently wash under cold running water. Pat dry with some kitchen paper or a clean cloth. Remove the skin with a filleting knife, then spread the Dijon mustard over the other side of the salmon. Sprinkle the chopped dill on top, re-wrap tightly in cling film and chill for 1 hour.

For the salad, bring a small pan of water to the boil, add the quail's eggs and boil for 2 1/2 minutes. Drain and refresh in iced water. When cold, peel carefully. Cut them in half and season with a little sea salt and black pepper.

Divide the chervil and dill into small sprigs and the tarragon and parsley into single leaves. Cut the chives into 1cm batons. Cut the shiso cress with a pair of scissors. Put all the herbs and cress in a bowl with the frisée lettuce.

With a sharp serrated carving knife, cut the salmon into 20 thin slices. Lay 5 in the middle of each serving plate and arrange the quail's eggs in the centre. Toss the salad with the vinaigrette and place on top of the eggs.

MATJES HERRINGS WITH A WARM POTATO AND SHALLOT SALAD

Serves 4

Another French brasserie classic, inspired by the famous Brasserie Lipp in Paris. We have always been intrigued to see that many of the waiters there wear a badge bearing a number. On our last visit, we finally discovered that this related to length of service, with the waiter who has been there longest achieving number one.

1 free-range egg
300g waxy new potatoes, preferably Ratte
2 shallots, finely chopped
4 tablespoons extra virgin olive oil
8 Matjes herrings
2 tablespoons finely chopped chives
4 sprigs of flat-leaf parsley
sea salt and mignonette pepper

Hard-boil the egg, then drain, cool under cold running water and peel. Separate the yolk and white and press them through a sieve into separate bowls. Set aside.

Cook the potatoes in a pan of boiling salted water until tender, then drain. Peel and slice them while still warm and toss with the shallots, olive oil and some seasoning.

Arrange the potato mixture in a mound in the centre of 4 serving plates and place the herring fillets on the top. Sprinkle the herring with the sieved egg white and yolk and then scatter over the chives. Finish with a sprig of parsley and serve.

CURED SALMON WITH CRAB, FENNEL AND AVOCADO CREAM

Serves 6

A recipe inspired by Anton Mosimann. Full of light, fresh flavours, it's ideal for a dinner party, as you can plate the salmon in advance and just add the garnish before serving. We use Loch Duart organic salmon, which, although farmed, is as close to wild as you'll get.

700g piece of organic salmon fillet from the thick end, skin on
500g rock salt
500g caster sugar
200g lemongrass, finely chopped
25g white peppercorns
25g coriander seeds
1/2 bunch of coriander, chopped
finely grated zest of 1 lemon
sea salt and freshly ground white pepper

For the lemon dressing
1 tablespoon olive oil
1 shallot, finely diced
finely grated zest and juice of 1 lemon
25ml Chardonnay vinegar or white wine vinegar
50ml Lemon Oil (see page 57)

For the avocado cream
2 very ripe avocados
1/2 teaspoon lemon juice

To serve
1 head of fennel, trimmed
50g white crab meat, preferably from the south coast of England
1 tablespoon chopped chives
a little olive oil
10g farmed caviar, such as Sevruga (optional)
a little coriander cress or a few coriander leaves

Clean any scales off the fish skin with the back of a large knife, then score the skin at 3cm intervals, being careful not to cut too far into the salmon flesh. Wash the salmon, check for any remaining bones and then place it in a deep dish. Mix together the rock salt, sugar, lemongrass, spices, coriander and lemon zest and sprinkle this mixture over the fish. Cover with cling film, place in the fridge and leave for 12 hours, turning after 6 hours.

Remove the salmon from the cure, rinse well and pat dry. Place on a plate, cover with a clean cloth and leave in the fridge for 2 hours. Then use a long, thin knife to slice the salmon down and off the skin, leaving the dark blood line on the skin. Arrange the slices on each serving plate in a circle, cover with cling film and return to the fridge.

To make the lemon dressing, heat the olive oil in a small pan, add the shallot and sweat until softened but not coloured. Add the lemon zest and juice and simmer until the liquid has reduced by half. Add the vinegar and simmer until reduced by a third. Remove from the heat and whisk in the lemon oil. Adjust the seasoning and then chill.

For the avocado cream, halve, stone, peel and chop the avocados. Toss with the lemon juice, then place in a food processor or blender and blend to a smooth purée; if it is too thick to blend, you can add a few drops of water to help keep it moving. Season with sea salt and place in a piping bag (it's not absolutely necessary to pipe the avocado cream but storing it in a piping bag helps it keep its colour). Place in the fridge.

Cut the fennel lengthwise in half and shred it very finely, preferably with a mandolin. Toss the fennel with a teaspoon of the lemon dressing, season with sea salt and set aside.

To serve, spoon a teaspoon of lemon dressing on to each portion of salmon and rub it all over the fish. Put the crab in a small bowl with the chives, a little olive oil and some salt and pepper and mix well. Sprinkle the crab over the plates of salmon, place the fennel on top, then add 5 dots per plate of the avocado purée, followed by the caviar, if using. Garnish with the coriander and then serve.

ESCABECHE OF YELLOWFIN TUNA WITH AUBERGINE PURÉE AND HERBS

Serves 6

This is a signature dish at La Chapelle – it's not been off the menu since we opened. Line-caught yellowfin tuna is a more sustainable fish than the endangered blue fin. Although this recipe looks complex, the escabeche actually benefits from being made two or three days in advance, as the flavours mellow.

2 x 250g pieces of yellowfin tuna loin, 15cm long and 4.5cm wide
1 tablespoon olive oil
$^1/_2$ teaspoon Dijon mustard
10 coriander leaves, roughly chopped
10g tarragon, roughly chopped
10g chervil, roughly chopped
10g flat-leaf parsley, roughly chopped
sea salt and freshly ground white pepper

For the escabeche
150g new carrots
400ml olive oil
1 small onion, finely sliced
1 small red onion, finely sliced
3 garlic cloves, finely sliced
150ml white wine
2 tablespoons white wine vinegar
30 coriander seeds, roasted in a dry frying pan and then crushed
a pinch of saffron strands
juice of $^1/_2$ lemon

For the tuna marinade
300ml still mineral water
200g Maldon sea salt
200g caster sugar
finely grated zest and juice of 1 lemon
3 black peppercorns, crushed
3 coriander seeds, crushed
10 coriander leaves

For the aubergine purée
1 aubergine
1 garlic clove, finely sliced
2 tablespoons olive oil
leaves from a sprig of thyme
1 tablespoon crème fraîche
juice of $^1/_2$ lemon
a pinch of ground cumin

For the herb salad
30g frisée lettuce, white part only
10g chervil sprigs
10 small tarragon leaves
10g flat-leaf parsley leaves
2 tablespoons Simple Vinaigrette (see page 50)
10g coriander cress

First prepare the escabeche. Slice the carrots 1mm thick at a 45-degree angle, using a mandolin if you have one. Put them in a heavy-based pan, add 100ml of the olive oil and cook gently for 5 minutes, until they start to soften. Add the onions and garlic and cook for a further 5 minutes or until the onions have begun to collapse. Add the white wine, vinegar, coriander seeds, saffron and the rest of the olive oil. Bring to the boil, then reduce the heat to a simmer and cook for $1^1/_2$ hours. Remove from the heat and leave to cool, then add the lemon juice and season with salt and pepper.

For the tuna marinade, put the water in a pan, add the salt and sugar and heat, stirring, until they dissolve. Remove from the heat and cool slightly, then stir in the remaining ingredients. Leave to cool completely, then chill.

Place the tuna in the marinade and leave for $1^1/_2$ hours. Remove from the marinade and rinse under cold water, then pat dry with kitchen paper. Wrap each piece of tuna tightly in cling film to form a sausage shape and chill for 1 hour. Unwrap the tuna.

(continued on page 94)

(continued from page 92)

Heat a non-stick frying pan until very hot, add the olive oil, then add the tuna and sear it all over – this should only take about 20 seconds on each side, rolling it constantly in the pan. Transfer to kitchen paper to drain. Spread the outside of the tuna with the Dijon mustard to give a thin coating and then roll it in the chopped herbs. Wrap each piece tightly in cling film to form a sausage and tie with string at both ends. Place in the fridge for at least 3 hours to firm up.

For the aubergine purée, cut the aubergine lengthwise in half, score the flesh in a criss-cross fashion and insert the garlic slices. Place cut-side down on a hot griddle pan and cook for 5–8 minutes, until the flesh is almost black. Transfer the aubergines to a baking tray lined with foil, drizzle with the olive oil, sprinkle with the thyme and season with salt and pepper. Place in an oven preheated to 160°C/Gas Mark 3. Bake for 1 hour 20 minutes, then remove from the oven and leave to cool. Scoop out the flesh and purée in a blender or food processor until smooth. Pass the mixture through a fine sieve into a mixing bowl and whisk in the crème fraîche, lemon juice and cumin. Season to taste with salt and pepper.

To serve, slice the tuna with a sharp serrated knife into 3mm-thick discs, allowing 5 per portion – remember to remove the cling film after you have cut the discs. Stir the escabeche well, because the oil and vinegar will have separated, then place a large tablespoon of it in the middle of each serving plate. With a teaspoon, place the aubergine purée on the plates. Arrange the tuna slices neatly on top of the escabeche.

For the salad, in a small bowl, toss the frisée and herbs with the vinaigrette. Take a little of the coriander cress and place on top of the tuna, then arrange the salad at the top of each plate. Finally drizzle a little of the escabeche around.

ENDIVE SALAD WITH MOZZARELLA, BLOOD ORANGES AND SPECK

Serves 4

A delicious salad, best eaten between January and March, when blood oranges are in season. The citrus juice cuts the fattiness of the speck.

2 heads of red endive
1 radicchio
1 radicchio di Treviso
2 x 125g balls of unpasteurised buffalo
   mozzarella, each cut into 6 slices
2 tablespoons extra virgin olive oil
8 very thin slices of speck
2 blood oranges, peeled and divided into
   segments
2 tablespoons pomegranate seeds
12 sprigs of chervil
sea salt and freshly ground white pepper

For the dressing
1 teaspoon honey
1 teaspoon Dijon mustard
25ml balsamic vinegar
75ml olive oil

To make the dressing, mix the honey, mustard and balsamic vinegar together, then gradually whisk in the olive oil. Season with a pinch of salt and pepper.

Cut the bottom off the endive and radicchios and separate the leaves. Lightly toss the leaves with a little of the dressing.

Drizzle the mozzarella with the olive oil and season with salt and pepper.

Make a small bed of leaves on each serving plate, lay a slice of speck on top, then 3 slices of mozzarella and place a few orange segments around. Curl the remaining slice of speck on top and scatter the pomegranate seeds over the salad. Garnish with the chervil sprigs and finish by drizzling a tablespoon of dressing around.

The new season's garlic harvest at Rungis Market, just outside Paris.

BALLOTINE OF MACKEREL AND TARTARE WITH SOFT-BOILED QUAIL'S EGGS AND BONE MARROW AND PARSLEY CUSTARD

Serves 4

Here, a single type of fish is treated in two very contrasting ways. The bone marrow custard works surprisingly well with mackerel, as it is a very meaty fish. The best mackerel are Cornish line-caught in the spring. Ask your fishmonger to fillet and pin bone them for you if you are not confident.

2 handfuls of coarse sea salt
finely grated zest of 1 lemon
4 medium mackerel, filleted, pin bones removed
4 quail's eggs
12 small parsley leaves
finely grated zest of 1 lime
2 tablespoons rice wine vinegar
2 tablespoons extra virgin olive oil, plus extra for drizzling

For the bone marrow and parsley custard
50g bone marrow
250ml whipping cream
30g flat-leaf parsley leaves
2 free-range egg yolks
sea salt and freshly ground white pepper

For the pickled kohlrabi
1 kohlrabi
200ml still mineral water
20ml rice wine vinegar
20g dried seaweed

Place the bone marrow in a container of cold water and leave to soak in the fridge for 24 hours.

Next, prepare the kohlrabi. Peel it and slice in half, then use a mandolin or a sharp knife to slice it very thinly. Cut out the slices with a round cutter to even the shape. Put the water, vinegar and seaweed in a blender and blend on high speed. Strain the mixture through a fine sieve over the kohlrabi and leave in the fridge overnight.

Place the coarse sea salt on a large tray and sprinkle the lemon zest on top. Place the fish fillets skin-side down on the mixture and leave for 30 minutes. Brush off the salt and, with a sharp filleting knife, skin the fish fillets – the skin will have hardened and it should come away easily, leaving behind a silvery snakeskin pattern.

Lay out 2 large pieces of cling film on a work surface and place 2 of the mackerel fillets on each piece, head to tail. Starting at a short end, roll each pair of fillets into a small sausage shape, keeping them wrapped tightly in the cling film, then tie at each end. Bring a large pan of water to just below boiling point, remove it from the heat and drop in the fish ballotines.

Poach for 4 minutes, then remove from the water and place in a large bowl of iced water. Leave for 4 hours.

Bring a pan of water to the boil for the quail's eggs, add a pinch of salt and then gently place the eggs in the pan. Cook for $2^{1}/_{2}$ minutes, then remove the eggs and place straight into iced water. When the eggs are cold, peel carefully and set aside.

Bring a pan of water to the boil, add a pinch of salt and drop in the 12 small parsley leaves. Boil for 45 seconds, then drain the parsley through a colander and immediately place it in some iced water to chill. Drain before using.

Lay the remaining mackerel fillets on a clean tray and place in the freezer for 20–30 minutes, until set firm (this makes it easier to dice them evenly – do not let them freeze solid). Using a sharp knife, cut the fish into 5mm dice. Place in a small bowl and sprinkle over the lime zest, followed by the vinegar and olive oil. Mix well, then correct the seasoning to your taste with lime juice, more vinegar and sea salt. Set aside in the fridge, but do not make this more than 30 minutes before serving.

(continued on page 100)

(continued from page 98)

For the bone marrow and parsley custard, drain the bone marrow, then roughly chop it into cubes about 5mm in size. Bring the cream to a simmer in a pan, add the chopped bone marrow and simmer for 3–4 minutes. Transfer to a blender or food processor, add the flat-leaf parsley leaves and blend until smooth and a good green colour. Add the egg yolks and blend again, then return to the pan. Cook gently over a medium heat, stirring, until the custard is thick enough to coat the back of a spoon – do not let it boil or the custard will split. Pass the custard through a fine sieve and season to taste.

Slice the mackerel ballotines across into 5cm sections, peel off the cling film and place the portions of ballotine on 4 serving plates. Arrange the pickled kohlrabi (about 3 slices per portion), mackerel tartare and quail's eggs around, then at the last moment pour around the warm custard. Drizzle a little olive oil over the mackerel and garnish with the parsley leaves.

SALADE LYONNAISE

Serves 4

Lyons is famous for its saladiers – little bowls of salad ingredients that you can make up your own salad with. Consequently, there are many versions of salade lyonnaise. In this one, the sausage, egg, fish and beans come together to make a beautifully balanced dish. Serve as a substantial starter or a light main course.

12 slices of baguette, cut about 2mm thick on the bias
olive oil, for brushing
100g Morteau sausage
200g waxy new potatoes, preferably Ratte
4 free-range eggs
50g fine French beans
1 curly endive, yellow part only
2 tablespoons Classic Vinaigrette (see page 50)
4 Matjes herrings, cut into diamonds or lozenges
3 tablespoons chopped chives
3 tablespoons chopped curly parsley
sea salt and mignonette pepper

Brush the baguette slices with olive oil. Place on a baking tray and bake in an oven preheated to 160°C/Gas Mark 3 for 5–8 minutes, until golden. Remove from the oven and leave to cool.

Put the sausage in a pan, cover with cold water and bring to the boil. Remove from the heat and leave to cool in the liquid, then drain and slice.

Cook the potatoes in a pan of boiling salted water until tender, then drain. Peel and slice them while still warm and then sprinkle with a little salt.

Boil the eggs for 6–8 minutes, then drain, run under cold water and peel. Cut them into quarters. Blanch the French beans in boiling salted water for 2 minutes, then drain and refresh in cold water.

Toss the curly endive and French beans in the vinaigrette and divide between 4 serving plates. Place the boiled egg quarters on top and then add the Matjes herrings. Arrange the sausage slices attractively on the plate, add the potatoes and sprinkle with the baguette croûtons. To finish, season with a little salt and pepper, then scatter over the chives and parsley.

PISSALADIÈRE WITH ROCKET SALAD

Serves 4

Pissaladière is the famous street snack of Nice, where you can buy it wrapped in paper and eat it as you wander around the narrow streets of the Old Town. It's one of the first dishes we put on the menu at the Café à Vin, and it works perfectly with a glass of wine. You could also cut it into small squares and serve as a canapé.

1 quantity of Pizza Dough (see page 53)
24 smoked anchovy fillets, cut lengthwise
   into quarters
30 stoned black olives, cut in half
a small sprig of thyme
a large bunch of wild rocket
extra virgin olive oil

For the onions
40g unsalted butter
2 large onions, very finely sliced
sea salt and freshly ground white pepper

To cook the onions, melt the butter in a heavy-based saucepan, add the onions and some salt and pepper and cook slowly (with a tight-fitting lid on initially, then when the onions have collapsed, without the lid) over a low heat for about $1^1/_2$ hours, until golden brown and very soft. Remove from the heat and leave to cool.

Roll the dough out into four 20cm x 8cm rectangles about 2mm thick. Prick them all over with a fork and place on a baking sheet. Spread the onions over the bases, leaving a 1cm border all around. Arrange the anchovies in a crisscross pattern on top, putting the olive halves in the gaps, then sprinkle over the thyme leaves.

We cook these in a wood-fired oven at 350°C for $2^1/_2$ minutes; at home, preheat your oven to 250°C/Gas Mark 10 and cook on the top shelf on a pizza tray or, even better, a baking stone, for 5 minutes, until the edges are golden.

Lightly toss the rocket in a little olive oil and arrange on top of the pissaladière. Finish by adding a drizzle of olive oil.

THE CARVED DUCK

Because we were taught to cook in a strictly classical manner, we always try to ensure that there are elements on the menu that reflect this. We particularly like tableside work by the waiters, since we feel it adds theatre, plus an opportunity for waiter and guest to interact.

One such dish was a roast duck, served for two and carved at the table. First the waiter had to remove the legs and return them to the kitchen to cook a little more, so they could be served later in the meal, beautifully arranged on a fresh herb salad. The next task was to take off the breast, carve it and lay it over a Tatin of endive with a jus made from the liver and duck heart poured around the plate. Simple ...

All waiters develop their own style, as do chefs. One waiter had the increasingly annoying habit of taking the legs off with the animation of someone conducting the Royal Philharmonic Orchestra before treating the breast with equal gusto. The climax was a swashbuckling raising of the carcass high in the air while crying, '*Voilà!*' It should be said at this point that the duck was a *canard au sang*, which meant a fairly bloody carcass.

On the fateful day, service was in full flight when a group of waiters came running into the kitchen trying desperately to suppress their laughter. This break in discipline drew my attention and needed to be stopped. I asked the senior member of the pack what on earth was going on, and he managed to blurt it out. The flamboyant waiter in question had been carving the duck for a large table of eight guests. All was going well until he decided to end with a more than usually enthusiastic '*Voilà!*' and the carcass left the end of his fork, sailed through the air and landed in a customer's handbag. The staff attending the table froze, not knowing what to do, until they slowly realised that no one had noticed. This, they thought, was their opportunity to make a hasty retreat to the kitchen.

'Where is it now?' I demanded.

'Still in Madame's bag,' came the reply.

The service was going on all around us with its usual mayhem and now I had this to deal with too.

I summoned the manager, who had an idea: 'We will remove it without Madame knowing,' he said.

This struck me as nonsense but he insisted it was perfectly possible. 'The culprit is vertically challenged, so he is near the ground anyway. He can pass by the table, swoop down and try to retrieve the duck.'

If it had happened on television I would have thought it hilarious, but right then it was the worst thing that had ever happened in my career. 'We need to discreetly tell the guest,' I said.

'Too late,' came the reply, 'he is on the first sweep!'

The hapless waiter was, of course, caught with his hand in the bag clutching the bloody, fatty duck carcass, and it took a while to convince Madame that he wasn't a pickpocket but was simply trying to retrieve his duck. The outcome? The handbag was Louis Vuitton, it cost our insurers a lot of money and us a lot of soul searching. The person responsible was banned from ever carving again and, from that day on, showmanship was kept to a minimum.

PISSALADIÈRE WITH SNAILS, HERB BUTTER AND BACON

Serves 8

We used to have special escargot dishes at the Bistrot but when they all got broken we decided to serve the snails like this instead. A pissaladière is a good vehicle for other ingredients – we have paired it with confit chicken wings; sliced rare tuna with spring onion and coriander; caramelised endive and roast duck.

48 tinned Burgundy snails, drained
2 tablespoons olive oil
6 onions, finely sliced
2 garlic cloves, finely sliced
4 sprigs of thyme
2 plum tomatoes, skinned, deseeded and diced
250g Puff Pastry (see page 53)
2 free-range egg yolks, lightly beaten
10 anchovy fillets, cut into matchsticks
10 Provençal olives, stoned and cut into quarters
2 rashers of unsmoked streaky bacon, cut into thin strips

For the snail butter
200g slightly softened salted butter
20g garlic cloves, finely chopped
75g flat-leaf parsley leaves
15g ground almonds
25ml Pernod
a small pinch of cayenne pepper

For the garnish
1 tablespoon chives, snipped into 1cm lengths
1 tablespoon snipped chervil
1 teaspoon snipped tarragon
1 tablespoon snipped flat-leaf parsley
2 tablespoons Brown Chicken Jus (see page 45) (optional)

Beat all the ingredients for the snail butter together, then transfer the mixture to a disposable piping bag. Snip the tip off and pipe 48 marble-sized pieces on to a sheet of greaseproof paper. While the butter is still soft, place a snail into the centre of each piece. Refrigerate until firm.

Heat a heavy-based pan over a medium heat, then add the olive oil, onions, garlic and thyme and cook, stirring, until the onions start to colour. Cover the pan and cook, stirring occasionally, until the onions are soft and a uniform golden colour. Add the tomatoes and cook for a few minutes longer, until the tomatoes start to meld with the onions.

Roll the pastry out on a lightly floured surface into a 60cm x 20cm rectangle about 3mm thick. Cut out 8 smaller rectangles from the pastry sheet, each 15cm x 10cm. Fold the edges of each pastry rectangle over by 3mm to form a border, then decoratively crimp it on the diagonal with the back of a knife. Heavily prick the base of the pastry rectangles all over with a fork, then brush with egg yolk. Leave to rest in the fridge for 1 hour, then remove and brush again with egg yolk before returning to the fridge for a further 30 minutes.

Place the pastry rectangles on a baking sheet and bake in an oven preheated to 200°C/Gas Mark 6 for 10–12 minutes, until golden. Remove from the oven, transfer to a wire rack and leave to cool completely.

Spread the onion mixture over each tart base, then arrange the anchovies on top in a criss-cross pattern and sprinkle with the olive quarters.

Scatter the bacon strips over a baking tray and cook under a hot grill until crisp. Drain off any fat, place the bacon on kitchen paper, set aside and keep warm.

To serve, divide the snails enrobed in butter between 8 small heatproof dishes and place under a hot grill for 6–8 minutes, until the butter is bubbling and has turned a good golden colour. Meanwhile, put the tarts into a hot oven for a couple of minutes to warm through. Place the warmed tarts on plates and tip each portion of snails in their butter over a tart. Sprinkle with the bacon and snipped herbs, then drizzle over the chicken jus, if using.

Choosing crayfish, Rungis Market.

BAYONNE HAM WITH CELERIAC REMOULADE

Serves 4

An absolutely classic French dish. The hallmark of a good celeriac remoulade is that it should taste noticeably mustardy, to give it punch.

¹/₄ celeriac
75ml Mayonnaise (see page 51)
1 tablespoon crème fraîche
1 tablespoon capers
1 teaspoon Dijon mustard
¹/₄ teaspoon English mustard
¹/₄ anchovy fillet, finely chopped
12 thin slices of Bayonne ham
4 sprigs of flat-leaf parsley
12 caper berries
a drizzle of extra virgin olive oil
sea salt and freshly ground white pepper

Peel the celeriac and cut it into thin slices on a mandolin, then cut these into fine shreds with a large knife. Place in a mixing bowl. Add the mayonnaise, crème fraîche, capers, mustards and chopped anchovy and mix well. Adjust the seasoning, adding salt and pepper if necessary.

To serve, mound the celeriac remoulade in the centre of 4 serving plates, drape the slices of Bayonne ham over it and garnish with the flat-leaf parsley and caper berries. Drizzle with a little olive oil.

PURPLE FIG SALAD WITH MOZZARELLA, BRESAOLA, ROCKET AND MINT

Serves 4

This recipe relies heavily on the figs being very ripe and the mozzarella being unpasteurised. The figs should be heavy and oozing a little syrup from the base – the time to buy them is late July to September.

2 balls of unpasteurised buffalo
   mozzarella
200g wild rocket
50g pine nuts, lightly toasted in a dry
   frying pan
20 mint leaves, roughly chopped
4 tablespoons Classic Vinaigrette (see
   page 50)
20 slices of bresaola
8 very ripe purple figs, cut into quarters
a drizzle of extra virgin olive oil
sea salt and freshly ground white pepper

Tear the mozzarella into strands and put them into a large mixing bowl with the rocket, pine nuts and mint. Toss with the vinaigrette and season with salt and pepper.

Lay the bresaola slices in the middle of each serving plate, overlapping them to form a rosette. Build the mozzarella mixture up on top of this, then place the figs around the edge. Finish with a drizzle of olive oil.

TARTE FLAMBÉE

Serves 4

This is a classic tart from Alsace. It's so simple to make but people always love it. If you can get ventreche bacon from Alsace, that is the one to use here. It's cured and smoked and has a fantastic flavour. Otherwise, any good smoked bacon will do

1 quantity of Pizza Dough (see page 53)
100ml crème fraîche
100g fromage blanc
2 pinches of freshly grated nutmeg
1 small onion, finely diced
120g smoked bacon, preferably Alsace, cut into small lardons
olive oil, for drizzling
sea salt and freshly ground white pepper

Divide the dough into 4 portions and roll out each piece into a 20cm x 8cm rectangle, about 2mm thick. Prick them all over with a fork.

Put the crème fraîche, fromage blanc, nutmeg and a little salt and pepper in a bowl and mix well. Spread this evenly over the bases, leaving a 1cm border all around, then scatter the onion and bacon over the top. We cook these in a wood-fired oven at 350°C for 2$^{1}/_{2}$ minutes; at home, preheat your oven to 250°C/Gas Mark 10 and cook on the top shelf on a pizza tray or, even better, a baking stone for 5 minutes, until the edges are golden. Cut each tart into 4 and serve immediately on wooden boards or plates, drizzled with olive oil. These must be eaten straight from the oven.

STEAK TARTARE WITH TOASTED COUNTRY BREAD

Serves 4

A lot of people use fillet of beef for this but it doesn't have the greatest flavour. We prefer rump, which is full of flavour and better value for money. Tell your butcher how you are planning to serve it and they should be able to sort you out.

500g lean beef, such as rump, chuck or
  even bavette
4 free-range egg yolks
4 slices of country bread

For the tartare dressing
50g cornichons, finely chopped
15g shallot, finely chopped
25g fine capers, chopped
30g Dijon mustard
1 anchovy, finely chopped
1/2 teaspoon paprika
2–3 drops of Tabasco sauce
5 drops of Worcestershire sauce
1 tablespoon olive oil
1 tablespoon chopped *fines herbes*
  (mixed chervil, tarragon, parsley and
  chives)
sea salt and freshly ground white pepper

Finely chop the meat into 3mm dice with a very sharp knife. Place all the ingredients for the dressing in a bowl and mix together thoroughly. Add the chopped meat and season with salt and pepper.

Divide the meat mixture into 4 portions and, using a 9cm round metal ring, mould each portion of meat into a round on a serving plate. Make an indentation in the centre of each one and place an egg yolk in it. Toast the bread and serve immediately with the steak tartare.

PORK RILLETTES WITH TOASTED COUNTRY BREAD

Serves 8-10

If you can get hold of Middle White pork, that is the one to use here. It has the best flavour and a high fat ratio, which is important for rillettes.

400g pork back fat, diced
175ml white wine
100ml water
1kg good-quality free-range pork shoulder
750g good-quality free-range pork belly
1 head of garlic, cut horizontally in half
1 largish carrot, peeled
1 onion, peeled
200g goose fat
1 teaspoon Quatre-épices (see page 58)
1 teaspoon sea salt
2 bay leaves
5 sprigs of thyme
1 sprig of rosemary

To serve
country bread, toasted
cornichons

Place the pork back fat, white wine and water in a large, heavy-based casserole and bring to a gentle boil. Reduce to a simmer and leave until the fat has melted. Add all the remaining ingredients, tying the herbs together into a bundle. Cover with a tight-fitting lid or foil, place in an oven preheated to 110°C/Gas Mark $^1/_4$ and cook for 3–4 hours, until the meat is soft enough to cut with a spoon. Remove from the oven and leave until cool enough to handle.

Discard the herbs, onion and carrot; the garlic flesh will be very soft and can be squeezed back into the mixture. Pour the contents of the pan into a bowl placed over ice, then by hand or with 2 forks, shred and rub the meat into grains. The ice helps to keep it at the right temperature, but you will need to stir the mixture fairly often, otherwise the fat will start to emulsify. Once all the meat has been shredded, you should have created a rough paste. Do not over work it, it is meant to be rough and fibrous. Adjust the seasoning and then place in the fridge to set.

Remove from the fridge 30 minutes before serving. Serve the rillettes with the toasted country bread and cornichons.

RAVIOLI OF BEEF SHIN WITH CELERIAC PURÉE AND HORSERADISH

Serves 8

This is an excellent winter dish. Shin is a relatively cheap cut but when it's marinated and cooked slowly in this way, it is tender and flavoursome.

800g beef shin
50ml vegetable oil
3 litres Brown Chicken Stock (see page 44)
1 tablespoon roughly chopped flat-leaf parsley
1 quantity of Pasta Dough (see page 52)
2 free-range egg yolks, lightly beaten
sea salt and freshly ground white pepper

For the marinade
100ml red wine
50ml port
1 carrot, roughly chopped
1 stick celery, roughly chopped
1/4 onion, roughly chopped
1/4 leek, roughly chopped
3 garlic cloves, chopped
1 sprig of thyme
1 bay leaf
2 black peppercorns, crushed

For the celeriac purée
250g celeriac, peeled and roughly diced
50g unsalted butter
130ml milk
1 tablespoon double cream
a pinch of sea salt

For the horseradish foam
75ml double cream
100ml milk
10g fresh horseradish, peeled and finely grated
a few drops of lemon juice

Mix together all the ingredients for the marinade in a bowl, add the beef shin and leave to marinate in the fridge for 24 hours.

The next day, drain the mixture in a colander with a bowl underneath to catch the liquid. In a very hot, heavy-based frying pan, sauté the beef and the vegetables from the marinade in the vegetable oil until golden brown and well caramelised. Meanwhile, pour the liquid from the marinade into a saucepan and boil until reduced by half.

Place the browned beef and vegetables in a casserole and cover with the reduced marinade and the chicken stock. Bring to the boil, cover with a lid or a piece of foil and transfer to an oven preheated to 110°C/Gas Mark 1/4. Braise for 3 1/2 hours, until the meat is really tender. Remove from the oven and leave the meat to cool in the liquid, then take the meat off the bone and set aside. Pass the cooking liquor through a fine sieve and set aside 125ml for the horseradish foam. Place the rest in a saucepan and boil until reduced to the consistency of runny honey. Remove from the heat and leave to cool.

Bind the cooked meat with the reduced cooking liquor and add the flat-leaf parsley. Adjust the seasoning and mix until the beef has broken down into fine shreds. Divide the mixture into 8 balls and chill until firm.

To make the ravioli, roll the pasta out on a lightly floured surface until it is thin enough to go through the thickest setting on a pasta machine. Feed the dough through the machine, reducing the setting by one notch each time, until it is so thin that you can see your fingers through it –

this may well take 8–10 rolls through the machine. Brush the pasta with the beaten egg yolks. Using an 11cm pastry cutter, cut out 8 discs of pasta, then cut out 8 discs with a 13.5cm cutter. Place the filling in the centre of the smaller discs, then put the remaining pasta discs on top, expelling any air and sealing by pressing with your fingers. Cut out with an 11cm pastry cutter. Place the ravioli on a tray and set aside in the fridge.

For the celeriac purée, place all the ingredients in a saucepan and bring to the boil. Reduce the heat to a simmer, cover the pan with a tight-fitting lid and cook for 20 minutes or until the celeriac is tender. Purée the mixture in a blender or food processor until smooth, then pass through a fine sieve and adjust the seasoning. Reheat gently just before serving.

To make the horseradish foam, put the cream, milk and horseradish in a small pan with the 125ml of reserved beef shin stock and simmer for 7 minutes. Season with the lemon juice and some salt and pepper, then pass through a sieve lined with a piece of muslin. Keep warm.

Cook the ravioli in a large pan of boiling salted water for 8 minutes. Remove and place on a clean cloth to drain.

Place a tablespoon of hot celeriac purée in each of 8 warm soup plates and put the ravioli on top. Whisk the warm horseradish sauce with a handheld electric blender until frothy. Spoon the horseradish foam over the ravioli and serve.

PRESSED TERRINE OF LAMB WITH ANCHOIADE DRESSING

Serves 10

This seems like a lot of work but it is a great summery starter for a party or picnic and can be made well ahead of time. Chris was inspired to create this dish by a similar one he cooked when he worked at L'Oustau de Baumanière restaurant in the South of France.

3.5kg lamb shoulder on the bone
10 garlic cloves, sliced
10 sprigs of thyme
5 stems of rosemary
50g sea salt
1 litre goose fat
500ml red wine
200ml olive oil
4 aubergines, cut lengthways into slices 5mm thick
20 button onions
30g unsalted butter
20 stoned black olives, cut in half
28 Oven-dried Tomatoes (see page 56)
4 tablespoons flat-leaf parsley leaves, blanched in boiling water for 1 minute, then drained and refreshed in iced water
sea salt and freshly ground black pepper
10 small sprigs of basil, to garnish

For the anchoiade dressing
100g stoned black olives
80g anchovies in oil, drained
6 garlic cloves, peeled
2 tablespoons Cabernet red wine vinegar
2 tablespoons water
2 tablespoons extra virgin olive oil

Using the tip of a small, sharp knife, make even incisions all over the lamb shoulder. Into each cut, place a piece of garlic, thyme and a tiny sprig of rosemary leaves. Rub the lamb all over with the sea salt.

Heat a thin layer of the goose fat in a deep casserole, add the lamb shoulder and sear all over. Reduce the heat, add the rest of the goose fat and the wine and bring to the boil. Cover and place in an oven preheated to 110°C/Gas Mark 4. Cook for $3^1/_4$ hours or until the meat is falling off the bone. Remove from the oven and leave the meat to cool in the liquor.

Heat the olive oil in a frying pan and fry the slices of aubergine until just taking on a light colour. Season and then drain on kitchen paper.

Put the button onions in a small pan, add the butter, a pinch of salt and enough water just to cover, then bring to the boil. Simmer until tender and then drain.

Line a large terrine, with a capacity of about 1.3 litres, with a double layer of cling film, leaving a good 10cm overhanging the sides, then line with the aubergine slices, overlapping the slices by 5mm and leaving a 3cm overhang at the top of the terrine; you will need this to wrap over the top at the end.

Drain the lamb and pull the meat off the bone, separating the meat from any fat or sinew. Press a layer of lamb along the bottom of the terrine, pushing it down into the corners. Sprinkle on some olives, button onions, dried tomatoes and parsley, lightly seasoning with black pepper and salt. Press as you go and build the terrine up to the top, repeating each step to make 4 layers of meat and 3 layers of onion, tomato, olives and parsley. Finally, wrap with the overhanging aubergine, then wrap again with the excess cling film. Place an even weight of about 1kg on top of the terrine, place in the fridge and leave overnight to set.

To make the anchoiade dressing, simply whiz the olives, anchovies and garlic to a paste in a food processor, moisten with the vinegar and water, then gradually add the olive oil.

To serve, turn out the terrine and cut it into 1cm-thick slices. Peel off the cling film and place each slice on a serving plate. Spoon a little anchoiade dressing around the plate and place a basil sprig on each slice.

Valle de Baux olive oil from Maussane-les-Alpilles in Provence: the wonderful fruity oil we use in our restaurants.

POACHED LAMB'S TONGUES WITH BEETROOT AND MÂCHE

Serves 4

Don't be put off by the idea of lamb's tongues – you really should give this a try. It's extremely popular at the Bistrot. Lamb's tongues are very tender, and slightly sweeter than ox tongue. The ravigote dressing adds a welcome touch of acidity.

8 lamb's tongues
1.5 litres water
50g coarse sea salt
3 beetroots
3 sprigs of thyme
1 tablespoon olive oil
1.5 litres Chicken Stock (see page 44)
2 tablespoons Ravigote Dressing (see page 50)
100g mâche (lamb's lettuce)
1 tablespoon Classic Vinaigrette (see page 50)
1 tablespoon fine capers
sea salt and freshly ground white pepper

Place the tongues in a container and leave under a slowly running cold tap for 1 hour – it just needs to be a slow trickle.

To make the brine, place the water and coarse sea salt in a large pan and bring to the boil. Remove from the heat and leave to cool, then chill. Drain the tongues, then place in a container large enough to take the brine. Pour the cold brine over the tongues and refrigerate for 24 hours.

Drain the tongues, then rinse them under a trickle of running cold water, as before, for 1 hour.

Put the beetroots on a large piece of foil, add the thyme, olive oil and some salt and pepper and wrap up loosely in the foil. Place in an oven preheated to 150°C/Gas Mark 2 and bake for 1 hour or until tender. Remove from the oven, leave until cool enough to handle, then rub off the skin, which should come off easily (this is a good way of telling if they are cooked). Cut into orange-segment-sized pieces.

Heat the chicken stock in a heavy-based pan until just simmering. Add the rinsed tongues and poach gently for 1 hour 20 minutes. Remove from the heat and leave in the liquor until cool enough to handle. Remove the tongues one by one and peel off the outer layer of skin. This will be an easy task when warm but devilish when cold!

Arrange the segments of beetroot in a spiral fashion on each serving plate. Cut the tongues into 3mm-thick slices and arrange on top of the beetroot, then sprinkle a little seasoning on top. Spoon the ravigote dressing over the tongues. Lightly toss the mâche with the vinaigrette and place on top, add a sprinkling of fine capers and serve.

DUCK RILLETTES WITH SHALLOT CHUTNEY AND WATERCRESS AND WALNUT SALAD

Serves 6

This is something to keep tucked away in your fridge for a snack – the rillettes will keep for a good month, and the chutney too can be made well in advance. Rillettes were originally a means of preserving meat, and are a great way to use up duck legs if you are using the breasts for another dish.

4 large duck legs (about 1.8kg in total)
1 large carrot
2 garlic cloves, peeled and left whole
1 sprig of rosemary
750g duck fat
sea salt and freshly ground white pepper

To cure the duck
500g coarse sea salt
1/2 bunch of thyme
6 garlic cloves, peeled
1 teaspoon black peppercorns, crushed

For the shallot chutney
1 tablespoon olive oil
250g shallots, diced
2 garlic cloves, chopped
5 tablespoons sherry vinegar
50g soft brown sugar
12 cherry tomatoes, quartered
2 tablespoons water

For the walnut dressing
1 teaspoon Dijon mustard
1 teaspoon white wine vinegar
90ml vegetable oil
25ml walnut oil
25ml double cream

To serve
200g watercress
100g pickled walnuts
12 slices of sourdough bread

To cure the duck, blitz the salt, thyme, garlic and peppercorns to a coarse powder in a food processor. Cover the duck legs in this mixture and leave in the fridge for 24 hours.

The next day, rinse off the salt mixture and pat the duck legs dry with kitchen paper. Put them in a casserole with the whole carrot, garlic cloves and rosemary. Melt the duck fat in a pan and pour enough into the casserole to cover the legs. Gently heat the casserole on the hob to bring the fat to a simmer, then cover with a lid and transfer to an oven preheated to 140°C/Gas Mark 1. Cook for about 3 hours, until the meat falls easily from the bone. Remove from the oven and leave the legs to cool in the fat.

Remove the legs from the duck fat and shred the meat with 2 forks, discarding the bones (but save the duck skin and the fat). Place the meat in a large mixing bowl set over ice and beat 250g of the duck fat into it with a wooden spoon a little at a time until emulsified – or you can use your hands, like rubbing butter into flour. Finely grate the carrot and garlic that were cooked with the duck and add to the mixture. Mix well and adjust the seasoning. Divide the mixture between 6 sterilised 200ml Le Parfait jars, press down firmly to give an even layer, then clean the smear marks from the jars with a damp piece of kitchen paper, seal and chill. (Alternatively, you can just put the mixture in a single large serving dish.)

To make the chutney, heat the olive oil in a saucepan, add the shallots and garlic and cook for about 15 minutes, until golden brown. Add the vinegar, sugar, tomatoes and water and cook gently for another 15 minutes, until the juices form a thick syrup. Season with a pinch of salt and set aside to cool.

Put the duck leg skin on a baking tray and bake in an oven preheated to 180°C/Gas Mark 4 for 15 minutes or until golden and crisp. Remove from the oven, leave to cool and then cut into small pieces.

For the dressing, first make sure all the ingredients are chilled. Place the mustard and vinegar in a small blender or food processor with a small pinch of salt. With the machine running, slowly pour in the vegetable oil, then the walnut oil. The dressing should be quite thick and emulsified. Finally, mix in the double cream and adjust the seasoning. Chill before using.

Remove the jars from the fridge 30 minutes before serving. Put the watercress and walnuts in a bowl and toss with 3 tablespoons of the dressing. Put the jars on serving plates with the salad alongside, then scatter the crisp duck skin over the salad. Toast the sourdough bread and add to the plates, together with a spoonful of the chutney.

BALLOTINE OF FOIE GRAS WITH PEACHES AND PAIN D'ÉPICES

Serves 8

This sounds complex but it's really worth having a go at home. Once you've managed to get top-quality foie gras, the process is relatively straightforward. The peaches make a good foil for the richness of the foie gras but it's imperative that they are properly ripe. In France you will often find pain d'épices served with foie gras – sometimes it is used as a breadcrumb coating before searing it.

Sel rosé is a preserving salt containing nitrates that helps the foie gras keep its colour. If you can't find any, it's not absolutely essential.

1 lobe of foie gras, weighing 500–600g
8g sea salt
a pinch of white pepper
a pinch of sel rosé
50ml Armagnac
50g Pain d'épices (see page 58)
fleur de sel, for sprinkling (optional)

For the garnish
2 peaches
50g caster sugar
50ml water
1 teaspoon lemon juice
vegetable oil, for deep-frying
24 mint leaves

Leave the foie gras out of the fridge for 2 hours to soften. Pull the smaller lobe from the bigger lobe and cut the larger one in half lengthways. Using a small knife, carefully pull out any veins. Place the de-veined foie gras on a tray lined with cling film, then evenly sprinkle the sea salt, white pepper and pink salt over the top. Drizzle the Armagnac over, cover with cling film and leave to marinate at room temperature for 3 hours.

On a clean work surface, spread out a large piece of cling film, about 60cm x 40cm, making sure it is completely flat, then repeat to form a double layer. Press any air out with a clean tea towel. Lay the foie gras in the middle of the cling film, trying to keep it as whole as possible. Roll it into a sausage shape in the cling film and then tie one end with string. Twist the other end really tight, then tie.

Heat a large pan of water to 65°C, add the ballotine and poach for 3 minutes. Remove and plunge into iced water for 3 minutes, then drain. Leave in the refrigerator overnight.

Blitz the pain d'épices to a fine powder in a food processor and then spread it out on a tray. Carefully remove the cling film from the ballotine and roll the ballotine in the powdered crumbs, then re-wrap in cling film and return to the fridge.

For the garnish, blanch the peaches in boiling water for 10 seconds, then drain and refresh in iced water. Drain again, peel off the skins and reserve for the syrup. Cut the peaches in half and remove the stones. Set aside. Put the sugar, water, peach skins and lemon juice in a small pan and bring to the boil, stirring to dissolve the sugar. Simmer until reduced to a thick syrup, then remove from the heat, leave to cool, strain and then chill.

Heat the vegetable oil to 150°C in a deep-fat fryer or a deep saucepan. Deep-fry the mint leaves for 1 minute and then drain on kitchen paper.

To serve, cut the peaches into 2mm-thick slices and arrange in a rosette on 8 serving plates. With a hot knife, cut the ballotine into 8mm-thick slices and place a slice in the middle of the peaches. Drizzle the syrup around. Arrange the deep-fried mint leaves around the peaches and sprinkle some of the leftover pain d'épices powder around the edge of each plate. Finish the foie gras with a little fleur de sel, if you like.

SALAD OF GREY-LEG PARTRIDGE WITH POMEGRANATE AND MAPLE SAUCE

Serves 4

Grey-leg partridges are the indigenous British variety and have a much finer flavour than the French red-leg, which tend to be farmed. Pomegranate with game might seem an unusual combination but it is quite common in Italy. The maple syrup contrasts well with the smokiness of the pancetta.

2 grey-leg partridges
200g duck fat
1 tablespoon honey
1 teaspoon wholegrain mustard
½ pomegranate
100ml Brown Chicken Jus (see page 45)
50ml maple syrup
50ml sherry vinegar
50ml cranberry juice
30g unsalted butter
50g shallots, finely diced
50g smoked pancetta, finely diced
30g focaccia bread, cut into 5mm cubes
1 tablespoon vegetable oil
sea salt and freshly ground white pepper

For the herb salad
30g frisée lettuce, white part only
10g chervil
10g flat-leaf parsley leaves
10 small tarragon leaves
2 tablespoons Simple Vinaigrette (see page 50)

Cut the legs off the partridges and set the birds aside. Season the legs with salt and pepper. Heat the duck fat to 80°C in a saucepan and add the legs (they should be completely immersed in the fat). Keeping the fat at this temperature, cook the legs for about 1 hour; they are ready when the thighbone can be pulled out with little resistance. Remove from the heat and allow to cool in the fat.

Boil the honey in a small saucepan until it begins to caramelise. Remove from the heat and leave to cool, then mix in the mustard. This will be used to glaze the legs.

Hold the pomegranate half over a plate and gently tap the back of it with a spoon so the seeds fall out. Pick out any pith and set the seeds aside.

Heat the chicken jus and then set aside. Put the maple syrup and vinegar in a small pan and boil until reduced by half. Add the cranberry juice and reduce by half again. Add this mixture to the chicken jus and reduce a little more, until the sauce is thick enough to coat the back of a spoon.

Melt 10g of the butter in a small saucepan, add the shallots and cook over a low heat for 5–6 minutes, until soft but not coloured. Remove from the heat and set aside. Heat a frying pan until very hot, then add 10g of the butter and the pancetta and cook for 2–3 minutes, until golden and crisp. Drain on kitchen paper.

Add the fried shallots and pancetta to the sauce, then add the pomegranate seeds just before serving.

Heat the remaining butter in a frying pan until it is foaming, then add the focaccia cubes and fry until golden and crisp. Season with a pinch of salt, then drain on kitchen paper.

Heat an ovenproof frying pan over a high heat, then add the vegetable oil. Season the partridge crowns, add them to the pan and cook until the skin is a deep golden colour. Turn the birds the right way up and place the pan in an oven preheated to 180°C/Gas Mark 4. Roast for 4 minutes until the breasts are just cooked. Remove from the oven and leave to rest in a warm place for 10 minutes, then remove the breasts and slice each one into 3.

Meanwhile, remove the legs from the fat with a slotted spoon and crisp them up in a hot, non-stick frying pan. When the skin is golden and crisp, brush the legs with the honey and mustard mixture to glaze.

For the herb salad, lightly toss the lettuce and herbs in a bowl with the vinaigrette.

Place a sliced breast on each serving plate with a leg on top. Spoon a neat pile of salad at the back of the plate, spoon over the maple sauce (reheating it first, if necessary) and finish with the focaccia croûtons.

CHILLED ENGLISH ASPARAGUS WITH TRUFFLE VINAIGRETTE

Serves 4

We often like to serve asparagus chilled with a vinaigrette, particularly on a hot day. This truffle vinaigrette is very thick, with an almost mayonnaise-like consistency. Truffle juice is available in tins from some delis.

40 large spears of English asparagus
75ml truffle juice
1 tablespoon Brown Chicken Jus
   (see page 45)
1 teaspoon sherry vinegar
table salt
200ml groundnut oil
50ml black truffle oil
1 tablespoon extra virgin olive oil
12 shavings of black truffle
4 sprigs of chervil
coarse sea salt

Trim the asparagus by snapping off the base of the stems, then peel the spears from just below the tip. Blanch in a large pan of boiling salted water for 3–4 minutes, then drain. Refresh in iced water until completely cold, then drain again and spread out on a clean cloth. Place in the fridge.

For the vinaigrette, boil the truffle juice, chicken jus and vinegar together until reduced by half and then pour into a blender or food processor. Add a small pinch of table salt and then start to add the groundnut oil very slowly; the mixture should come together and start to thicken. When all the groundnut oil has been incorporated, add the truffle oil in the same manner. Finally, adjust the seasoning and the consistency, adding a little water if it is too thick; it should be thick enough just to hold its shape.

Cut the asparagus into 14cm spears, put them in a mixing bowl and toss with the olive oil, using just enough to coat. Season with table salt.

To serve, lay the asparagus spears neatly on serving plates, place the truffle shavings on top and, using 2 tablespoons, place a quenelle (oval shape) of the thick vinaigrette to the side. Garnish with the chervil sprigs and a pinch of sea salt.

Heirloom tomatoes at Rungis Market.

SALAD OF HEIRLOOM TOMATOES, GOAT'S CHEESE AND BASIL

Serves 4

By Heirloom tomatoes, we mean old-fashioned varieties that are packed with flavour. This is a perfect summer starter.

900g Heirloom tomatoes
200g goat's cheese log, such as Ragstone,
    Dorstone or Aisy Cendre
4 sprigs of basil
4 tablespoons extra virgin olive oil
sea salt and freshly ground black pepper

Thinly slice the tomatoes – some will just need cutting into quarters – and arrange on your most beautiful plates. Sprinkle lightly with sea salt.

Slice the goat's cheese evenly and arrange it on top of the tomatoes. Grind some black pepper over the top, then drop on the basil sprigs.

Finally, splash some olive oil over each plate to lubricate. This is really delicious served with crusty baguette.

SALAD OF WOOD-FIRED VEGETABLES WITH WALNUTS AND GOAT'S CHEESE

Serves 4

Wood-fired ovens seem to have taken over from the barbecue as a means for men to show off their cooking prowess. Whether you cook the vegetables in a wood-fired oven or a conventional one, the important thing is to make sure you drive off all the moisture and concentrate the flavours.

1 large beetroot, peeled and finely sliced
12 baby carrots, trimmed
12 baby beetroots
4 garlic cloves, finely sliced
4 sprigs of thyme
about 100ml extra virgin olive oil
12 baby leeks, trimmed
8 asparagus spears, trimmed
3 cooked baby artichokes, quartered
6–8 tablespoons Simple Vinaigrette (see page 50)
12 goat's cheese balls (or slices of fresh goat's cheese)
12 walnut halves
16 red chard leaves
sea salt and freshly ground white pepper

For the pickling liquor
250ml distilled malt vinegar
155g caster sugar
$1/2$ lemon, sliced
a pinch of sea salt
1 garlic clove, thinly sliced
$1/2$ teaspoon crushed coriander seeds

First prepare the pickling liquor. Put the vinegar and sugar in a small pan and boil until reduced by half. Remove from the heat and add the lemon, salt, garlic and coriander seeds.

Place the sliced beetroot in a bowl, cover with half the hot pickling liquor and leave for 24 hours.

The next day, reheat the remaining pickling liquor. Blanch the baby carrots in boiling salted water until just tender, then drain and cover with the hot pickling liquor.

Put the baby beetroots on a large sheet of foil, add the garlic, thyme, some salt and pepper and a tablespoon of the olive oil and wrap loosely in the foil to make a parcel. Roast in the back of a wood-fired oven, where it is cooler, or place in a conventional oven preheated to 160°C/Gas Mark 3 and roast for 1 hour, until tender. Remove from the oven and leave to cool, then peel off the skin and cut the beetroots in half.

Lightly coat the leeks, asparagus and artichokes in a little olive oil and roast separately in a wood-fired oven until lightly charred. If you don't have a wood-fired oven, cook the vegetables separately in a hot griddle pan on the hob.

Just before serving, drain the sliced beetroot and the baby carrots. Toss all the vegetables separately in a little of the vinaigrette and season to taste.

Arrange the vegetables, goat's cheese and walnuts attractively on serving plates. Toss the chard in the remaining vinaigrette and place on the salad, then drizzle olive oil around each serving.

SALAD OF HERITAGE BEETROOT, WATERMELON, TOMATO SEEDS AND WHIPPED GOAT'S CURD

Serves 4

A lovely light dish that makes a delicious late-summer starter. It's worth buying heritage beetroot – i.e. interesting old varieties – as they generally have a good concentration of flavour. If possible, look out for organic ones.

It's unusual to use the tomato seeds here, but with perfectly ripe tomatoes they taste wonderful and are very refreshing.

3 red heritage beetroots
50g acacia honey
3 black peppercorns, crushed
1 star anise, crushed
1 cardamom pod, crushed
2 tablespoons Cabernet Sauvignon
   vinegar
200ml port
2 golden heritage beetroots
$1/2$ watermelon
6 ripe plum tomatoes
vegetable oil, for deep-frying
100g fresh goat's curd or soft goat's
   cheese
a few drops of champagne vinegar or
   good white wine vinegar, to taste
50g baby salad leaves, such as chard,
   mizuna, sorrel and purslane
1 tablespoon extra virgin olive oil, for
   drizzling
sea salt and freshly ground white pepper

Peel 2 of the red beetroots, then slice them very thinly on a mandolin into a bowl. Heat a pan over a medium heat, add the honey and let it caramelise lightly, then remove from the heat. Add the crushed spices and let them toast in the honey for 20 seconds, then pour in the Cabernet Sauvignon vinegar and port. Return to the heat, bring to the boil and boil until reduced by a third. Pour the reduced liquid over the sliced beetroots, then place in a cool place and leave to marinate for 6 hours.

Wrap the golden beetroots individually in foil, put them on a baking tray and bake in an oven preheated oven to 160°C/ Gas Mark 3 for 1–1$1/2$ hours, until tender (test to see if the beetroots are cooked by piercing them with a small knife). Remove from the oven, take off the foil and peel the beetroots with a small knife while they are still hot – the skin should peel off easily. Cut each beetroot into 8 wedges and set aside in a small bowl. Let them cool to room temperature.

Peel the watermelon and cut out the most seeded part, then cut out 8 large dice from the flesh, each about 3cm square, and put these in a cool place. Cut each tomato in half, then with a small teaspoon, scoop out the central part containing the seeds and juice (in a good

tomato this will be almost a jelly and has the most amazing flavour). You won't need the tomato flesh here but you can save it for another dish.

Peel the remaining red beetroot and slice it very thinly, then deep-fry in a pan of hot vegetable oil until crisp. Drain on kitchen paper and season with salt.

Put the goat's curd in a large bowl, add the champagne vinegar and whisk together until well mixed, then season to taste with salt and plenty of pepper. Transfer the mixture to a piping bag fitted with a plain nozzle.

Wash all the salad leaves and spin dry, then place in a large bowl.

Drain the marinated red beetroot slices, reserving the juice, and arrange on serving plates. Toss the golden beetroot wedges and salad leaves with some of the reserved red beetroot juice and season. Arrange the golden beetroot wedges, watermelon and tomato seeds and jelly on the plates, pipe the goat's curd mixture around, then add the salad leaves and beetroot crisps. Drizzle with some more of the red juice and finally the olive oil.

CEP OMELETTE

Serves 2

An omelette makes a fabulous starter, as it is so versatile and a great vehicle for many ingredients, from asparagus to cheese and ceps. It's also very good with a little seared duck liver.

A word of warning: don't choose this dish if you have a lot of guests or you will be making omelettes all night – as we discovered in the restaurant! Best just to save it for a quiet dinner for two.

6 free-range eggs
2 tablespoons Clarified Butter (see page 51)
2 nut-sized pieces of unsalted butter
1 teaspoon chopped parsley
2 tablespoons Brown Chicken Jus
  (see page 45) (optional)
sea salt and freshly ground white pepper

For the filling
40g Clarified Butter (see page 51)
1 garlic clove, crushed
1 shallot, finely chopped
50g fresh ceps, sliced
$^1/_2$ teaspoon chopped parsley

First cook the filling. Heat the clarified butter in a small pan, add the garlic and shallot and allow to sizzle. Add the ceps, increase the heat a little and toss until golden and tender. Season to taste and remove from the heat. Stir in the parsley, then turn the mixture out of the pan on to kitchen paper to drain. Keep warm.

Make one omelette at a time: beat 3 of the eggs together until the yolks and whites are amalgamated and season with salt and pepper. Heat an omelette pan, add a tablespoon of the clarified butter and, when it is foaming, add a nut of butter (using clarified butter for frying means it is less likely to burn, but adding a little whole butter improves the flavour). Pour the beaten eggs into the pan and cook over a medium heat, drawing the mixture from the sides of the pan to the centre with a fork as it sets and tilting the pan to allow the uncooked egg to run to the edges.

When the omelette is very softly set, add a quarter of the cep mixture. Roll the omelette into a cigar shape and slide it on to a plate, then cut a slit along the top and spoon another quarter of the cep mixture in. Sprinkle half the chopped parsley over. Keep warm while you make a second omelette in the same way. Serve with the chicken jus drizzled around, if using.

IMAM BAYALDI

Serves 4

This is one of those dishes that taste even better on day two or day three. There are many ways of serving aubergine in Turkey and there are lots of stories about the origins of this one. The name means 'the imam fainted' – either because of the deliciousness of the dish or because of the extravagant quantity of olive oil it traditionally involves.

3 tablespoons olive oil
2 aubergines, diced
1 Spanish onion, diced
2 garlic cloves, finely chopped
1 teaspoon ground allspice
a pinch of cayenne pepper
1 teaspoon ground cumin
1 teaspoon ground coriander
100g plum tomatoes, skinned, deseeded
  and chopped
50g currants
1 tablespoon tomato passata
1 teaspoon extra virgin olive oil, plus
  extra to drizzle
1 sprig of mint, chopped
1 tablespoon chopped coriander
2 tablespoons chopped flat-leaf parsley
2 tablespoons thick natural Greek
  yoghurt
sea salt and freshly ground white pepper
20 pieces of coriander cress, to garnish

Heat the olive oil in a heavy-based pan over a high heat, add the aubergines and allow to caramelise a little. Turn them over and continue to cook until they are an even light golden colour all over. Transfer to a colander with a slotted spoon and set aside.

Add the onion to the hot oil and cook for 2 minutes or until slightly softened. Add the garlic and ground spices, reduce the heat and cook gently until the spices are toasted and the onion is golden brown. Add the tomatoes and cook over a medium heat for 3–4 minutes, then add the currants and gently stir in the aubergine. Remove from the heat and leave to cool.

Season the mixture to taste and add the passata just to moisten it a little. Stir in the extra virgin olive oil, followed by the chopped herbs. Divide the mixture into 4 portions and, using a 6cm round metal ring, mould each portion into a round on a serving plate and press down with a tablespoon.

Spoon the Greek yoghurt on top, garnish with the coriander cress, then drizzle with extra virgin olive oil. Serve with crusty bread.

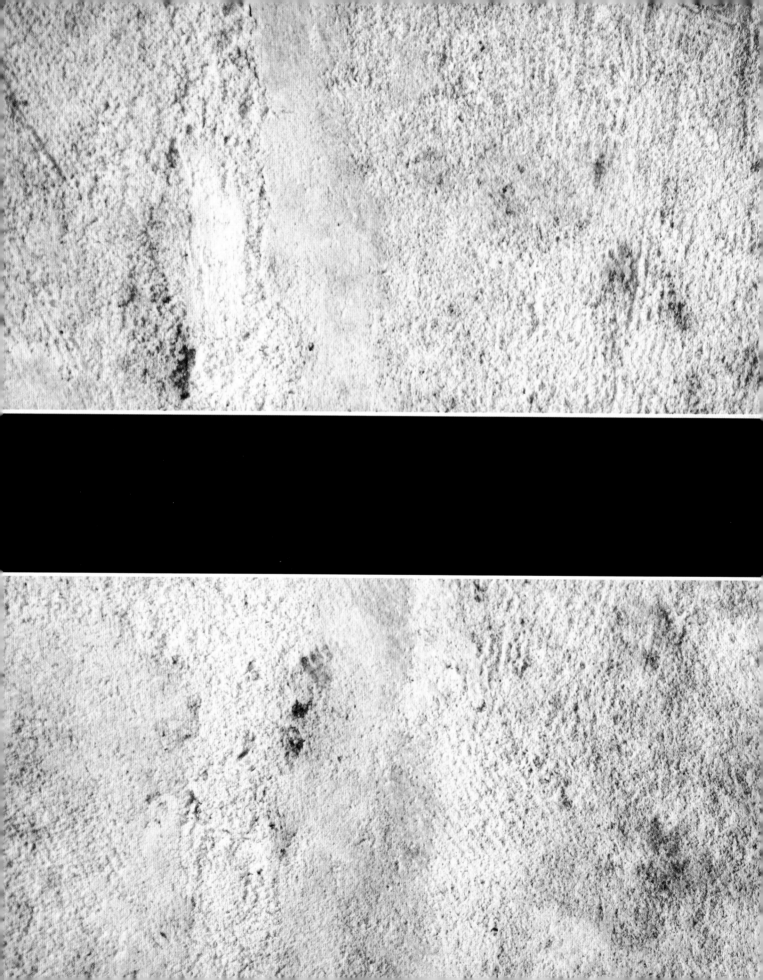

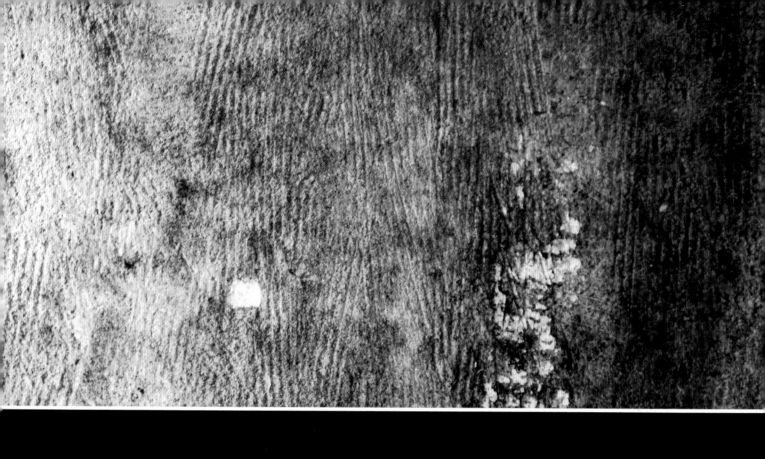

MAIN COURSES

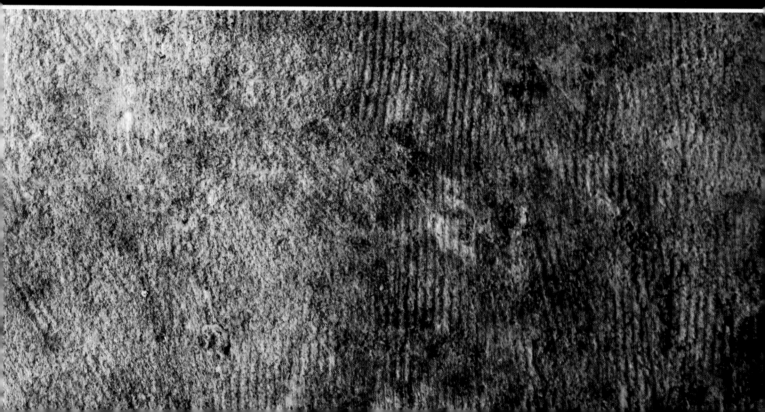

STEAMED HALIBUT WITH CARAMELISED CHICORY AND ITALIAN ARTICHOKES

Serves 4

This is a very light, delicate dish. We like to use the little Italian violet artichokes here, but other small, young artichokes will do.

6 Italian baby artichokes
1 lemon, cut in half
1 teaspoon olive oil
30g unsalted butter
1 small sprig of thyme
4 portions of halibut fillet (about 120g each)
sea salt and freshly ground white pepper
1 quantity of Red Wine Jus (see page 47), to serve
20 baby sorrel leaves, to garnish (optional)

For the Jerusalem artichoke purée
50g unsalted butter
250g Jerusalem artichokes, peeled and diced
40ml milk
2 tablespoons double cream

For the potatoes
200ml duck fat
6 Charlotte potatoes or similar waxy new potatoes, cut in half lengthwise
1 garlic clove, cut in half
1 sprig of thyme
1 tablespoon olive oil

For the chicory
6 chicory heads (use the heart only – you can save the outer leaves for a salad), cut in half lengthwise
400ml orange juice
2 tablespoons caster sugar
20 coriander seeds, roasted, then crushed
2 teaspoons olive oil

First make the Jerusalem artichoke purée. Melt the butter in a pan, add the Jerusalem artichokes and sweat for 10 minutes or until tender, being careful not to let them colour. Add the milk and cream and simmer for about 2 minutes. Transfer the mixture to a blender or food processor and blend until silky smooth. If the purée is too thick, add an additional splash of milk to loosen it. Season to taste.

For the potatoes, put the duck fat in a saucepan and bring to the boil. Add the potatoes, garlic and thyme and simmer gently for 20 minutes or until the potatoes are tender. Remove from the heat and allow the potatoes to cool slightly for 10 minutes in the fat, then remove with a slotted spoon. Place the potatoes cut-side down in a hot frying pan with the olive oil and cook over a high heat on one side only, until golden and crisp. Season, then drain on kitchen paper.

Put the chicory in a heavy-based saucepan and add the orange juice, sugar, coriander seeds and a good pinch of salt. Bring to the boil, then simmer over a medium heat for about 10 minutes. Remove the chicory from the cooking liquor and drain on kitchen paper. Heat the olive oil in a non-stick frying pan, add the chicory and cook on both sides until golden. Season with salt and pepper.

Prepare the baby artichokes as directed on page 57, rubbing them with the lemon halves as you go. Cut them in half from top to bottom, then heat a frying pan until quite hot. Add the olive oil and place the artichokes in the pan cut-side down. Season with a little salt and pepper and cook for about 2 minutes, until golden. Turn the artichokes over, add the butter and thyme and increase the heat a little so that the butter starts to foam. Continue cooking for 4 minutes or until tender. The trick is to keep the pan hot enough for the butter to stay foaming, but not so hot that it burns. Remove the artichokes from the pan and keep warm.

Lay each fish portion on a piece of greaseproof paper cut 1cm larger than the fish. Place them in a steamer and cook for 6–8 minutes. You can check the fish is cooked by sticking a cocktail stick through it – if you feel some resistance in the flesh, the fish will need to be cooked a little longer. Remove the fish from the steamer, squeeze a little lemon juice over and season with a pinch of salt. Drain on kitchen paper.

Reheat the Jerusalem artichoke purée. Spoon it on to the centre of each serving plate and arrange the chicory, artichokes and potatoes around it. Place the fish on top of the purée and spoon the red wine jus around the outside. Garnish with the sorrel leaves, if using.

POACHED COD WITH PAYSANNE OF LEEKS AND CHARLOTTE POTATOES

Serves 4

Paysanne means peasant-style – in this case roughly chopped potatoes and leeks. They give a wonderfully earthy flavour to the cod. The poaching liquor from the fish is used to form the sauce, with cream and butter added to enrich it.

6 Charlotte potatoes or similar waxy new potatoes
2 leeks, light green part only, cut into 2cm dice
50g softened unsalted butter, plus 50g chilled unsalted butter, diced
2 shallots, very finely chopped
4 thick portions of cod fillet (about 120g each), skinned
250ml Fish Stock (see page 46)
125ml dry white wine
75ml whipping cream
4 tablespoons chopped chives
a small bunch of chervil
sea salt and freshly ground white pepper

Cook the potatoes in a pan of boiling salted water until tender, then drain. When cool enough to handle, peel and cut into 3mm-thick slices. Cook the leeks in boiling salted water for 1 minute or until just tender, then drain and refresh in cold water. Drain well again and set aside.

Use the softened butter to grease a heavy-based casserole suitable for poaching the cod. Sprinkle in the shallots and then place the cod on top. Add the fish stock and wine and place on the hob. Bring to the boil, add some salt and cover with a piece of buttered greaseproof paper. Transfer the dish to an oven preheated to 180°C/Gas Mark 4 and cook for 8–10 minutes, until the cod is just cooked through.

Remove from the oven and drain off the juices through a sieve into a clean pan. Keep the buttered paper on the fish and set aside in a warm place. Boil the cooking liquor until reduced to 150ml, then add the cream. Bring back to the boil, let it reduce a little, then whisk in the chilled butter, a few pieces at a time, until you have a smooth, emulsified sauce. Taste and adjust the seasoning.

Add the potatoes and leeks to the sauce, turning up the heat a little as they will cool the sauce. When the mixture is almost at a simmer, spoon it into warm bowls and place the cod on top. Sprinkle the chives around, then use scissors to snip lots of chervil over the top.

WHOLE PLAICE MEUNIÈRE WITH BROWN SHRIMPS, CAPERS AND NEW POTATOES

Serves 4

We always use line-caught or harpooned plaice, as this really makes a difference to the flesh. In large trawler nets, the fish get damaged and the flesh tends to be mushy.

300g new potatoes, peeled
1/2 bunch of mint
30g unsalted butter
6 tablespoons olive oil
4 whole plaice (about 500g each), scaled, heads removed and gutted
50g plain flour, seasoned with salt and pepper
200g salted butter, cut into 1cm dice
100g cooked brown shrimps
a few drops of lemon juice
75g fine capers, drained
2 tablespoons chopped parsley
sea salt and freshly ground black pepper

To cook the potatoes, place them in a saucepan and cover with cold water, then add the mint and a good pinch of salt. Bring rapidly to the boil, reduce the heat and simmer for 15–20 minutes or until tender. Drain and return to the pan, add the unsalted butter, season with a little salt and keep warm.

Heat the olive oil in a large heavy-based frying pan. Dust the plaice all over with the seasoned flour, tapping off any excess. Lay the plaice in the pan skin-side down (you will probably have to cook them 1 or 2 at a time – or use 2 frying pans). Cook the plaice over a high heat for 2–3 minutes without moving them, then turn over and cook for a further 3 minutes. The best way to tell if it is cooked is to push a cocktail stick into the thickest part of the fish – if it comes out without resistance, the fish is cooked.

Remove the fish and drain on kitchen paper, then transfer to serving plates and keep warm. Drain off the excess oil from the pan and return the pan to the heat. Add the salted butter and allow it to melt and foam, then continue to cook until it is golden brown. Remove from the heat and pass it through a fine sieve. Return the butter to the pan, drop in the shrimps and bring the butter to the boil. Add the lemon juice, capers and parsley.

Remove from the heat and spoon the shrimp mixture over the plaice. Serve with the hot, minted new potatoes.

ROASTED BALLOTINE OF COD WITH ARTICHOKES, AIOLI AND PEA SHOOTS

Serves 8

This is a posh version of brandade of cod. We use a whole fillet of cod, lightly salt the thickest part and make a purée with the trimmings. We then roll up the lightly salted cod to make a ballotine and serve with the brandade and aioli.

1 fillet of cod, weighing about 1.5kg, skinned and pinbones removed
200g rock salt
1 free-range egg white
2 baby aubergines
vegetable oil, for deep-frying
10 violet artichokes
1 lemon, cut in half
1 teaspoon olive oil, plus extra for drizzling
30g unsalted butter
1 small sprig of thyme
2 punnets of pea shoots
sea salt and freshly ground white pepper

For the cod brandade
300g salt cod
1 litre milk
100ml double cream
3 garlic cloves, finely sliced
1 bay leaf
a sprig of thyme
1 large potato (about 250g), peeled and cut into quarters
2 tablespoons olive oil
freshly ground black pepper

For the aioli
1 free-range egg yolk
1 garlic clove, finely chopped
a pinch of saffron strands
90ml olive oil
50g mashed potato
90ml vegetable oil
lemon juice, to taste

First make the brandade. Put the salt cod in a large container of cold water and leave to soak in the fridge for 24 hours, changing the water several times. The next day, take the cod from the fridge, drain and leave under a trickle of cold running water for 1 hour.

Put the milk, cream, garlic, bay leaf and thyme in a pan, bring to the boil and simmer for 5 minutes. Remove from the heat and leave to infuse for 20 minutes. Meanwhile, cook the potato in boiling salted water until tender, then drain, pass through a fine sieve and keep warm. Bring the milk mixture back to the boil, add the cod and poach for 6–8 minutes, depending on the thickness of the fish. Be careful not to let it boil or to overcook the fish. Remove from the heat and leave to cool for 10 minutes.

Strain the cod, reserving the cooking liquor. Mix the fish with the warm potato, then beat in the olive oil with a wooden spoon, adding enough of the strained cooking liquor to give a soft but not runny consistency. Season with black pepper, and with salt if necessary, but it rarely requires any salt. Set aside.

Trim the tail end and belly off the cod fillet, just to square off the shape of the fillet. Reserve the trimmings. Put the fillet on a large plastic tray, scatter over the rock salt and leave for 5 minutes. Rinse off the salt and pat dry with a clean cloth.

Purée the fish trimmings in a blender or food processor until smooth, then add the egg white and blend together. Cut the cod fillet in half widthwise. Spread 2 tablespoons of the cod purée on 1 piece of fillet and place the other piece of fillet on top.

Take a piece of cling film about 80cm x 50cm and lay it out flat. Repeat to form a double layer, then press out any air with a clean cloth. Lay the cod in the middle of the cling film, trying to keep it as even as possible. Roll up into a sausage shape in the cling film and then tie up one end with string. Twist the other end very tightly and tie with string. Leave in the fridge for 3 hours to firm up.

For the aioli, blend the egg yolk, garlic and saffron with a pinch of salt in a blender or food processor, then slowly add the olive oil, as if making mayonnaise. Add the mashed potato and blend until smooth. Gradually mix in the vegetable oil. If the aioli becomes too thick, thin it down with a little warm water. Correct the seasoning with salt and lemon juice.

To make the aubergine crisps, slice the aubergines into very thin rounds, preferably on a mandolin. Sprinkle with salt and leave for 5 minutes, then rinse and pat dry on kitchen paper. Heat the vegetable oil in a deep-fat fryer or a deep saucepan to 170°C and deep-fry the aubergine slices, in batches, until golden.

(continued on page 144)

(continued from page 143)

Drain on kitchen paper, season with salt and set aside.

Prepare the baby artichokes as directed on page 57. Rub the prepared artichokes with one of the lemon halves as you go to prevent them turning black. To cook the artichokes, cut them into quarters, top to bottom, then heat a frying pan until quite hot. Add the olive oil, then place the artichokes in the pan cut-side down. Season with a little salt and pepper, then fry for about 2 minutes, until golden. Turn the artichokes over, then add the butter and thyme and increase the heat a little so that the butter starts to foam. Continue cooking for 4 minutes or until tender. The trick is to keep the pan hot enough for the butter to stay foaming, but not so hot that it burns. Remove the artichokes from the pan and keep warm.

Cut the ballotine into 8 slices, each about 2cm thick, keeping the cling film on. Cook in a hot, ovenproof, non-stick frying pan for 2 minutes, until golden on one side – the cling film will shrivel slightly but it helps the cod to keep its shape. Transfer the pan to an oven preheated to 200°C/Gas Mark 6 and cook for 3 minutes. Remove from the oven, turn over carefully, remove the cling film and cook in the oven for another 2 minutes. Remove from the oven, brush with olive oil and squeeze over the juice of the remaining lemon half. Put the fish on kitchen paper to soak up any juices and excess oil and season with salt.

Lightly toss the pea shoots with a little olive oil. Place the cod in the centre of 8 serving plates and arrange the artichokes, aubergine crisps and pea shoots around it. Using 2 tablespoons, shape the brandade into ovals and place on top of the cod. Serve accompanied by the aioli.

Bunched shallots from Nantes.

JOHN DORY WITH ORANGE-GLAZED ENDIVE, CAULIFLOWER PURÉE, CURRY OIL, PINE NUTS AND SULTANAS

Serves 4

This is a really well balanced dish that would be great with any white fish. We often change the fish and just buy what is plentiful and fresh and we encourage you to do the same.

4 fillets of John Dory (about 140g each), skin on
juice of 1/2 lemon
sea salt and freshly ground white pepper

For the curry oil
50g medium curry powder
300ml groundnut oil or very light olive oil (not extra virgin)

For the dressing
40g sultanas
20g pine nuts, lightly toasted
10g baby salted capers
40ml curry oil (see above)
10 leaves of coriander

For the cauliflower purée
1 cauliflower
100g unsalted butter
100ml milk
50ml single cream

For the glazed endive
2 Belgian endive (chicory)
20g icing sugar
40g unsalted butter
2 oranges
1 lemon
2 tablespoons red wine vinegar

Make the curry oil. Heat a large frying pan over a medium heat until hot, then add the curry powder and cook, stirring constantly to prevent burning, for about 2 minutes to toast the spice and bring out the aromas. When toasted, add the oil and heat to a temperature of around 60°C, then remove from the heat and pour into a suitable container. Cool, cover and keep for 2 days to mature.

Start the dressing. Place the sultanas in a bowl and cover with boiling water. Leave to soak overnight.

For the cauliflower purée, cut the cauliflower into small florets, discarding all the outer leaves and excess stalk. Heat a large pan over a medium heat and melt the butter, then add the cauliflower and sweat for 3–4 minutes or until tender. Add the milk and increase the heat a little, then cover with a lid and cook until the cauliflower is very tender. Drain, discarding the milk, then place the cauliflower in a blender or food processor and blend while slowly adding the cream. Season to taste, then pass the purée through a fine sieve into a bowl. Cover with cling film and keep hot until you are ready to serve.

For the glazed endive, trim any dead outer leaves from the endive, then cut in half lengthwise and dust the cut sides very well with the icing sugar. Heat a large frying pan over a medium heat and add the butter. When the butter is foaming, add the endive sugared-side down and cook slowly until caramelised. Finely grate the zest of 1 orange and the lemon on a microplane and add to the pan. Cook, turning the endive every 2 minutes, until they are well coloured and caramelised. Juice both the oranges and the lemon and add to the caramelised endives with the vinegar. Reduce the heat and cook very slowly until the endive is tender when pierced with a knife and the caramel is glazed and sticky. Season with salt and pepper and keep warm.

Finish the dressing. Drain the soaked sultanas and put in a pan with all the remaining ingredients, except the coriander. Warm together very gently.

Coat the fish fillets in some curry oil 10 minutes prior to cooking. Heat a large non-stick pan over a high heat until very hot, drain the fillets, then add them to the hot pan skin-side down, using the curry oil left over from coating the fish as your cooking oil. Let the skin crisp without moving it for 2–3 minutes, depending on the thickness of the fish, then reduce the heat to medium, turn the fish and cook for a further minute. Remove from the pan and drain on kitchen paper.

To serve, put a piece of endive on each plate and fan out slightly, then put the fish on top. With a tablespoon, make a swipe of cauliflower purée at the top and bottom of each plate. Add the coriander to the warm dressing and spoon it over the fish.

WHOLE SEA BREAM ROASTED WITH FENNEL STICKS AND CHARRED LEMON

Serves 4

It's lovely to cook fish, or meat for that matter, on the bone. I think we used to be frightened at the prospect of eating a whole fish, but people are more familiar with it now. The advantage is a much more moist and flavoursome result.

40g dried fennel stalks
2 large unwaxed lemons
4 sea bream (about 200g each), gutted
6 tablespoons extra virgin olive oil, plus extra for drizzling
4 sprigs of thyme
a squeeze of lemon juice
coarse sea salt and freshly ground black pepper

Soak the fennel stalks in cold water for 1 hour, then drain.

Cut the lemons into 3mm-thick slices. Place over a charcoal grill, or on a very hot griddle pan, and cook for a minute on each side or until well charred but not black.

To prepare the fish, ensure that there are no scales left by scraping towards the head with the back of a knife. Cut off all of the fins and trim the tails to a v-shape. Using a large, sharp knife, slash the fish on the diagonal several times on either side.

Brush the fish with olive oil on the outside and in the belly. Season with salt and pepper, then stuff the cavity of each fish with the fennel sticks and thyme. Put the fish in a single layer in an ovenproof dish and lay the charred lemon slices on top. Bake in an oven preheated to 200°C/ Gas Mark 6 for 14 minutes or until cooked through. Remove from the oven and leave to rest in a warm place for 5 minutes.

Serve with a drizzle of olive oil and a squeeze of lemon juice. We like to accompany this with a green salad and some boiled Jersey Royal potatoes.

ROAST HAKE WITH CLAMS, MUSSELS AND TOMATO FONDUE

Serves 4

Hake, which is used heavily by the Spanish, was an underrated fish in the UK but is now becoming more popular. It is imperative that it is extremely fresh. It makes a great combination with the shellfish here.

8 tablespoons olive oil
4 large shallots, finely chopped
2 garlic cloves, finely chopped
350ml white wine
1 teaspoon sherry vinegar
5 tablespoons tomato passata
4 ripe tomatoes, skinned, halved,
   deseeded and diced
1 teaspoon caster sugar (optional)
400g fresh clams
400g fresh mussels
1 small sprig of thyme
1 small sprig of flat-leaf parsley
4 pieces of hake fillet (about 150g each),
   skin on, pin bones removed
50g plain flour, seasoned with salt and
   pepper
a squeeze of lemon juice
2 tablespoons chopped parsley
sea salt and freshly ground white pepper

Heat 3 tablespoons of the olive oil in a heavy-based saucepan, add 2 of the chopped shallots and cook, stirring, until soft and very light golden. Add half the garlic and cook until it becomes a light golden colour, stirring occasionally. Add 125ml of the white wine and the vinegar, bring to the boil and boil until reduced by half, then add the passata. Bring back to the boil and simmer for 2–3 minutes, then add the diced tomatoes. Add seasoning to taste and add the sugar, if necessary (this is usually only necessary when the tomatoes are not fully ripe). Cook for 3 minutes, then remove from the heat and reserve.

To prepare the shellfish, wash the clams and mussels thoroughly under cold running water, discarding any open ones that don't close when tapped lightly on a work surface. Pull off any beards from the mussels and wash again carefully.

To cook the shellfish, heat another 3 tablespoons of olive oil in a heavy-based saucepan over a medium heat, add the remaining shallots and garlic plus the thyme and parsley sprigs and sweat until the shallots start to soften without colouring. Add the remaining wine, increase the heat and bring to the boil, then add the clams and cover with a lid. Cook for 2–3 minutes, until the clam shells open. Immediately pour them into a colander with a bowl beneath and drain, reserving the clams and cooking liquor separately. Cover the clams with a damp cloth, then repeat the process to cook the mussels, using the same cooking liquor.

Leave the clams and mussels to cool, then remove them from their shells, discarding any with unopened shells. Carefully pour the cooking liquor through a fine strainer or a piece of muslin cloth, leaving the sediment behind. Reserve the liquor to finish the dish.

To cook the hake, heat the remaining 2 tablespoons of olive oil in a large, heavy-based frying pan. Dip the hake fillets skin-side down in the seasoned flour, dust off any excess then place the fish skin-side down in the hot oil. Reduce the heat a little and cook for 3 minutes, until you can see a golden edge forming and the flesh of the fish starts to turn white from the base up. When it reaches halfway up, turn the fish over, season and continue cooking for about 2–3 minutes. To test if the fish is cooked, take a cocktail stick and push it into the thickest part of the fish about halfway through. When extracting the cocktail stick, it should just slide out with little resistance; if it tugs a little, this means the fish requires more cooking. Once cooked, remove the fish from the pan, season with a squeeze of lemon juice and keep warm.

Reheat the tomato fondue in a pan and moisten with a little of the mussel/clam stock to produce a sauce consistency. Add the clams and mussels and gently warm together, then stir in the parsley. Serve the tomato fondue in large bowls with the hake placed in the centre.

BRANDADE OF POLLACK WITH RUNNER BEANS AND SOFT-BOILED EGGS

Serves 4

This is a very popular Bistrot plat du jour. It's a thrifty dish, as we use leftover cod or pollack trimmings, and a little goes a long way.

600g pollack fillet, cut from the head end
200g rock salt
1 litre milk
100ml double cream
6 garlic cloves, peeled and left whole
1 bay leaf
1 sprig of thyme
2 large floury potatoes, such as Maris Piper (about 500g in total), peeled and cut into chunks
200ml olive oil
4 free-range eggs
300g runner beans, trimmed and cut on the bias into 1cm lengths
30g unsalted butter
12 black olives, stoned and halved
sea salt and freshly ground white pepper
extra virgin olive oil, for drizzling
3 tablespoons chopped chives

Put the pollack on a plastic tray, cover with the rock salt and leave in the fridge overnight. The next day, rinse the fish under cold running water and pat dry.

Put the milk, cream, garlic, bay leaf and thyme in a large pan and bring to the boil. Simmer for 5 minutes, then remove from the heat and leave to infuse for 20 minutes. Meanwhile, cook the potatoes in boiling salted water until tender, then drain, pass through a fine sieve and keep warm.

Bring the milk mixture back to the boil and add the pollack. Return to the boil again, then reduce the heat and poach for 6–8 minutes, depending on the thickness of the fish – be careful not to overcook it or let it boil. Remove from the heat and leave for 10 minutes.

Strain the pollack, reserving the cooking liquor and removing the skin and any bones. Mix the fish with the warm potato, then gradually beat in the olive oil with a wooden spoon, adding enough of the reserved cooking liquor to give a soft but not runny consistency. Season with black pepper and salt if necessary, but taste first, as it rarely requires any salt.

Boil the eggs for 4 minutes, then drain, peel and cut into quarters. Meanwhile, cook the runner beans in a pan of boiling salted water for 4–5 minutes, until just tender. Drain well, then return the beans to the pan, season with salt and pepper and add the butter. Toss to coat the beans in the butter.

To serve, divide the beans between 4 serving plates, put a large mound of brandade on top, then arrange the boiled egg quarters and the olives around the edge. Drizzle extra virgin olive oil over the brandade and finish with the chopped chives.

SEARED FILLET OF SEA BASS WITH SQUID, FLAT-LEAF PARSLEY AND CAPERS

Serves 4

Chris learned to make this dish when he worked at the celebrated L'Oustau de Baumanière in the South of France. It's very easy to make at home, as it can all be done in one pan. Be careful not to set fire to the kitchen, though, as Chris almost did when he cooked it on BBC Television's 'Saturday Kitchen'.

3 garlic cloves, thinly sliced
175ml dessert wine, preferably Banyuls
50g flat-leaf parsley leaves
2 shallots, finely sliced
25g black olives, stoned and cut in half
25g tinned piquillo peppers, drained, peeled and cut into strips
10g fine capers, drained
1 lemon, peeled and cut into segments
20g orzo pasta, cooked and drained
olive oil, for dressing and cooking
4 x 175g pieces of line-caught sea bass fillet
a few drops of lemon or lime juice
200g cleaned baby squid, sliced into very thin rings
1 tablespoon extra virgin olive oil
sea salt and freshly ground white pepper

Blanch the garlic in boiling water for 2 minutes, then drain and set aside. Boil the dessert wine in a pan until reduced to 1 tablespoon. Remove from the heat and set aside.

Mix the parsley, shallots, olives, piquillo peppers and capers together. Add the lemon and then stir in the cooled orzo pasta. Add 2 tablespoons of olive oil and toss to mix, then season to taste.

Heat 1 teaspoon of olive oil in a large, non-stick frying pan over a fairly high heat and lay the bass in it skin-side down. Cook without moving the fish for 1 minute, then reduce the heat to medium and leave for another 2 minutes. You will notice the opaque colour of the fish change to white, rising from the bottom of the fish. When this reaches just over half way, turn the bass and cook for about a minute longer. Remove from the heat, brush the top of the fish with a little more oil and season with salt and pepper and a few drops of lemon or lime juice. Leave in a warm place to rest.

Heat a little olive oil in a heavy-based frying pan until smoking, add the squid and drained garlic and sear quickly for about 1 minute. Season, remove from the heat and place on kitchen paper to drain. Add to the parsley salad and divide between 4 serving plates. Place the sea bass next to the salad. Pour a little extra virgin olive oil in a ring around each plate and finally add a thread of the reduced dessert wine. Serve at once.

ROAST MONKFISH WITH FRESH COCO BEANS, WOOD-ROASTED PEPPERS AND ANCHOVY DRESSING

Serves 4

Coco beans come from Paimpol in Brittany and they're beginning to make their way into the UK – London's Borough Market often has them in the summer months. In French supermarkets, they are easy to find, sold in their pods in large nets. On our trips to France, it's not unusual to spot elderly ladies walking out with a large sackful slung over one shoulder.

Dried coco beans, or even dried haricot beans, could be used instead but will need pre-cooking.

2 red peppers
3 tablespoons olive oil, plus extra for cooking the monkfish
1 shallot, finely sliced
a pinch of smoked paprika
1 garlic clove, very finely chopped or crushed
25g unsalted butter, diced
4 monkfish tails (about 160g each)
$^1/_2$ lemon
sea salt and freshly ground white pepper

For the coco beans
250g shelled fresh coco beans (about 500g unshelled weight)
$^1/_4$ onion, sliced
1 carrot, sliced lengthwise in half
$^1/_2$ stick celery, sliced in 3
500ml Chicken Stock (see page 44)
1 small sprig of thyme

For the anchovy dressing
120ml extra virgin olive oil
$^1/_2$ garlic clove
1 tablespoon red wine vinegar
7 anchovy fillets
$^1/_2$ lemon
freshly ground black pepper
2 tablespoons chopped mixed herbs, such as parsley, tarragon and chervil

Place all the ingredients for the coco beans in a saucepan. Bring to the boil, then reduce the heat and simmer for about $1^1/_2$ hours until the beans are tender. Top up with water if the liquid gets low during cooking. Remove from the heat and leave the beans to cool in the liquid, then remove and discard the onion, carrot, celery and thyme. Drain the beans, reserving 100ml of the cooking liquor (the rest would make great stock for a soup). Set aside.

Place the red peppers on a baking tray, then roll them in 2 tablespoons of the olive oil and sprinkle with a pinch of salt. Place them in the hottest part of a wood oven. Cook for about 2 minutes, until the skin has blistered, then turn over and cook for another couple of minutes. Remove from the oven. If you don't have a wood oven, an ordinary oven is okay but the cooking time will be much longer – say, 20 minutes at 200°C/Gas Mark 6.

When the peppers are cool enough to handle, remove the skin, which should come off easily – if not, you need to cook them for a little longer. Cut the peppers in half, remove the stalks and seeds, then cut the flesh into strips about 1–2mm thick.

Heat the remaining tablespoon of olive oil in a saucepan. Add the peppers, shallot, paprika and garlic and cook over a medium heat for 5 minutes. Add the coco beans and reserved cooking liquor, bring to a simmer, then add the butter, a little at a time, and stir it in to form an emulsion that coats the beans. Adjust the seasoning.

To make the anchovy dressing, gently heat the olive oil, garlic, vinegar and anchovies together in a small saucepan until just warm, then blitz in a blender until smooth. Add a squeeze of lemon juice and a twist of black pepper. Stir in the chopped herbs just before serving.

Heat a large, ovenproof frying pan until very hot, add a drizzle of olive oil, then add the monkfish tails. Cook until golden on both sides, then transfer the pan to an oven preheated to 200°C/Gas Mark 6. Roast for 6 minutes, turning halfway through, then remove from the oven and leave to rest for a couple of minutes. Season the fish with a pinch of salt and a squeeze of lemon.

To serve, place the coco beans in the centre of 4 serving plates, then slice each monkfish tail into 5 and place on top of the beans. Spoon the warm dressing over the fish.

This page: arriving at the vast, world-famous Rungis Market, just outside Paris, home to some of the most wonderful produce available.

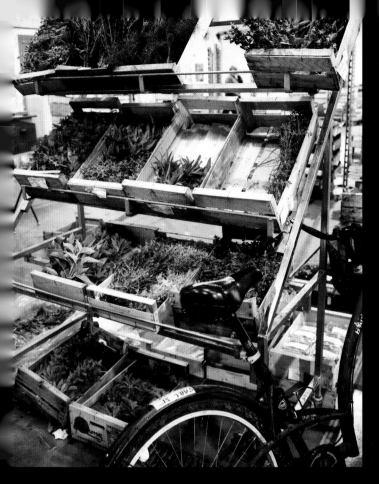

This page, top: produce from the Growers' Market at Rungis, grown on the allotments of the Somme, north of Paris; *bottom:* enjoying casse-croûtes (a light snack) with some of the growers at Rungis.

POACHED MONKFISH CHEEKS WITH GINGER, CARROTS AND WATERCRESS

Serves 4

Another Bistrot plat du jour. Fishermen tell us that if they've had a really good catch, they throw the monkfish heads away; if they haven't, they'll take out the cheeks to sell for extra cash. Fresh monkfish cheeks are lovely – sweet and juicy with quite a meaty texture.

50g softened unsalted butter
50g shallots, very finely chopped
20g fresh ginger, cut into very fine strips
600g trimmed monkfish cheeks
75ml Fish Stock (see page 46)
125ml white wine
4 tablespoons crème fraîche
a few drops of lemon juice
sea salt and freshly ground white pepper
a bunch of watercress, trimmed and separated into 4 small bunches, to garnish

For the carrots
4 carrots, cut into long, thin strips
50ml water
15g unsalted butter
1 teaspoon caster sugar

Use the butter to grease the base of a heavy-based, shallow, flameproof dish suitable for poaching the fish. Sprinkle with the shallots and ginger, then place the monkfish cheeks on top, sprinkle with a pinch of salt and cover with a piece of buttered greaseproof paper. Place the dish on the hob, add the fish stock and wine and bring to the boil. Transfer the dish to an oven preheated to 180°C/Gas Mark 4 and cook for 4–5 minutes, until the fish is just cooked.

Meanwhile, cook the carrots. Put the carrots in a pan with the water, butter, sugar and a pinch of salt and boil rapidly for 1 minute or until the carrots are cooked and shiny.

Divide the fish between 4 shallow bowls. Add the crème fraîche to the sauce in the dish and bring to the boil on the hob, then add a few drops of lemon juice and adjust the seasoning.

Coat the fish in the sauce, spooning the ginger and shallots over. Arrange the carrots on top of the monkfish cheeks and finish with a small bunch of watercress in the centre of each portion.

SEARED FILLET OF YELLOWFIN TUNA BASQUAISE

Serves 4

There is some beautiful pole-caught tuna in the Bay of Biscay. Here it is combined with another classic Spanish element, pipérade. Pipérade is rather like risotto – chefs can never agree on how it should be cooked.

1 tablespoon olive oil
4 pieces of thick yellowfin tuna loin
   (about 150g each)
sea salt and freshly ground white pepper

For the tapenade
1 tablespoon fine capers, drained
1 garlic clove, peeled
a pinch of thyme leaves
2 anchovy fillets
100g black olives, stoned
1 teaspoon Cognac
2 tablespoons extra virgin olive oil

For the pipérade
2 tablespoons olive oil
1 large onion, finely sliced
1 garlic clove, crushed
1 green pepper, peeled, deseeded and
   sliced
2 red peppers, peeled, deseeded and
   sliced
a pinch of piment d'Espelette (or smoked
   paprika)

To finish
20 small flat-leaf parsley leaves
2 tablespoons extra virgin olive oil
1 teaspoon thick aged balsamic vinegar

First, make the tapenade. Pulse the capers, garlic, thyme and anchovies in a small blender or food processor until smooth (or pound them using a pestle and mortar). Add the olives and Cognac and pulse for 30 seconds, then add the olive oil and pulse for 5 seconds. Taste and adjust the seasoning, then set aside.

To make the pipérade, heat the olive oil in a small, heavy-based pan, add the onion and cook gently until soft and lightly coloured. Add the garlic and green pepper, cook for 2 minutes, then add the red pepper and sprinkle on the piment d'Espelette. Cook gently, uncovered, for 20 minutes, then remove from the heat and season to taste.

Heat a non-stick griddle pan until extremely hot, then add the olive oil. Sear the tuna in the hot oil over a high heat for 45 seconds, then sprinkle with salt and turn over. Cook the second side for another 45 seconds to give rare tuna.

Divide the pipérade between 4 serving plates and shape into a neat circle slightly larger than the fish. Place the tuna on top. Put a spoonful of tapenade on each piece of fish and finish with 5 small flat-leaf parsley leaves around the pipérade. Drizzle the olive oil and balsamic vinegar around.

CORNISH RED MULLET WITH FENNEL PURÉE AND BRANDADE OF COD

Serves 4

A robust, summery dish, where the sweetness of the red mullet and olives is underpinned by the meatiness of the cod. Salt cod can be hard to track down, unless you have a Portuguese or Caribbean food store nearby, but we have seen it in some supermarkets too.

12 red mullet fillets (about 70–80g each) scaled and pin bones removed
1/2 lemon
4 tablespoons extra virgin olive oil
6 stoned black olives, thinly sliced
1 tablespoon finely chopped chives
2 heads of red chicory, separated into leaves
sea salt and freshly ground white pepper

For the cod brandade
300g salt cod
1 litre milk
100ml double cream
3 garlic cloves, finely sliced
1 bay leaf
1 sprig of thyme
1 large potato (about 250g), peeled and cut into quarters
50ml extra virgin olive oil, plus extra for brushing
freshly ground black pepper
4 tinned piquillo peppers, peeled and deseeded

For the fennel purée
50g unsalted butter
2 fennel bulbs, finely chopped (you need 350g fennel)
100ml Chicken Stock (see page 44)

First, prepare the cod brandade. Put the salt cod in a large container of cold water and leave to soak in the fridge for 24 hours, changing the water several times. The next day, take the cod from the fridge, drain and leave under a trickle of cold running water for 1 hour.

Put the milk, cream, garlic, bay leaf and thyme in a large pan and bring to the boil. Simmer for 5 minutes, then remove from the heat and leave to infuse for 20 minutes. Meanwhile, cook the potato in a pan of boiling salted water until tender, then drain, pass through a fine sieve and keep warm. Bring the milk mixture back to the boil and add the cod. Return to the boil again, then reduce the heat and poach for 6–8 minutes, depending on the thickness of the fish. Be careful not to let it boil or to overcook the fish.

Remove from the heat and leave to cool for 10 minutes, then strain the cod, reserving the cooking liquor.
Mix the cooked cod with the warm potato in a clean saucepan, then using a wooden spoon, beat in the olive oil, then enough of the strained cooking liquor to obtain a soft but not runny consistency. Season with black pepper and salt if necessary, but taste first, as this dish rarely requires extra salt.

Using a small spoon, fill the peppers with the brandade. Stand the peppers up on an oiled baking tray and place in an oven preheated to 160°C/Gas Mark 3 for 3–4 minutes to heat through. Remove and brush with olive oil.

For the fennel purée, melt the butter in a saucepan, add the fennel and cook over a low heat for 5 minutes, without colouring. Add the chicken stock and simmer until the fennel is just tender. Purée in a blender or food processor until smooth, then pass the mixture through a fine sieve. Season to taste with salt and pepper. Keep warm.

Place the red mullet fillets skin-side up on an oiled baking tray, brush with a little oil and cook under a hot grill for 2–3 minutes, until just cooked through. Season with salt and a squeeze of lemon. Warm the olive oil and black olives together in a small pan, adding the chives at the last moment.

To serve, divide the fennel purée between 4 serving plates and top with the stuffed peppers. Add the red mullet fillets and red chicory leaves, then spoon the warm olive oil, black olives and chives around and over the fish and chicory.

ROAST SEA TROUT WITH GNOCCHI, BROWN SHRIMPS AND NEW-SEASON GARLIC

Serves 4

Sea trout and new-season garlic are both available in April, making it the perfect time to prepare this dish. If you want to cook it out of season, you could use some good salmon instead.

2 tablespoons olive oil
1 quantity of Parmesan Gnocchi
  (see page 52)
4 portions of wild sea trout fillet (about
  120g each), with skin on
½ lemon
sea salt and freshly ground white pepper
a few small sprigs of wood sorrel
  (optional), to garnish

For the garlic purée
100g new-season garlic, peeled
100ml double cream
50ml Chicken Stock (see page 44)

For the sauce
100g white mushrooms
200ml Chicken Stock (see page 44)
2 tablespoons double cream
50g chilled unsalted butter, diced
a squeeze of lemon juice
1 tablespoon olive oil
20g samphire
50g cooked and peeled brown shrimps

For the garlic purée, place the garlic in a small saucepan and cover with cold water. Bring to the boil, then remove from the heat, drain and refresh under cold running water. Drain again and repeat this whole process twice. Drain the garlic, place it in the same saucepan and cover with the cream and chicken stock. Bring gently to the boil, then simmer for 15 minutes. Transfer to a food processor and blend until smooth. Pass through a fine sieve, season to taste and set aside.

To make the sauce, blitz half the mushrooms in a blender or food processor, then put them in a piece of muslin cloth and squeeze out the juice into a saucepan. Discard the blitzed mushroom pulp. Add the chicken stock to the mushroom juice, bring to the boil and simmer until reduced by a third. Add the cream and boil for 2 minutes, then whisk in the cold butter, a few pieces at a time, until emulsified. Season with salt and a squeeze of lemon juice.

Slice the rest of the mushrooms and sauté them in the olive oil until tender. Drain well and add to the sauce, along with the samphire and brown shrimps. Check the seasoning, remembering that the samphire will add a little salt.

Heat half the olive oil in a frying pan, add the gnocchi and cook until golden brown all over. Keep warm.

Meanwhile, to cook the sea trout, heat the remaining olive oil in a large, ovenproof, non-stick frying pan. When it is very hot, add the trout skin-side down and cook for 1 minute. Transfer the pan to an oven preheated to 200°C/Gas Mark 6 and cook for 3–4 minutes. Turn the fish on to the flesh side and roast for a minute longer, then season with a squeeze of lemon and a pinch of salt.

Gently reheat the garlic purée and the sauce, if necessary. Divide the garlic purée between 4 serving plates, place the fish in the centre and then scatter the gnocchi around. Spoon the sauce into the gaps and garnish with the wood sorrel, if using.

PROVENÇAL TARTE FINE WITH GRILLED CORNISH SARDINES

Serves 4

This is classically Provençal but we believe that Cornish sardines are superior to any you get in the Mediterranean. It's a popular dish in the back garden of our café.

1 garlic clove, peeled and left whole
4 tablespoons olive oil
150g Puff Pastry (see page 53)
2 courgettes, cut into 5mm-thick slices
4 tomatoes, skinned, quartered and deseeded
1 teaspoon thyme leaves
6 green and 6 black olives, cut in half and stoned
4 salted anchovies, cut into thin strips
12 Cornish sardine fillets, scales removed
juice of 1 lemon
12 small basil sprigs
2 tablespoons extra virgin olive oil
sea salt and freshly ground black pepper
a few drops of Cabernet Sauvignon wine vinegar, to serve

Put the garlic clove in a small pan with 2 tablespoons of the olive oil and heat gently. Remove from the heat and leave to infuse.

Roll the puff pastry out on a lightly floured work surface into a 24cm square. Prick the pastry sheet all over with a fork and place it on a baking sheet. Place a sheet of greaseproof paper over the pastry, then place another baking sheet on top to stop it rising. Bake in an oven preheated to 200°C/Gas Mark 6 for 10–12 minutes or until golden brown. Remove from the oven, remove the top baking sheet and paper and leave the pastry to cool. When cool, cut four 10cm rounds from the pastry and set aside. Discard the pastry trimmings.

Reheat the garlic-infused olive oil in a heavy-based pan until hot, then add the courgette slices and cook for about 1 minute each side or until they take on a little colour. Remove from the heat and drain on kitchen paper.

Divide the courgette slices and tomato quarters between the 4 pastry rounds, arranging them in an overlapping pattern. Sprinkle the tarts with the thyme, olives and anchovies, season lightly with salt and pepper, then drizzle with a little of the remaining olive oil. Place the tarts on an oiled baking tray. Reduce the oven temperature to 150°C/Gas Mark 2 and place the tarts in the oven for 5 minutes.

On a separate oiled baking tray, lay the sardine fillets out side by side and skin-side up. Brush with the remaining olive oil, then season and place under a hot grill for 2 minutes or until just cooked; there is no need to turn them.

To serve, remove the tarts from the oven and place each one in the centre of a serving plate. Place 3 sardine fillets over the top of each tart, sprinkle a little lemon juice over, then the basil sprigs, followed by a little salt and the extra virgin olive oil. To finish, drizzle over a few drops of wine vinegar.

ROAST CÔTE DE BOEUF WITH TRUFFLE MACARONI AND HERMITAGE JUS

Serves 2

Côte de boeuf is a single rib of beef, just right for serving two. At the restaurant this is carved at the table. Hermitage is a famous red wine from the Rhône, but any full-bodied Côtes du Rhône can be used.

2 x 6cm pieces of beef bone marrow
1 bulb garlic
olive oil
a 550g côte de boeuf
1 tablespoon duck fat
sea salt and freshly ground white pepper
1 bunch of watercress, to garnish

For the sauce
180g beef trimmings
15g duck fat
15g unsalted butter
375ml red Côtes du Rhône wine
70g shallots, sliced
3 garlic cloves, roughly chopped
3 sprigs of thyme
1 bay leaf
40g button mushrooms, thinly sliced
30g smoked streaky bacon, diced
50ml port
200ml Brown Chicken Stock (see page 44)
3 black peppercorns

For the truffle macaroni
100g macaroni
1 tablespoon olive oil, plus extra for drizzling
35g unsalted butter
35g plain flour
250ml milk
70g Philadelphia cream cheese
80g Cheddar cheese, grated
125ml whipping cream
3 free-range egg yolks
15g Parmesan cheese, finely grated
25g Gruyère cheese, finely grated
1/2 teaspoon truffle oil
1 teaspoon chopped truffle
6 slices of truffle

Cover the bone marrow with salted cold water and leave for 24 hours to remove the blood. The next day, wash and scrape the outside of the bone clean. Set aside.

For the sauce, put the beef trimmings, half the duck fat and half the butter in a pan and cook until caramelised. Add 40ml of the red wine and cook for a minute or so, stirring and scraping the base of the pan to deglaze it. In a separate pan, sweat the shallots in the remaining duck fat and butter until soft, then add the garlic, thyme and bay leaf and cook until lightly caramelised. Drain the shallot mixture in a colander, reserving the fat and shallot mixture separately. Put the fat back in the pan, add the mushrooms and bacon and cook until caramelised. Combine all the caramelised ingredients and add 120ml of the remaining red wine and all the port. Bring to the boil, then boil until the mixture is reduced to a thick syrup. Add the remaining red wine, return to the boil and boil until reduced by two-thirds. Add the chicken stock and peppercorns, bring to the boil, then reduce the heat and simmer very gently for 2 hours.

Pass the sauce through a fine sieve, ensuring all the liquid is squeezed out of the beef and mirepoix (caramelised vegetables). Return the liquid to the pan and bring slowly back to the boil, skimming well, then boil until reduced to a coating consistency. Season to taste.

Trim the top of the garlic bulb, leaving the cloves exposed, brush with a little olive oil and sprinkle with a pinch of salt. Wrap in foil and roast in an oven preheated to 200°C/Gas Mark 6 for about 35 minutes or until golden and tender.

For the truffle macaroni, cook the pasta in a pan of boiling salted water with the tablespoon of oil added, until al dente. Strain in a colander, making sure you shake the pasta to remove water lodged inside. Drizzle a little olive oil over the pasta, transfer to a flat tray and leave to cool.

Melt the butter in a saucepan. Remove from the heat and stir in the flour, then return the pan to a very low heat and cook, stirring constantly with a wooden spoon, for 3 minutes. Remove from the heat and cool slightly, then gradually whisk in the milk. Return to the heat and cook, stirring, until the sauce is thickened and smooth. Reduce the heat and simmer very gently for 10 minutes. Remove from the heat again and stir in the Philadelphia and Cheddar cheeses, then adjust the seasoning. Mix the sauce with the cooked pasta and transfer to an ovenproof dish. Bake in an oven preheated to 180°C/Gas Mark 4 for 10 minutes.

Whip the cream in a bowl to form soft peaks, then fold in the egg yolks, Parmesan and Gruyère cheeses, the truffle oil and chopped truffle. Add a pinch of salt and a little pepper.

Spoon this glaze over the macaroni cheese and place under a hot grill until golden brown. When serving, garnish with the remaining sliced truffle and a drizzle of the sauce.

About 30 minutes before cooking the beef, take it out of the fridge to bring it to room temperature. Melt the duck fat in a very hot ovenproof frying pan, add the beef and cook for 2 minutes on each side, until well caramelised. Transfer the pan to an oven preheated to 220°C/Gas Mark 7 and cook for 8 minutes. Remove from the oven and leave to rest in a warm place for 10–15 minutes.

Meanwhile, put the bone marrow in an ovenproof pan with a little olive oil and cook in an oven preheated to 200°C/Gas Mark 6 for 8 minutes, then remove and keep warm.

Carve the beef into 10 slices, divide between 2 serving plates and season with a little sea salt. Garnish the plates with the roast bone marrow, watercress and roast garlic. Serve the macaroni and the sauce separately.

SLOW-COOKED SHORT-RIB OF BEEF WITH SHALLOT PURÉE, HONEY-ROAST PARSNIPS AND HERMITAGE WINE SAUCE

Serves 4

Short-ribs, also known as Jacob's ladder, are a very good-value piece of beef that requires long, slow cooking. The honey-roast parsnips are a lovely little dish that would work well for any Sunday lunch.

For the beef
50ml vegetable oil
8 beef short-ribs (about 125g each)
1 carrot, roughly chopped
1 stick celery, roughly chopped
$\frac{1}{2}$ leek, roughly chopped
$\frac{1}{2}$ onion, roughly chopped
25g button mushrooms, sliced
1 garlic clove, chopped
25g smoked streaky bacon, diced
1 sprig of thyme
1 bay leaf
250ml Crozes-Hermitage red wine
250ml Chicken Stock (see page 44)
375ml Brown Chicken Jus (see page 45)

For the shallot purée
60g unsalted butter
300g shallots, finely sliced
50ml double cream
200ml Chicken Stock (see page 44)
sea salt and freshly ground white pepper

For the honey-roast parsnips
a little olive oil, for cooking
2 large parsnips, peeled, core removed
   and cut into 8cm batons
1 teaspoon honey

For the beef, heat about half of the vegetable oil in a heavy-based pan over a high heat. Seal the beef on all sides until caramelised – do this in small batches as it will stop the pan losing temperature and the beef from stewing. Once all the beef is coloured, transfer it to a casserole. Add the remaining oil to the pan, then add the chopped vegetables, sliced mushrooms, garlic and bacon and cook until caramelised. Transfer this mixture into the casserole along with the herbs.

Pour the wine into the pan and let it bubble, stirring and scraping the base of the pan with a wooden spoon to deglaze it. Pour this over the beef, then pour over the chicken stock and jus and bring to the boil. Cover with a tight-fitting lid, transfer the casserole to an oven preheated to 110°C/Gas Mark $\frac{1}{4}$ and cook for 2–2$\frac{1}{2}$ hours or until the beef is tender. Remove from the oven and leave it to cool in the casserole.

Once cooled, remove the beef from the dish and place it in a small tray. Strain the liquid through a fine sieve into a saucepan, then bring to the boil and cook over a medium heat until it has reduced enough to coat the back of a spoon. Add the beef to the sauce and heat through, basting until it is nicely glazed all over.

Meanwhile, make the shallot purée. Melt the butter in a pan, add the shallots and sweat gently for 1 hour until soft and golden brown. Add the cream and stock and cook for a further 5 minutes, then purée in a blender or food processor. Pass the purée through a fine sieve and season to taste.

In the meantime, prepare the honey-roast parsnips. Heat a little olive oil in an ovenproof frying pan until very hot. Add the parsnips and cook for 2–3 minutes until they start to caramelise, then transfer the pan to an oven preheated to 200°C/Gas Mark 6 and roast for 3 minutes. Season and stir the parsnips, then roast for a further 3 minutes. Pour over the honey and continue to cook for another 3 minutes.

Divide the shallot purée between 4 serving plates. Add the parsnips and lay 2 ribs alongside. Finally spoon the sauce around the dish.

BAVETTE OF BEEF WITH MACARONI CHEESE AND BORDELAISE SAUCE

Serves 4

This is a good wintry dish. You could use rump or entrecote steak instead of bavette, if you like. Be sure to use a good quality wine for the sauce.

For the macaroni cheese
100g macaroni
1 tablespoon olive oil
250ml milk
1/4 onion, with a clove and a bay leaf studded in it
35g unsalted butter
35g plain flour
70g Philadelphia cream cheese
80g Cheddar cheese, grated

For the bavettes
1 tablespoon vegetable oil
4 bavettes (skirt steak), weighing about 150g each
freshly ground black pepper
10g unsalted butter
1 sprig of thyme

For the Bordelaise sauce
40g unsalted butter
3 white peppercorns
50g shallots, finely chopped
125ml good-quality red Bordeaux wine
100ml Brown Chicken Jus (see page 45)
sea salt and freshly ground white pepper

For the spinach
20g unsalted butter
400g baby spinach leaves, rinsed and well drained

For the bone marrow
200g beef bone marrow, removed from the bone (ask your butcher to do this), sliced into 5mm-thick discs and soaked in cold water for 24 hours, then drained
coarse sea salt
1 tablespoon chopped parsley, to garnish

For the macaroni cheese, cook the macaroni in a large pan of boiling salted water with the olive oil added, until tender (but keep a little bite to the pasta). When cooked, drain, refresh under cold water and drain very well, then place in a large bowl and set aside.

To make the sauce to bind the pasta, put the milk and studded onion in a pan and bring to the boil, then remove from the heat and leave to infuse for 5 minutes. Remove the studded onion and discard. Melt the butter in a separate heavy-based saucepan, stir in the flour and cook gently, stirring, for 1–2 minutes. Remove from the heat and gradually add the hot milk, whisking continuously. Return to the heat and cook, stirring, until the sauce is thickened and smooth, then reduce the heat and simmer very gently for 10 minutes, stirring occasionally. Remove from the heat again, stir in the Philadelphia and Cheddar cheeses and season. Stir the sauce into the cooked macaroni. Transfer the mixture to an ovenproof dish and bake in an oven preheated to 180°C/Gas Mark 4 for 20 minutes.

To cook the steaks, heat a large cast-iron frying pan until it is really hot, then add the vegetable oil. Season the bavettes with plenty of black pepper, then carefully place them into the pan. Still over a high heat, colour the meat on both sides until golden. Add the butter and thyme, then when the butter starts to foam, transfer the pan to an oven preheated to 200°C/Gas Mark 6 and roast for about 2 minutes on each side (depending how thick your bavettes are). Bavette is most tender when it is served rare. Remove from the oven, place the meat on a warm plate and leave to rest in a warm place for 20 minutes.

For the Bordelaise sauce, heat 10g of the butter in a pan, add the peppercorns and shallots and cook for 5 minutes, until the shallots are soft but not coloured. Add the wine and boil until reduced by two thirds. Remove the peppercorns. Add the chicken jus, bring to the boil, then reduce the heat and simmer for 5 minutes. Just before serving, reheat the sauce until boiling, dice the remaining butter and gradually whisk it in. Adjust the seasoning.

To cook the spinach, melt 10g of the butter in a saucepan, then add the spinach. Cook briefly over a high heat until the spinach starts to collapse, then remove from the heat and squeeze out any liquid. Remove the spinach to a plate. Melt the remaining butter in the same pan, add the spinach and reheat. Season to taste and keep warm.

Place the bone marrow in a small saucepan of cold water with a pinch of coarse sea salt added and gently bring to the boil, then drain. Keep warm.

To serve, spoon some macaroni cheese on to each serving plate, then make a bed of spinach alongside. Cut the beef across the grain into 5mm-thick slices, then sprinkle with coarse sea salt. Place the beef on the spinach, then the bone marrow on top. Spoon the sauce over the bone marrow and beef, then sprinkle the parsley and a pinch of coarse sea salt over the top.

The wonders of Rungis Market: cheese, meat, fish and poultry all under one roof.

ROAST BEEF FILLET AND SLOW-COOKED OX CHEEK WITH CHARD, WATERCRESS AND TRUFFLE MASH

Serves 4

To all intents and purposes, beef and ox are the same animal, so the terminology can be a little confusing. The term ox is used for thriftier cuts such as tail and cheeks. Whatever you call it, this is a wonderful dish, contrasting the rich meat of slow-cooked cheeks with flash-roasted, tender beef fillet.

For the ox cheek
2kg ox cheek, cleaned of all sinew
250ml red Beaujolais wine
125ml port
1 carrot, roughly chopped
1 stick celery, roughly chopped
100g onion, roughly chopped
80g leek, roughly chopped
3 garlic cloves, chopped
1 sprig of thyme
1 bay leaf
2 black peppercorns, crushed
100ml vegetable oil
2 litres Brown Chicken Stock (see page 44)
200g Swiss chard, stalk cut into 5mm dice and green leafy part finely shredded
$^1/_2$ bunch watercress, leaves only

For the truffle mash
600g Desiree potatoes or similar floury potatoes, peeled and halved
300g chilled unsalted butter, diced
100ml double cream
100ml full-fat milk
1 tablespoon chopped winter truffle
1 teaspoon truffle oil
12 slices of winter truffle

For the beef fillet
600g beef fillet
1 tablespoon vegetable oil
15g unsalted butter
1 sprig of thyme
sea salt and freshly ground white pepper

Combine the ox cheek, red wine, port, chopped vegetables, garlic, herbs and peppercorns in a non-metallic dish and leave to marinate in the fridge for 24 hours. Strain through a colander with a bowl set underneath to catch the liquid.

Heat a heavy-based frying pan until very hot, then add the vegetable oil, ox cheek and vegetables and sauté until golden brown and nicely caramelised. In a saucepan, bring the strained marinade liquid to the boil, then boil until reduced by half.

Place the browned ox cheek and vegetables into a casserole and cover with the reduced marinade and the chicken stock. Bring to the boil, then cover with a lid or foil and transfer to an oven preheated to 110°C/Gas Mark $^1/_4$. Braise for $3^1/_2$–4 hours or until the meat is really tender. Remove from the oven and allow the mixture to cool in the dish.

Once cooled, remove the meat from the dish and chill, then cut into 1cm dice. Pass the cooking liquor through a fine sieve into a saucepan, bring to the boil and simmer until reduced to the consistency of honey. Remove from the heat, allow to cool, then refrigerate.

For the truffle mash, cook the potatoes in a pan of boiling salted water until tender. Drain well, then return to the pan and place over a low heat to drive off any remaining moisture. Pass the potatoes through a fine sieve or ricer or mash well, then return to a clean saucepan. Using a whisk, beat in the butter, then the cream and milk and reheat gently. If at any time the mash splits, just add an extra 100ml of milk and whisk until it comes back together. Finally add the chopped truffle and truffle oil.

Season the beef fillet with salt and pepper. Heat an ovenproof frying pan until very hot, add the vegetable oil and beef and seal the fillet on all sides and on each end. Add the butter and thyme. Transfer the pan to an oven preheated to 200°C/Gas Mark 6 and roast for 6–8 minutes, turning and basting the meat every 2 minutes. When cooked to medium-rare, the meat will feel slightly springy when squeezed. Remove from the oven and leave to rest in a warm place for at least 12 minutes.

To cook the Swiss chard, blanch the leaf part in a pan of boiling salted water for 1 minute, then remove with a slotted spoon and set aside. Add the chard stalks to the water and cook for 2–3 minutes, until tender. Drain well.

To serve, heat the ox cheek up in the reduced cooking liquor, add the chard leaves and stalks, then at the last moment, add the watercress leaves. Divide between 4 serving plates. Carve the beef fillet into 4 even slices and place on top of the ox cheek. Using 2 metal spoons to shape the mash into quenelles (oval shapes), place a quenelle of truffle mash on the side of each plate and finish with 3 slices of truffle on top of each.

TÊTE DE VEAU WITH SAUCE RAVIGOTE

Serves 6

This dish is the braised boneless head of a veal calf. It's a real Bistrot classic. Calf's head may prove difficult to buy in the UK but it's worth asking a specialist butcher to source one for you.

For the tête de veau
1 calf's head, boned and rolled (ask your butcher to do this)
2 large carrots, cut into quarters
1 onion, cut into quarters
1 leek, cut in half
1 stick celery, cut in half
2 garlic cloves, peeled and left whole
1 sprig of thyme
4 litres Chicken Stock (see page 44)

For the garnish
6 large new potatoes, peeled
20g unsalted butter
6 new carrots, cut into 5cm pieces
3 sticks celery, cut into 5cm pieces
salt and freshly ground white pepper

1 quantity of Ravigote Dressing (see page 50)

To cook the calf's head, place all the ingredients in a large pan and bring to the boil, skimming well. Reduce the heat and simmer for 2½ hours, then remove from the heat and leave the calf's head to cool in its own liquor. Remove from the pan, being careful to keep it intact. Roll it into a sausage shape in cling film, then place in the fridge overnight to firm up. Pass the cooking liquor through a fine sieve into a clean pan and boil until it has reduced by one third.

To prepare the garnish, cook the potatoes in a pan of lightly salted boiling water until tender. Drain and keep warm. Just before serving, toss the potatoes in half the butter and some seasoning. Cook the carrots and celery together in a separate pan of water with a pinch of salt and the remaining butter added, until tender. Drain and keep warm.

Take the calf's head from the fridge and slice into 6 portions, leaving the cling film around the outside. Place in a large saucepan or roasting pan. Reheat the reduced cooking liquor and pour it over the calf's head. Bring back to the boil, then simmer for 10 minutes or until the meat is thoroughly hot throughout.

Place the calf's head portions in deep serving bowls and remove the cling film. Add the carrots, celery and potatoes. Pour over some of the cooking liquor and serve the ravigote dressing separately.

BRAISED VEAL CHEEKS, HAM AND TONGUE WITH POMMES PURÉES AND TRUFFLE MADEIRA SAUCE

Serves 4

Jeff used to cook this at the Savoy Hotel 20 years ago. It's so good that we still have it on the menu today. Ham, tongue, mushrooms and truffle together make up a classic French garnish known as zingara.

For the tongue
1 veal tongue
1 onion, sliced
1 carrot, sliced
2 garlic cloves, chopped
1 bay leaf
2 sprigs of thyme
1 litre Chicken Stock (see page 44)
2 tablespoons sherry vinegar

For the veal cheeks and sauce
2–3 tablespoons vegetable oil
12 veal cheeks (30–40g each), trimmed of fat and skin
1 onion, diced
2 carrots, diced
1 leek, diced
3 garlic cloves, chopped
125ml white wine
1 bay leaf
2 sprigs of thyme
600ml Brown Chicken Stock (see page 44)
200ml Brown Chicken Jus (see page 45)
1 teaspoon sherry vinegar
5g black truffle, finely chopped
2 tablespoons Madeira

To finish and serve
40g unsalted butter
200g ham, cut into 6cm batons
1 teaspoon chopped parsley
16 small button mushrooms, stalks trimmed off
sea salt
juice of ¼ lemon
1 quantity of Pommes Purées (see page 56)

Place the tongue in a casserole with the vegetables, garlic and herbs. Cover with the stock and vinegar – depending on the size of dish, you may need to top up with a little water. Cover with a lid and braise in an oven preheated to 140°C/Gas Mark 1 for 4 hours. Remove from the oven, then remove the tongue from the dish and peel off the skin whilst it is still hot. Discard the skin, return the tongue to the stock and leave it to cool in the liquid.

For the veal cheeks, heat the vegetable oil in a heavy-based ovenproof pan or casserole, add the cheeks and cook over a medium-high heat until sealed all over. When browned on all sides, remove the cheeks from the pan and set aside. Add the vegetables and garlic to the pan and cook over a high heat until caramelised. Add the wine and bubble rapidly until reduced by half. Return the cheeks to the pan with the herbs and cover with the stock and jus, then bring to the boil. Cover with a tight-fitting lid and braise in an oven preheated to 110°C/Gas Mark ¼ for 2–2½ hours or until tender.

Remove from the oven, leave the cheeks to cool in the liquor, then remove from the pan. Strain the cooking liquor into a clean saucepan, bring to the boil and simmer until reduced to a coating consistency. Reserve 200ml of this sauce. Add the cheeks to the remaining sauce and reheat gently.

Heat the reserved sauce in a small saucepan, add the vinegar and truffle and simmer for 2 minutes. Just before serving, add the Madeira.

Cut the tongue into batons the same size as the ham. Melt half the butter in a pan, add the tongue and ham and cook until thoroughly heated through. Stir in the parsley. Melt the remaining butter in a separate pan, add the mushrooms and cook for 2–3 minutes until tender, then season with salt and a little lemon juice.

To serve, spoon the potato on to 4 serving plates, then add the cheeks, the tongue and ham mixture and finally the mushrooms. Spoon the sauce over the meat and around the plate.

BAKED VACHERIN MONT D'OR WITH RATTE POTATOES AND CHARCUTERIE

This is very easy to prepare and makes a good dish for an informal Christmas meal with friends – Vacherin Mont d'Or is available in December and January. In France they often pour a little vin jaune from the Jura over the cheese just before serving.

2 x 350g Vacherin Mont d'Or cheeses
600g waxy new potatoes, preferably Ratte
40g unsalted butter
12 slices of Bayonne ham
12 slices of Jésus de Lyon salami
12 slices of saucisson sec
12 slices of rosette saucisson
12 caper berries
150g cornichons
150g cocktail onions
sea salt

Soak the cheeses, still in their boxes, in cold water for 3 hours. When the cheeses are baked, the steam from the moisture absorbed into the wooden boxes gives them a lovely wood scent. Remove the cheese from the cold water and wrap the boxes (with lids still on and cheese inside) in foil. Place on a baking tray in an oven preheated to 180°C/Gas Mark 4 and bake for 25 minutes.

Meanwhile, put the potatoes in a pan of cold salted water, bring to the boil and simmer for 15–20 minutes or until tender. Drain well, then add the butter and season with salt.

To serve, remove the foil from the cheese and place on a large wooden board, then neatly arrange the charcuterie around them. Scatter the caper berries, cornichons and onions over the meats. Accompany with the warm buttered potatoes. Eat like a fondue, dipping the accompaniments into the molten cheese using a fork.

SAUTÉED VEAL KIDNEYS WITH GLAZED ONIONS, CHANTERELLES AND GRAIN MUSTARD

Serves 4

We always buy kidneys that are still encased in their own fat, as this ensures no oxidisation of the kidney. If you are buying kidneys out of the fat, make sure they are bright red in colour rather than brown. You will enjoy them more if they are cooked medium-rare.

For the pommes mousselines
200g Desiree potatoes or similar floury potatoes, peeled and halved
100g chilled unsalted butter, diced
50ml double cream
50ml full-fat milk

For the sauce
¼ onion, chopped
½ garlic clove, chopped
1 sprig of thyme
20g unsalted butter
75ml white wine
1 tablespoon white wine vinegar
150ml double cream
1 tablespoon Brown Chicken Jus (see page 45)
2 teaspoons Dijon mustard
1 teaspoon English mustard
2 teaspoons wholegrain mustard
a small squeeze of lemon juice
sea salt and freshly ground white pepper

For the glazed onions
12 baby onions, peeled
25g unsalted butter
1 teaspoon caster sugar

For the carrots
3 tablespoons water
10g unsalted butter
1 large carrot, peeled and cut into 6cm batons using a mandolin

For the kidneys
1 teaspoon vegetable oil
440g veal kidneys, cleaned and cut into 1cm cubes
a knob of unsalted butter

To finish
10g unsalted butter
100g yellow chanterelle mushrooms

For the pommes mousselines, cook the potatoes in a pan of boiling salted water until tender. Drain well, then return to the pan and place over a low heat to drive off any remaining moisture. Pass the potatoes through a fine sieve or ricer or mash well, then return to a clean saucepan over a low heat. Using a whisk, beat in the butter, then the cream and milk. If at any time the mash splits, just add a little extra milk and whisk until it comes back together. Keep hot.

To make the sauce, sweat the onion, garlic and thyme in the butter in a small saucepan over a medium heat for 5 minutes; do not colour. Add the wine and vinegar and boil until reduced by three-quarters, then add the cream, chicken jus and Dijon and English mustards and simmer for 2 minutes. Remove from the heat and strain through a fine sieve. Return to the saucepan, add the wholegrain mustard, then season with a pinch of salt and a small squeeze of lemon juice. Keep warm.

For the glazed onions, place the baby onions in a small saucepan and cover with water, then add the butter and sugar. Bring to the boil, then reduce the heat and simmer until the liquid evaporates and the onions are evenly browned. Keep warm.

For the carrots, place the water in a small saucepan, along with the butter and bring to the boil. Once emulsified, add the carrot batons and a pinch of salt and boil for 30 seconds. Remove from the heat, drain and keep warm.

For the kidneys, heat a large frying pan until very hot, add the vegetable oil, then the kidneys and sauté for 2 minutes. Add the butter and cook for a further 30 seconds, making sure the kidneys are coloured on the outside but still pink inside. Season with salt and pepper, then drain the kidneys on a clean cloth.

To finish, heat the butter in a small frying pan until it is just starting to brown, then add the chanterelles and cook for about 1 minute or until soft. Season and drain.

Divide the pommes mousselines between 4 large serving bowls. Place the kidneys on top, then put the onions and chanterelles around the outside. Spoon the hot sauce over the kidneys and place the carrots on top to finish.

SLOW-COOKED PORK CHEEKS AND BELLY WITH BOULANGÈRE POTATOES AND SAVOY CABBAGE

Serves 8

These are two of our favourite cuts of pork, and two of the cheapest – or at least they used to be, but now that thrifty cuts are becoming fashionable the price seems to be creeping up. The boulangère potatoes are also very good with fish, if you substitute fish stock for the chicken stock. Most of the work for this dish can be done well in advance.

For the pork belly
300g rock salt
10 sprigs of thyme, chopped
1 teaspoon black peppercorns, crushed
6 garlic cloves, crushed
1kg pork belly
1.5 litres duck fat

For the boulangère potatoes
20g unsalted butter
1 onion, very finely sliced
800g potatoes, peeled
100ml boiling Chicken Stock (see page 44)
50g Clarified Butter (see page 51), for brushing
sea salt and freshly ground white pepper

For the pork cheeks
2 tablespoons vegetable oil
24 pork cheeks
olive oil, for cooking
1 carrot, sliced
1 onion, sliced
2 sticks celery, chopped
$^1/_2$ leek, chopped
3 sprigs of thyme
4 garlic cloves, crushed
100ml white wine
2 litres Brown Chicken Stock (see page 44)

For the cabbage
1 tablespoon duck fat
1 Savoy cabbage, finely shredded
4 tablespoons boiling water

For the pork belly, put the rock salt, thyme, peppercorns and garlic into a blender or food processor and process to mix. Spread half of this mixture over the base of a deep, non-metallic tray, large enough to just hold the pork belly. Place the pork belly on top, then cover with the remaining salt mixture and leave in the fridge for 24 hours.

Remove the pork belly and thoroughly rinse off the salt under cold running water. Pat dry with kitchen paper.

Melt the duck fat in a large heavy-based casserole, making sure it does not come too close to the top. Add the rinsed belly, then gently bring the fat to a simmer. Put the lid on and cook in an oven preheated to 110°C/Gas Mark $^1/_4$ for $1^1/_2$–2 hours or until the meat is very tender. Remove from the oven and leave to cool. Take out the pork belly and place it in between 2 trays with a small weight placed on top. Leave in the fridge for at least 6 hours, preferably overnight.

For the potatoes, melt the unsalted butter in a heavy-based saucepan over a low heat, then add the onion and some salt and pepper. Cook slowly for 1–$1^1/_2$ hours or until the onion is golden brown and very soft, stirring occasionally. Spread the warm cooked onion between 2 sheets of greaseproof paper (32cm x 12cm in size) in a tray and roll to an even layer.

Slice the potatoes thinly on a mandolin on to a tray. Do not wash them after they are sliced. Arrange half the potato slices, slightly overlapping each other, in a buttered and greaseproof paper-lined baking tin or dish (32cm x 12cm in size) and season with salt and pepper. Carefully remove the top sheet of paper from the cooked onions, invert the onions on top of the potatoes, then remove the tray and the sheet of greaseproof now covering the onions. Arrange the remaining potato slices, slightly overlapping each other, over the onion layer. Pour over the boiling stock and brush with some of the clarified butter.

Bake in an oven preheated to 180°C/ Gas Mark 4 for 15 minutes, then remove from the oven, press the potatoes down with a fish slice and brush with a little more clarified butter. Return to the oven and bake for a further 15 minutes. When cooked, it should be golden on top. Remove from the oven and leave to cool slightly, then cover with a sheet of greaseproof paper. Place a tray of a similar size on top and press down. Place a small weight on top, then chill in the fridge for 24 hours.

To cook the pork cheeks, heat a heavy-based frying pan until it is very hot, add the vegetable oil, then add the cheeks in small batches and cook until coloured all over and nicely caramelised. Remove to a plate and set aside.

Heat a little olive oil in a large casserole, add the vegetables and fry until golden brown. Add the thyme, garlic, white wine and pork cheeks, then pour in the stock to cover. Bring back to a gentle simmer, cover with a tight-fitting lid and transfer to an oven preheated to 140°C/Gas Mark 1. Cook for $1\frac{1}{2}$ hours or until the meat is tender. Remove from the oven and leave to cool, then remove the meat to a plate and strain the cooking liquor through a fine sieve. Return the cooking liquor to the pan and cook over a high heat until reduced and thickened enough to coat the back of a spoon.

Before you are ready to serve, turn the chilled potato mixture out on to a chopping board and cut it into rectangles, each about 8cm x 6cm. Place these on a baking sheet and reheat in an oven preheated to 180°C/Gas Mark 4 for 10 minutes.

Cut the pressed pork belly into 16 strips, each about 6cm x 3cm and 1cm thick. Heat a little olive oil in a frying pan until hot, then add the belly strips and fry until golden on both sides. Drain on kitchen paper.

For the cabbage, heat the duck fat in a large saucepan until it is very hot. Keep the heat on high, then add the cabbage and boiling water. Stir the cabbage continuously as it will cook very quickly. The idea is that by the time the cabbage is cooked, the water has evaporated. If you think the cabbage is starting to colour but is not quite cooked, add another tablespoon of boiling water. Once cooked, season the cabbage and remove it from the pan.

Reheat the reduced cooking liquor in a large pan, add the pork cheeks and simmer gently for 8–10 minutes, until thoroughly heated.

To serve, divide the cabbage between 4 serving plates and top with a portion of potato. Place 3 cheeks on top of the potato, then place 2 pork belly strips in between the cheeks. Lastly spoon the reduced cooking liquor around the plate.

Opposite: Monsieur Baudino, farmer, and his AOC Sisteron lamb, famed for its flavour and tenderness.

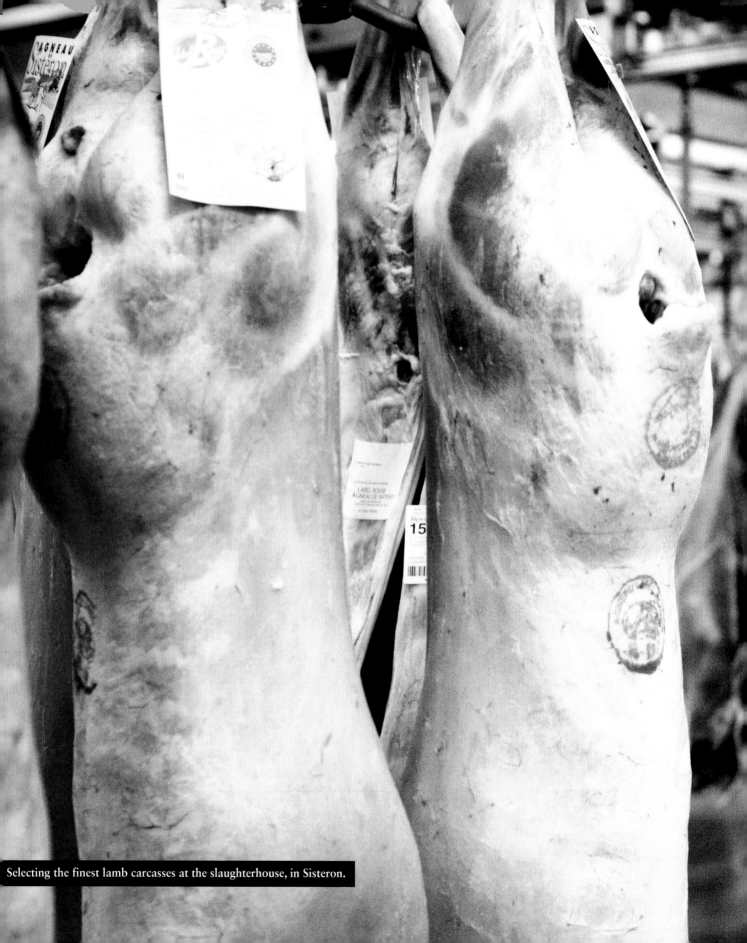

Selecting the finest lamb carcasses at the slaughterhouse, in Sisteron.

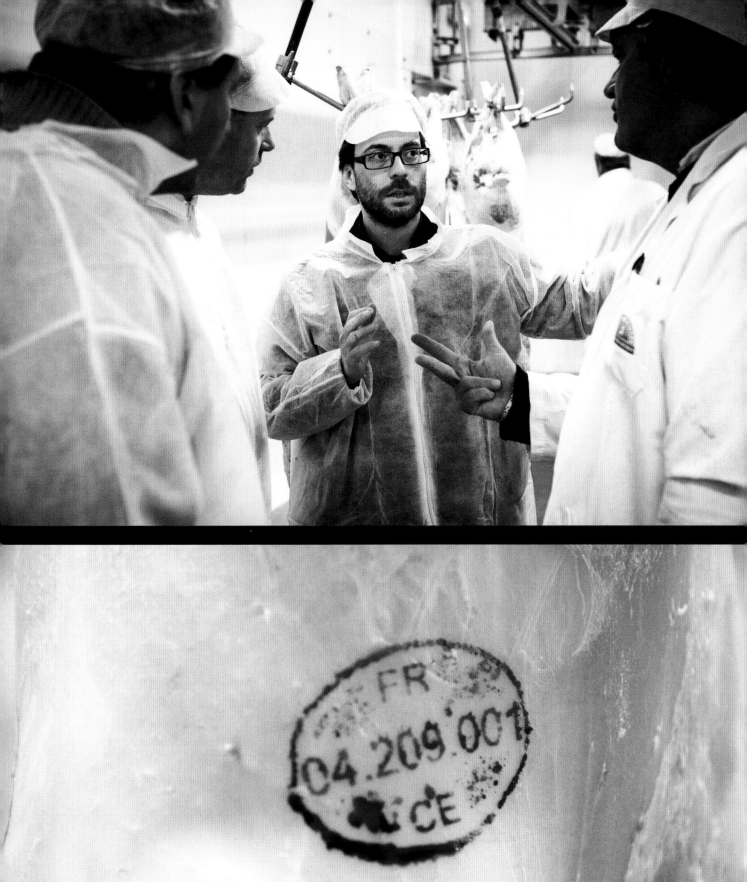

SLOW-COOKED PYRENEES LAMB SHOULDER WITH PIPÉRADE AND GOAT'S CHEESE RAVIOLI

Serves 4

Pyrenees milk-fed lambs have pale meat, a delicate flavour and a buttery texture. We buy them whole and are always looking for ways of using everything up. We devised a means of using the shoulders in this dish, where pipérade and goat's cheese add a lovely sweetness and acidity. You can, of course, use new-season lamb instead.

For the lamb
4 teaspoons vegetable oil
1 Pyrenees lamb shoulder, boned and
    rolled (about 1kg)
40g carrot, roughly chopped
20g onion, roughly chopped
20g celery, roughly chopped
20g leek, roughly chopped
2 garlic cloves, chopped
50ml white wine
1 sprig of thyme
1 sprig of rosemary
2 litres Brown Chicken Stock (see page 44)

For the pipérade
300g onions, finely sliced
1 garlic clove, finely sliced
50ml olive oil
300g piquillo peppers (from a tin or jar),
    drained and finely sliced
sea salt and freshly ground white pepper

For the ravioli
60g good quality goat's cheese, such as
    St Maure
1 tablespoon chopped mixed herbs, such
    as chervil, parsley and tarragon
1/2 quantity of Pasta Dough (see page 52)
1 free-range egg yolk
olive oil

For the garnish
10 stoned black nicoise olives, cut in half
20 flat-leaf parsley leaves

For the lamb, heat a large, heavy-based frying pan until it is extremely hot, add the vegetable oil, then cook the lamb until it is golden all over – this should take at least 5 minutes. Once the lamb is well browned, transfer it to a casserole.

Fry the vegetables and garlic in the same frying pan until golden, then add them to the lamb. Pour the wine into the frying pan and let it bubble, stirring and scraping the base of the pan with a wooden spoon to deglaze it, then add this to the lamb. Lastly add the herbs and stock to the casserole and bring to the boil, skimming off any scum from the surface.

Cover the casserole with a lid and transfer it to an oven preheated to 110°C/Gas Mark 1/4. Cook for 2–2 1/2 hours or until tender. A good test for braised meat is that you should be able to put the handle of a dinner knife through it without much resistance.

Remove from the oven and leave to cool. Remove any string from the lamb, then wrap the lamb tightly in cling film to form a round sausage shape about 5–6cm thick. Refrigerate for 24 hours.

Pass the cooking liquor through a piece of muslin cloth or a fine sieve, then boil it until it is reduced to a light coating consistency. Cool and refrigerate until required.

For the pipérade, sweat the onions and garlic in the olive oil in a wide saucepan with no lid on. Initially the onions will release some liquid, which will evaporate. Continue to cook over a low heat for 1 hour, stirring occasionally. The onions should start to colour as the sugars in them caramelise. When they are golden brown and very soft, add the piquillo peppers and cook for a further 10 minutes. Season with salt and pepper and keep warm.

To make the ravioli, mix the goat's cheese and chopped herbs together, then transfer this mixture to a piping bag fitted with a plain nozzle. Roll the pasta dough out to the thinnest setting using a pasta machine and then brush it with the egg yolk. Cut out 40 discs of pasta using a 3cm round pastry cutter. Pipe about 1/4 teaspoon of goat's cheese mixture on to 20 of the discs, then place the remaining discs on top to make the ravioli, sealing the edges with your fingers and pressing down well so there is no air left inside.

To serve, cut the lamb, still wrapped in cling film, into 4 even portions. Pour the sauce into a saucepan and bring to the boil, then reduce the heat, stand the lamb in the simmering sauce and cover with a lid. Simmer for about 10 minutes to reheat the lamb, then with a pair of scissors, carefully remove the cling film.

(Continued on page 188)

(Continued from page 186)

Simmer for a further 5 minutes, coating the lamb regularly with the sauce. The lamb should be nicely glazed by the time it is hot.

Cook the ravioli in a large pan of boiling salted water for 2 minutes, then drain. Roll it gently in a little olive oil and season with salt.

Spoon a circle of the hot pipérade on to each serving plate and place the lamb in the centre. Surround each portion of lamb with 5 ravioli, 5 olive halves and 5 parsley leaves. Drizzle a little of the lamb sauce around each plate and serve.

BRAISED LAMB SHOULDER WITH RUNNER BEANS, PEAS, CONFIT POTATOES, OLIVES AND MINT

Serves 4

This is a Café à Vin lunchtime favourite in early summer. Shoulder of lamb is a more economical cut than leg but the flavour is all there.

For the lamb
1 teaspoon vegetable oil
1 small lamb shoulder, boned and rolled (about 1kg)
40g carrot, roughly chopped
20g onion, roughly chopped
20g celery, roughly chopped
20g leek, roughly chopped
2 garlic cloves, chopped
50ml white wine
1 sprig of thyme
1 sprig of rosemary
2 litres Brown Chicken Stock (see page 44)

For the confit potatoes
200ml duck fat
6 Charlotte potatoes or other waxy new potatoes, cut in half lengthwise
1 garlic clove, cut in half
1 sprig of thyme
1 tablespoon olive oil
sea salt and freshly ground white pepper

To serve
200g shelled fresh peas
200g runner beans, cut into 1cm diamonds
1 tablespoon extra virgin olive oil
2 tablespoons chopped mint
75g stoned black olives, halved

For the lamb, heat a large, heavy-based frying pan until it is extremely hot, add the vegetable oil, then seal the lamb until it is golden all over – this should take at least 5 minutes. Once the lamb is well browned, transfer it to a casserole.

Fry all of the vegetables and chopped garlic in the same frying pan until golden, then add them to the lamb. Pour the wine into the frying pan and let it bubble, stirring and scraping the base of the pan with a wooden spoon to deglaze it, then add this to the lamb. Lastly add the herbs and stock to the casserole and bring to the boil, skimming off any scum from the surface. Cover with a lid and transfer to an oven preheated to 110°C/Gas Mark $^1/_4$. Cook for 2–2$^1/_2$ hours or until tender.

Remove from the oven and leave to cool. Remove any string from the lamb, then wrap the lamb tightly in cling film to form a roll. Refrigerate for at least 6 hours or overnight.

Strain the cooking liquor through a piece of muslin cloth or a fine sieve, then boil it until it is reduced to a light coating consistency. Cool and refrigerate until required.

For the potatoes, put the duck fat in a saucepan and bring to the boil. Add the potatoes, garlic and thyme and simmer gently for 20 minutes or until the potatoes are tender. Remove from the

heat and leave the potatoes in the fat to cool slightly, then remove them with a slotted spoon. Place the potatoes cut-side down in a hot frying pan with the olive oil and cook on one side only over a high heat until golden and crisp. Season, then drain on kitchen paper.

Cut the lamb, still wrapped in cling film, into 4 even portions. Put them in a saucepan in a single layer. Boil the sauce in a separate pan, then pour enough over the lamb to cover by three-quarters. Bring back to the boil, then reduce the heat, cover and simmer for 15 minutes. Carefully remove the cling film with a pair of scissors.

To serve, blanch the peas and runner beans in a large pan of boiling salted water for 3 minutes, drain well, then return them to the pan and add the olive oil. Heat through, then add the mint, olives and cooked potatoes and adjust the seasoning.

Divide the potato mixture between 4 large soup plates, place the glazed meat in the centre.

ASSIETTE OF CORNISH LAMB PROVENCALE

Serves 6

This is a very detailed dish, which we devised to use up all the cuts of the lamb.
If you don't feel up to cooking the whole thing it's fine to do just one or two elements,
such as the pastillas and the stuffed courgette flowers.

For the lamb pastillas
2 teaspoons vegetable oil
200g lamb shoulder
20g carrot, roughly chopped
10g onion, roughly chopped
10g celery, roughly chopped
10g leek, roughly chopped
1 garlic clove, chopped
25ml white wine
1 sprig of thyme
1 sprig of rosemary
1 litre Brown Chicken Stock (see page 44)
100g Dried Fruit Chutney (see pages 209–210)
100g filo pastry sheets
100g Clarified Butter (see page 51), melted
1 teaspoon olive oil

For the stuffed courgette flowers
100g onion, cut into 3mm dice
$\frac{1}{2}$ garlic clove, crushed
2 tablespoons olive oil, plus extra for brushing and drizzling
4 plum tomatoes, peeled, deseeded and cut into 3mm dice
1 aubergine, skin only, pared off with a 3mm-thick layer of flesh attached, cut into 3mm dice
2 red peppers, skinned, deseeded and cut into 3mm dice
2 yellow peppers, skinned, deseeded and cut into 3mm dice
1 courgette, skin only, pared off with a 3mm-thick layer of flesh attached, cut into 3mm dice
6 courgette flowers

For the lamb rumps
2 rumps of Cornish lamb (about 200g each)
1 tablespoon olive oil
10g unsalted butter
1 sprig of thyme
sea salt and freshly ground white pepper

For the lamb sweetbreads
12 lamb's sweetbreads, soaked in cold water overnight, then drained
50g plain flour
1 free-range egg, beaten
50g Japanese panko breadcrumbs
vegetable oil, for deep-frying

For the garnish
350g baby spinach leaves, washed and drained
20g unsalted butter
12 cherry tomatoes on the vine, skinned

For the lamb pastillas, heat a heavy-based frying pan until it is extremely hot, add the vegetable oil, then seal the lamb until it is golden all over. Transfer it to a small casserole.

Fry all of the vegetables and the garlic in the same frying pan until golden, then add them to the lamb. Pour the wine into the frying pan and let it bubble, stirring and scraping the base of the pan with a wooden spoon to deglaze it, then add this to the lamb. Lastly add the herbs and stock to the casserole and bring to the boil, skimming off any scum from the surface. Cover with a lid, transfer to an oven preheated to 110°C/Gas Mark $\frac{1}{4}$ and cook for 2–2$\frac{1}{2}$ hours or until tender.

Remove from the oven and leave to cool. Shred the meat into a bowl using 2 forks and then stir in the dried fruit chutney. Pass the cooking liquor through a fine sieve or a piece of muslin cloth into a clean pan and boil until it is reduced to the consistency of a thick jus. Mix this jus through the lamb, then spoon the mixture in a 9cm square in a tray lined with cling film. Press down firmly to expel any air. Cover with cling film and refrigerate overnight.

Turn the lamb mixture out onto a chopping board and remove the cling film. Cut the mixture into 1.5cm x 1.5cm x 9cm strips. Cut a sheet of filo into a 30cm x 14cm rectangle and brush it with clarified butter. Place a strip of the cooked lamb mixture on the filo and wrap it up, tucking the sides in as you go. Brush the outside lightly with the clarified butter. Repeat with the remaining filo pastry sheets to make 6 pastillas. Refrigerate until you are ready to cook them.

To make the ratatouille stuffing for the courgettes, first sweat the onion and garlic in 1 tablespoon of the olive oil until soft, then add the tomatoes and cook for 6 minutes or until any water from the tomatoes has evaporated. Meanwhile, in separate pans, cook the aubergine, peppers and courgette in 1 teaspoon of olive oil each until tender, then drain these on kitchen paper. Add the cooked aubergine, peppers and courgette to the tomato and onion mixture and season. Spoon the mixture into a piping bag fitted with a wide plain nozzle.

Blanch the courgette flowers in a pan of boiling salted water for 1 minute. Refresh in iced water, then drain well. Carefully open up each flower and pipe in some of the ratatouille, then close the flower. With a small knife, slice through the courgette stems several times to make a fan shape. Set aside.

To cook the lamb rumps, season the lamb and heat an ovenproof frying pan until very hot. Add the olive oil to the hot pan, then seal the seasoned lamb on all sides. Add the butter and thyme and transfer the pan to an oven preheated to 220°C/Gas Mark 7. Roast the lamb on the skin side for 6 minutes, then turn over and roast for a further 4 minutes, basting 4 or 5 times during cooking. Remove from the oven and leave to rest in a warm place for 10 minutes. Slice each rump into 3 and season with a little salt. Keep warm.

Blanch the lamb sweetbreads in a pan of boiling salted water for 1 minute, then drain and refresh in iced water. Peel off the membrane and fat to leave the meat part. Season well with salt and pepper. Coat the sweetbreads first in the flour, then in the egg and finally in the breadcrumbs. Heat the oil in a deep-fat fryer or a deep saucepan to 180°C. Deep-fry the sweetbreads until golden brown, then remove with a slotted spoon and drain on kitchen paper. Season with salt and keep warm.

To cook the pastillas, heat the olive oil in a non-stick frying pan, add the pastillas and cook for about 1 minute on each side or until golden. Keep warm.

Steam the stuffed courgette flowers for 4 minutes or until the ratatouille is hot, then brush each flower with olive oil and sprinkle with a little salt.

To cook the spinach, melt 10g of the butter in a saucepan, add the spinach and cook briefly over a high heat until it starts to collapse. Remove from the heat and squeeze out any liquid. Melt the remaining butter in the pan, add the spinach and reheat gently. Season to taste.

Drizzle a little olive oil over the tomatoes, place under a hot grill and cook for 3 minutes.

To serve, spoon the spinach on to 6 serving plates, then add a stuffed courgette flower to each plate. Add the pastillas, then neatly arrange the sweetbreads, slices of rump and cherry tomatoes on the plates.

CARAMELISED VEAL BRAINS WITH BROWN BUTTER AND CAPERS

Serves 4

This is a real Bistrot staple. Brains are very good for you, so order some from your butcher in advance and give this a go. It's delicious served with Pommes Mousselines (page 179).

4 calf's brains, the 2 lobes separated
2 litres Court Bouillon (see page 46)
100g plain flour, seasoned with salt and
   pepper
2 tablespoons olive oil
125g salted butter, diced
a few drops of lemon juice
80g fine capers, drained
2 lemons, skin, seeds and pith removed,
   segments cut into small pieces
2 tablespoons chopped parsley
sea salt and freshly ground white pepper

Soak the brains in cold water for 24 hours.

Remove the brains from the water, drain, then trim away any excess tubes from the base. Bring the court bouillon to a simmer in a pan, then add the brains, return to a simmer and poach for 10 minutes. Remove from the heat and leave to cool in the bouillon.

Remove the brains from the cool liquid and carefully remove the membrane covering each lobe. Pat the brains dry with kitchen paper, then dust them in the seasoned flour, lightly coating all over.

Heat the olive oil in a heavy-based frying pan until smoking hot, then place the brains into the pan rounded-side down. Cook for 2–3 minutes or until golden brown. Remove from the heat and pour off the oil, then return to the heat. Add the diced butter; after a minute or so it will start to foam and change colour to a hazelnut brown. At this point, turn the brains over and constantly spoon the butter over the top for 5 minutes.

Remove the brains from the pan to serving plates, then add the lemon juice to the foaming butter off the heat – the butter will really foam up at this stage. Pass the butter through a fine sieve into a small saucepan, then add the capers, chopped lemon and parsley. Check if the butter needs any seasoning, then spoon it over the brains.

GRILLED TRANCHE OF CALF'S LIVER WITH FLAT MUSHROOMS, BACON AND LYONNAISE ONIONS

Serves 4

This is one of the oldest combinations there is and remains as popular as ever. Our mother used to cook a wonderful liver and bacon dish with big chunks of lamb's liver. At the restaurant, we like to use French calf's liver, and French veal in general – the welfare standards tend to be much higher, resulting in a better flavour. Always try to choose veal products from calves that have been kept with their mother.

For the Lyonnaise onions
20g unsalted butter
300g onions, very finely sliced
a pinch of caster sugar
a pinch of sea salt
freshly ground white pepper

For the crisp parsley
1/2 teaspoon olive oil
12 flat-leaf parsley leaves
a pinch of sea salt

For the mushrooms
4 flat field mushrooms
1 tablespoon olive oil
10g unsalted butter

For the liver and bacon
4 slices of calf's liver (about 120g each)
20g plain flour, seasoned with salt and pepper
olive oil, for cooking and drizzling
12 very thin rashers of smoked streaky bacon

1 quantity of Pommes Purées (see page 56), to serve
1 quantity of Madeira Jus (see page 47), to serve

To cook the Lyonnaise onions, melt the butter in a heavy-based saucepan, then add the onions, sugar and salt. Cook slowly over a medium-low heat for about 1 hour or until the onions are golden brown and very soft, stirring occasionally. Initially the onions will release some liquid, then this will evaporate. They should start to colour as the sugars in them caramelise, but make sure they don't burn on the bottom of the pan. Adjust the seasoning to taste. Keep warm.

For the crisp parsley, place a sheet of cling film over a plate and stretch it tightly. Rub the cling film with the olive oil, then arrange the parsley leaves on top so that they are completely flat. Microwave on full power for 2 minutes or until they are crisp. Season the leaves with a pinch of salt and set aside.

For the mushrooms, peel off the skin and cut the stalks off level with the mushroom caps. Cut each mushroom into 4 fairly thick slices. Heat the olive oil and butter in a hot frying pan and add the mushrooms. Fry until golden brown on both sides, then season with salt and pepper. Drain on kitchen paper and keep warm.

To cook the liver, first pat it dry with kitchen paper. Dip each slice of liver into the seasoned flour, coating all over, then pat off any excess. Heat a ridged griddle pan over a high heat, brush with a little olive oil, then add the liver and cook for 2 minutes on each side so that it is medium-rare. Season with salt and pepper. Leave the bacon under a hot grill until cooked but not too crisp.

To serve, shape the pommes purées into quenelles using 2 metal spoons by scooping it from one spoon to another to form a three-sided oval. Place the quenelles on 4 serving plates, spoon the Lyonnaise onions alongside, then put the liver slices on top. Arrange the mushrooms and bacon on top of the liver along with the crisp parsley. Finally, spoon the Madeira jus around and finish with a drizzle of olive oil.

BISTROT DE LUXE CASSOULET

Serves 10

Every cassoulet is different and this is our version. There's quite a lot of work involved, but the beauty of it is that everything is there in one dish and you just serve it up at the table. It can be assembled well in advance, then cooked before serving.

1kg dried haricot blanc (lingot) beans
1 ham hock
55g duck fat
4 large onions, chopped
12 large garlic cloves, thinly sliced
400g pork rind, rolled and tied
800g carrots, cut into 5mm-thick slices
1 large onion, cut into quarters
2 bay leaves
1 sprig of thyme
4 Toulouse sausages
1kg shoulder of lamb on the bone,
  trimmed of sinew and cut into 10
  pieces
4 Confit Duck Legs (see page 200),
  broken into large pieces
800g piece of unsmoked back bacon, cut
  into rashers 1cm thick
3 tablespoons chopped parsley
sea salt and freshly ground white pepper

Soak the dried beans in cold water for 12 hours, draining and changing the water 3 times during this period. Soak the ham hock in cold water for 12 hours, then drain.

Heat 30g of the duck fat in a heavy-based pan over a medium heat, add the chopped onions and cook slowly for 10–15 minutes or until caramelised. Add the garlic, reduce the heat and cook for a further 10 minutes or until the mixture is almost a purée. Remove from the heat and set aside.

Place the drained haricot beans in a large, heavy-based saucepan with the pork rind, carrots, onion quarters, ham hock, bay leaves and thyme. Cover with water to the level of 2 fingers above the beans, then bring to the boil. Reduce the heat and simmer for about 1 hour, until the beans are par-cooked, then drain, reserving the cooking liquor and bean mixture separately. Discard the bones from the ham hock and discard the onion quarters and herbs. Put the bean mixture in a bowl. Chop the pork rind to a purée and stir it into the bean mixture, together with the onion/garlic purée.

Heat half the remaining duck fat in a separate pan over a fairly high heat, then add the sausages and cook for about 1 minute or until coloured all over. Remove the sausages and drain. When they are cool enough to handle, cut into 4cm-thick slices.

Heat the pan again and add the remaining duck fat. Add the lamb shoulder pieces and cook until just golden all over, then season, remove from the pan and drain.

Spoon about one third of the bean mixture into a large, earthenware cassoulet dish. Add the lamb shoulder in an even layer and cover this evenly with another third of the bean mixture. Add the sliced sausages, duck confit and back bacon rashers, then add the final layer of the bean mixture. Pour enough reserved bean cooking liquor over the top so that everything is just covered.

Cook in an oven preheated to 160°C/ Gas Mark 3. After 1 hour, check the level of liquid; if it has almost evaporated you will have to moisten with more hot bean cooking liquor or boiling water. You will need to repeat this process several times until a crust has formed on top of the cassoulet – this will take $2^{1}/_{2}$–3 hours. The cassoulet is ready when it has a melting resistance if pierced with the point of a knife and the crust is deeply caramelised. Sprinkle with the chopped parsley and serve.

BOUDIN BLANC WITH CARAMELISED APPLES

Serves 4

You could buy a good-quality boudin blanc to use here, but if you're up for a challenge, do make it yourself. It's not difficult and, rather than using natural casings, we pipe the mixture out on to cling film and wrap it up tightly to form the sausages.

For the boudin blanc
50g fresh white breadcrumbs
200ml milk
100g chilled foie gras
25ml Armagnac
2 skinless boneless chicken breasts
150g lean rump of veal
2 free-range eggs
150ml double cream
olive oil, for brushing
softened unsalted butter, for brushing
sea salt and freshly ground white pepper

For the caramelised apples
100g caster sugar
50g unsalted butter
2 eating apples, such as Braeburn or
   Cox's Orange Pippin, peeled, quartered
   and cored

To serve
1 quantity of Pommes Purées (see page
   56)
2 tablespoons chopped parsley
4 tablespoons Brown Chicken Jus (see
   page 45)

For the boudin blanc, soak the breadcrumbs in the milk for 30 minutes until the mixture forms a paste. Place 50g of the foie gras in a shallow bowl, sprinkle over the Armagnac and set aside.

Put the chicken and veal into a chilled food processor bowl and pulse for 30 seconds or until you have a very smooth purée. Add seasoning, the eggs and the remaining foie gras and pulse for 15 seconds. Add the breadcrumb mixture and pulse for 10 seconds until incorporated. Finally, with the machine running, slowly add the cream. Transfer the mixture to a chilled stainless steel bowl. Cut the Armagnac-marinated foie gras into 5mm dice and fold it into the mixture. Cover with cling film and chill in the fridge.

To make the boudin, cut 8 sheets of cling film 30cm x 20cm, and brush them very lightly with olive oil. Place the chicken mixture into a piping bag fitted with a 2cm plain nozzle and pipe a sausage, 12cm x 3cm in size, on to each piece of cling film. Roll each one up, making sure it is rolled fairly tightly, and expel any air. Tie at both ends with string.

To cook the boudin, pour water into a heavy-based pan so that it is 10cm deep. Bring to the boil, then reduce the heat to a simmer. Drop the boudin into the simmering water, cook for 5 minutes, then remove on to kitchen paper. To check if they are cooked, either they

will spring back to the touch, or you can pierce the boudin with a cocktail stick, which should come out clean. Leave the boudin to rest for 1 minute, then snip one end off each one and slide the boudin out of the cling film. Brush the boudin with a little softened butter, then grill lightly to a pale golden finish under a hot grill.

Meanwhile, for the caramelised apples, sprinkle the sugar into a non-stick pan, then heat until it turns pale gold. Remove from the heat, add the butter and shake the pan to melt it, then add the apples, shaking the pan again. Be careful as the sugar is very hot at this point and can give you a nasty burn. Carefully toss the apples in the caramel and cook for about 2–3 minutes or until the point of a knife easily pierces the centre of the apples. Remove from the pan to a warm plate.

Spoon some pommes purées into the centre of 4 serving plates, place a boudin either side and spoon the caramelised apple on top of the mash. Sprinkle with chopped parsley and spoon a thread of chicken jus around.

CRISP CONFIT DUCK LEG, BLACK PUDDING AND SALAD LYONNAISE

Serves 6

It's worth noting that this dish takes 2 days' preparation, but the duck legs can be cooked well in advance. It is a relatively cheap dish, very French, and quite straightforward and easy to serve.

200g French beans, trimmed and cut into 4cm lengths
1 Morteau sausage (about 300g)
200g garlic sausage
200g unsmoked bacon lardons
10g unsalted butter
2 x 150g French black puddings
6 tablespoons Simple Vinaigrette (see page 50)
2 heads of curly frisée (white part only), leaves separated
2 tablespoons chopped parsley
100ml Red Wine Jus (see page 47)
3 tablespoons extra virgin olive oil
sea salt and freshly ground white pepper

For the duck confit
500g coarse sea salt
1 sprig of thyme
1 sprig of rosemary
4 garlic cloves
1 teaspoon black peppercorns, crushed
6 duck legs (about 160g each)
2kg duck fat

First, prepare the duck confit – this needs to be started 2 days in advance. In a blender or food processor, blend the salt, thyme, rosemary, garlic and peppercorns together until the herbs and garlic have completely broken down. Pour half of this mixture on to a tray large enough to hold all of the duck legs side by side, then place the duck legs on top. Cover the legs with the remaining salt mixture. Cover with cling film, then leave in the fridge for 24 hours.

Remove the legs from the salt, brushing off any excess, then discard the salt mixture. Rinse the legs thoroughly under cold running water.

Melt the duck fat in a large casserole, add the duck legs and return the fat to a slow simmer. Cover with a lid, transfer the casserole to an oven preheated to 120°C/ Gas Mark $^1/_2$ and cook for 3 hours or until the meat is tender (you should be able to remove the thigh bone easily with your fingers). Carefully remove the casserole from the oven and leave the duck legs to cool to room temperature in the fat. Using a slotted spoon, remove the legs to a cling-film-lined tray, placing them skin-side down, then refrigerate for 24 hours or until completely chilled.

Blanch the French beans in a large pan of boiling salted water for 5 minutes, then refresh in iced water, drain and set aside.

Put the Morteau sausage in a pan, cover with cold water and bring to the boil,

then immediately refresh under cold water for 5 minutes. Drain. Cut both the cooked Morteau sausage and the garlic sausage into quarters lengthwise, then cut them into 3mm-thick slices. Place the bacon lardons in a very hot frying pan with the butter and cook until golden, then drain and set aside.

To reheat the duck legs, place them in a very hot, ovenproof frying pan skin-side down (you don't need any fat in the pan) and cook over a high heat for 2 minutes, then transfer the pan to an oven preheated to 200°C/Gas Mark 6 for 12 minutes. Remove from the oven and use a fish slice to ease the skin from the bottom of the frying pan. If the skin isn't golden enough, cook over a medium heat on the hob until golden and crisp. Remove from the pan and keep warm.

Cut the black pudding into 1cm-thick slices. Lay the slices in a lightly oiled baking tray and cook under a medium grill for 4 minutes or until heated through.

To serve, heat the French beans, sausages and bacon lardons together in a saucepan over a medium heat until they are warmed through. Transfer to a mixing bowl, add the vinaigrette, frisée, parsley and some seasoning and gently toss together. Divide the salad between 6 serving plates, place the duck legs on top and the black pudding around. Spoon the red wine jus around the outside of the plates and finish with a drizzle of extra virgin olive oil.

POACHED LANDAISE CHICKEN WITH PISTOU VEGETABLES

Serves 4

Landaise chickens are reared in the south-west of France, where they roam freely round a vast forest near the coast, supplementing their diet of homegrown maize with worms and berries. The flavour is superb. Don't be too disheartened if you can't get them, though. There are some excellent British birds now, and we particularly like Reg Johnson's Goosnargh birds from Lancashire.

4 free-range chicken breasts (about 200g each), skin removed
about 400ml Chicken Stock (see page 44)
a small sprig of thyme
30g unsalted butter
50g Gruyère cheese, finely grated
sea salt and freshly ground white pepper

For the pistou
4 garlic cloves, peeled and left whole
½ bunch of basil
1 teaspoon pine nuts
125ml extra virgin olive oil

For the soup
100g French beans, cut into 1.5cm lengths
100g shelled small broad beans
100g shelled fresh peas
4 new carrots, cut into 1cm dice
2 courgettes, cut into 1cm dice
50g spaghetti, broken into 2cm lengths
100g Charlotte potatoes or other similar waxy new potatoes, cut into 1cm dice
50g unsalted butter
a squeeze of lemon juice
2 tomatoes, skinned, deseeded and diced

First, make the pistou. Pound the garlic to a paste using a pestle and mortar, then add the basil leaves and pine nuts and pound with the garlic. Slowly work in the olive oil, then season with salt. Set aside.

To poach the chicken, season the chicken breasts and place them in an earthenware dish or shallow casserole. Half cover with chicken stock and add the thyme and butter. Bring to just below boiling point, then cover with foil and transfer to an oven preheated to 190°C/Gas Mark 5. Cook for 8 minutes, then remove from the oven and leave to rest in the poaching liquor for 5 minutes. Just before serving, remove from the poaching liquor using a slotted spoon.

To make the soup, cook the beans, peas, carrots and courgettes separately in boiling salted water until tender, then drain, refresh in iced water and drain again. Do the same with the spaghetti. Put the potatoes in a pan of cold salted water, bring to the boil and simmer until tender, then drain and refresh.

Bring 350ml of the chicken poaching liquor to the boil in a pan, add the butter and pistou and blend with a handheld electric blender. Add the cooked vegetables and bring to the boil. Season with salt, pepper and a squeeze of lemon juice, then add the tomatoes just before serving.

Divide the soup between 4 large soup plates and sprinkle with the Gruyère, then place the chicken on top.

BREAST OF CORN-FED CHICKEN WITH FRESH PEAS, SHALLOT PURÉE, GIROLLES AND SMOKED BACON

Serves 4

Peas, bacon and girolle mushrooms make a perfect marriage of flavours. A great inspiration for this was Chez L'Ami Louis bistro in Paris, where they serve little copper pots of peas and girolles as an accompaniment. We've added the bacon as it goes so well with chicken and mushrooms.

160ml Chicken Stock (see page 44)
50ml white wine
40ml double cream
60g chilled unsalted butter, diced
20g chilled foie gras (or unsalted butter), diced
1 sprig of rosemary
a few drops of lemon juice
4 corn-fed chicken breasts, skin left on, wing bone attached (French trimmed)
1 teaspoon olive oil, plus extra for drizzling
250g shelled fresh peas
15g unsalted butter
125g girolle mushrooms, trimmed and cleaned
12 very thin rashers of smoked streaky bacon
sea salt and freshly ground white pepper

For the shallot purée
60g unsalted butter
300g shallots, finely sliced
50ml double cream
200ml Chicken Stock (see page 44)

First, make the shallot purée. Melt the butter in a pan, add the shallots, then cover and cook very gently for 1 hour or until very soft and golden. Add the cream and chicken stock and cook for 5 minutes. Transfer the mixture to a blender or food processor and purée until smooth. Pass through a fine sieve and season to taste. Set aside.

Put the chicken stock and wine in a saucepan and boil until reduced by two-thirds. Add the cream and boil for 1 minute, then take the pan off the heat. Gradually whisk in the chilled butter and foie gras, a few pieces at a time, then add the rosemary. Leave to infuse for 3 minutes, then season with salt and a little lemon juice. Pass the mixture through a fine sieve or a piece of muslin cloth into a clean pan and set aside.

Meanwhile, trim the chicken breasts neatly, removing any excess fat, then season with salt and pepper. Heat the olive oil in an ovenproof frying pan over a medium heat, add the chicken breasts skin-side down and cook for about 1 minute. Transfer the pan to an oven preheated to 180°C/Gas Mark 4. Cook for 8 minutes, then turn over and cook for a further 3 minutes. Remove from the oven and leave to rest for a few minutes.

Cook the peas in a pan of boiling salted water for 2 minutes, then drain. Return them to the pan with a drizzle of olive oil and a pinch of salt.

Melt the butter in a frying pan over a medium heat and as it foams up, add the girolles. Sauté until tender but not coloured, then season to taste. Grill the bacon under a hot grill for about 2 minutes.

To serve, reheat the shallot purée and sauce, if necessary, and blend the sauce with a handheld electric blender. Spoon the shallot purée into the centre of 4 serving bowls. Slice each chicken breast into 3 pieces and place on top. Scatter the peas and girolles evenly around. Finish with the sauce and bacon.

Opposite, top left: Emmy Lehmann-Miéral and farmer Jean Michel Sibelle with his prize poulet de Bresse, and, *below:* his family's incredible trophy room.
Bottom left: Bresse chickens are unique: fed on maize (seen growing in the background), which in turn is mixed with milk produced by cows from the same farm (in shot behind the maize).

PITHIVIER OF GAME WITH CARROT PURÉE AND GLAZED ONIONS

Serves 6

This is a great dinner party dish, as serving it is very easy. At the Bistrot it appears each year during the game season, but you could replace the game with wood pigeon and quail at other times of year.

500g Puff Pastry (see page 53)
plain flour, for dusting
4 free-range egg yolks, lightly beaten
Madeira Jus (see page 47), to serve

For the filling
250g mixed game, such as pheasant, wild
    duck and partridge breasts
250g veal shoulder
250g pork back fat or Italian lardo
6 partridge breasts
4 pheasant breasts
4 wild duck breasts
1 free-range egg
25g fresh white breadcrumbs
a pinch of ground allspice
1 tablespoon chopped herbs, such as
    parsley, chervil and tarragon
100g pig's caul
sea salt and freshly ground white pepper

For the carrot purée
50g unsalted butter
200g new carrots, roughly diced
2 tablespoons water

For the onions
30 small button onions, peeled
50g unsalted butter
1 tablespoon caster sugar

Roll the puff pastry out on a lightly floured work surface to 5mm thick. Lay the pastry sheet on a tray, cover with cling film and refrigerate for 2 hours.

For the filling, roughly cut the mixed game, veal shoulder and back fat or lardo into 2cm dice. Mince all the diced meat through a mincer fitted with a medium coarse blade. If you don't have a mincer, just chop the meat very finely. Cover with cling film and refrigerate.

Cut the partridge, pheasant and wild duck breasts into 1cm dice – take a lot more care with this dice as it will be on show when you cut open the pithiviers. Add the diced game to the mince, together with the egg, breadcrumbs, allspice and herbs. Season with salt and pepper and mix together really well. (If you want to check the seasoning, take a little of the mixture – about the size of a ping-pong ball – press it flat like a burger, fry it until cooked through, then taste and adjust the seasoning in the remaining mixture, if necessary.) Divide the meat mixture into 6 portions and shape them into slightly oval balls. Wrap each one in a single layer of pig's caul, place on a tray, cover with cling film and refrigerate.

Cut the puff pastry into twelve 10cm rounds using a pastry cutter (discard the pastry trimmings). Brush these pastry rounds with the egg yolks, then place a portion of prepared filling on top of 6 of them. Lay the remaining pastry rounds

egg-wash-side down on top of the filling, then press around each one to form a tight parcel with no air inside. Each parcel should have a 1cm or so border of pastry (this edge will not look particularly neat at this stage). Brush all over the parcels with egg yolk, then refrigerate (you want the egg to dry out, so do not cover). Remove after 15 minutes and brush with egg yolk one more time, then return to the fridge for a further 30 minutes. Cut the pithiviers out with the same (10cm) pastry cutter as before to achieve neat edges and a round shape, then score the top of each with a small knife for decoration. Chill again until ready to bake.

For the carrot purée, melt the butter in a saucepan over a medium heat. Add the carrots and water and bring to the boil, then reduce the heat to a simmer. Cover with a tight-fitting lid and cook slowly for 25 minutes or until the carrots are completely cooked through. Remove from the heat and blitz in a blender or food processor until silky smooth. Season with salt and pepper and keep warm.

Put the onions in a saucepan just big enough to hold them in a single layer. Add the butter and sugar and a little salt and pepper. Half cover the onions with cold water, then set the pan over a high heat. When the water comes to the boil, continue to cook over a high heat and eventually the liquid will evaporate and the onions will start to caramelise – it is very important to reduce the heat at this stage and colour the onions slowly until they are deep golden – this will take about 5 minutes. Remove the onions from the pan and keep warm.

Bake the pithiviers in an oven preheated to 190°C/Gas Mark 5 for 10 minutes, then remove from the oven and leave to rest in a warm place for 5 minutes.

To serve, spoon some carrot purée across each serving plate. Slice the cooked pithiviers in half and place on the plates, slightly opened out. Place the glazed onions around the outside and finally drizzle around a little Madeira jus.

TAGINE OF BRESSE PIGEON WITH COUSCOUS AND HARISSA SAUCE

Serves 8

This was inspired by the legendary La Maison Troisgros restaurant in Roanne, near Lyons, where Chris worked in the late 1990s. If you can't get Bresse pigeons, a good butcher should be able to get you squab pigeons instead. In France, pigeons au sang are sometimes used – these are pigeons that have been killed by wringing their necks so that they retain all the blood, and therefore all the flavour.

For the pigeons
200ml water
6 tablespoons coarse sea salt
1 tablespoon crushed black peppercorns
4 garlic cloves, crushed
1 sprig of thyme
2 tablespoons caster sugar
8 Bresse pigeons (600–650g each),
  legs and breasts removed (keep the
  carcasses for the sauce)
300g duck fat
1 teaspoon olive oil

For the Lyonnaise onions
20g unsalted butter
2 onions, very finely sliced

For the spice mix
3 cloves
10 black peppercorns
1 tablespoon cumin seeds
1/4 cinnamon stick
2 star anise

For the dried fruit chutney and pastillas
30g unsalted butter
1 teaspoon honey
1 teaspoon water
40g dried figs
40g dried dates
40g prunes
60g filo pastry sheets
melted unsalted butter, for brushing

For the roast garlic
8 garlic cloves, peeled and left whole
a little olive oil

For the sauce
the carcasses from the pigeons
200g chicken wings
2 teaspoons sherry vinegar
4 carrots, finely sliced on a mandolin
6 shallots, sliced
a little butter
3 garlic cloves, crushed
1 plum tomato, quartered
300ml Brown Chicken Jus (see page 45)
300ml Chicken Stock (see page 44)
1 teaspoon cumin seeds
1 fresh red chilli, deseeded and finely
  chopped
20 coriander leaves, finely shredded
sea salt and freshly ground white pepper

For the couscous
300g couscous
3 tablespoons lemon juice
1 tablespoon sherry vinegar
6 tablespoons olive oil
300ml boiling water
180g niçoise olives, stoned and quartered
6 tablespoons sultanas, soaked in hot
  water to plump up, then drained
6 tablespoons tinned piquillo peppers,
  drained and diced
6 tablespoons toasted almonds
2 tablespoons roughly chopped mint
2 tablespoons roughly chopped coriander

To finish and serve
8 quail's eggs
20g unsalted butter
450g baby spinach, washed and drained
1 quantity of Aubergine Purée (see pages
  92–94)

1 quantity of Preserved Lemons
  (see page 57)
Lemon Oil (see page 57), for drizzling
100g rose harissa

Mix together the water, salt, peppercorns, garlic, thyme and sugar in a large bowl, add the pigeon legs and leave for 24 hours. Rinse off the brine, then put the legs into a saucepan, cover with the duck fat and simmer for 2 hours. Leave the legs to cool in the fat, then remove. Take off the skin and pick all the meat from the legs. Set aside.

Meanwhile, cook the Lyonnaise onions. Melt the butter in a heavy-based saucepan and add the onions and some salt and pepper. Cook slowly over a low heat for about 1 1/2 hours or until golden brown and very soft.

Blitz all the ingredients for the spice mix together in a spice grinder. Reserve 1/2 teaspoon of the spice mix for the sauce.

To make the chutney, briefly fry the remaining ground spice mix in 10g of the butter in a small, heavy-based pan, until aromatic. Add the honey and water and bring to the boil, then add the dried fruits and cook slowly for 20 minutes. Remove from the heat and blend the chutney in a blender or food processor whilst it is still hot, otherwise the mixture will set firm.

(Continued on page 210)

(Continued from page 209)

Weigh the meat collected from the legs (it should be around 200g). Mix it with 100g of the cooked onions and 100g of the chutney and set aside.

For the roast garlic, put the garlic cloves on a piece of foil, add a little olive oil and a pinch of salt and enclose to make a parcel. Roast in an oven preheated to 180°C/Gas Mark 4 for 30 minutes or until soft. Remove from the oven and keep warm.

Meanwhile, to make the sauce, put the pigeon carcasses and chicken wings in a roasting tin and roast in an oven preheated to 180°C/Gas Mark 4 for 35 minutes or until golden brown. Remove from the oven and place the tin on the hob, then pour in the vinegar and let it bubble, stirring and scraping the base of the tin with a wooden spoon to deglaze it. Fry the carrots and shallots in a little butter in separate frying pans, adding the garlic to the shallots when soft. Combine the vegetables and bones in the shallot pan with the tomato and the reserved ½ teaspoon of spice mix. Cook over a medium heat until the tomato starts to break down. Add the chicken jus and stock, bring to the boil, then simmer until the meat on the chicken wings comes away easily.

Pass the mixture through a fine sieve, ensuring all the liquid is pressed out of the bones and vegetables, then pass the liquid through a fine sieve again or through a piece of muslin cloth into a clean pan. Bring to the boil, then reduce the heat and simmer, skimming occasionally, until reduced and thickened to a coating consistency. Season to taste, then stir in the cumin seeds, chopped chilli and fresh coriander. Keep warm.

To make the pastillas, divide the pigeon meat, onion and chutney mixture into 8 equal portions. Cut the filo pastry sheets into eight 11cm x 30cm rectangles and keep under a damp cloth to prevent them drying out. Brush 2 rectangles with melted butter and lay one on top of the other. Place 1 portion of the pigeon meat mixture on the filo pastry rectangles in a line 2cm from the top edge and 1cm clear of the sides. Fold over and tuck in the edges, then keep folding the pastry over until you have a parcel, brushing with melted butter to stick the edges together. Repeat with the remaining filo pastry rectangles and portions of pigeon meat mixture to make 8 parcels. Melt the remaining 20g butter in a frying pan over a medium heat, then add the pastillas and cook for 1–2 minutes on each side, until golden.

Prepare the couscous. In a bowl, mix together the couscous, lemon juice, vinegar and olive oil. Pour the boiling water over the couscous, add a pinch of salt and stir briefly. Cover with cling film and leave in a hot place for 10 minutes, then uncover and use a fork to break up any lumps. Stir in the olives, sultanas, piquillo peppers, almonds and herbs, then adjust the seasoning.

To finish, cook the quail's eggs in a pan of boiling water for 2½ minutes, then drain. Chill the eggs in a bowl of iced water, then peel them. Just before serving, gently heat up the eggs in a pan of boiling water for 1½ minutes. Drain well.

To cook the spinach, melt 10g of the butter in a saucepan, add the spinach and cook briefly over a high heat until it starts to collapse. Remove from the heat and squeeze out any liquid. Melt the remaining butter in the pan, add the spinach and reheat gently. Season to taste and keep warm.

To cook the pigeon breasts, heat the teaspoon of olive oil in a frying pan until hot. Add the pigeon breasts and cook until sealed all over. Place skin-side down in a roasting tin and roast in an oven preheated to 200°C/Gas Mark 6 for 5 minutes. Remove from the oven and allow to rest in a warm place for 10 minutes.

Use traditional tagine pots with lids to serve this dish in, if you have them. Spoon some couscous into the centre of each tagine, then place 2 spoonfuls of aubergine purée on either side of the couscous. Place a pastilla next to the couscous and spoon some spinach opposite it, then nest a quail's egg on top of the spinach. Lay a preserved lemon wedge and a roasted garlic clove alongside. Sit the pigeon breasts on top of the couscous and drizzle lemon oil around the dish. Serve with a pot of rose harissa and the sauce.

POT-ROAST SQUAB PIGEON, FARCI À GRATIN

Serves 4

Traditionally, farci à gratin is a mixture of poultry offal that is seared with bacon and shallots, mixed with Cognac and puréed to spread on toast and serve under roast game birds. Here we've made it more refined by substituting chicken breast and foie gras for the offal and using it to stuff the bird. It's a complex dish but well worth it.

4 squab pigeons (about 500g each), heads and feet attached
a little olive oil
100g salted butter
sea salt and freshly ground white pepper

For the stuffing
100g chicken breast fillet
1 small free-range egg white
130ml double cream
olive oil, for cooking
4 tablespoons chopped mixed wild mushrooms
100g fresh foie gras, cut into 2cm dice
1 tablespoon chopped flat-leaf parsley

For the black olive sauce
200g pigeon bones – also use the carcasses from the 4 pigeons (see above)
2 tablespoons rapeseed oil
2 garlic cloves, peeled and left whole
30g salted butter
1 shallot, finely chopped
1 litre Chicken Stock (see page 44)
3 tablespoons black olive stones
10g unsalted butter
2 tablespoons sliced black olives

The preparation of the pigeons is rather time consuming but with a little practice and good knife skills, you should be able to achieve it (or you could ask your butcher to do most of the work for you). Place each bird on a well-secured board with the breasts facing down. Using a very sharp small paring knife, cut a small incision along the back bone of each bird from the neck to the bottom. Then cut into the bird and follow the ribcage along each side until you can pull it out – cut the join of the legs and wing bones and take out the ribcage in one piece. Keep the birds in the fridge until you are ready to use them. From each ribcage, remove the hearts and livers and cut these up into 5mm dice, then refrigerate until needed. Keep the carcasses for the sauce.

For the stuffing, dice the chicken breast fillet, place in a blender or food processor with the egg white and blend to a fine purée. Transfer the chicken purée to a medium bowl and sit this bowl in a large bowl of iced water (making sure the water does not overflow into the medium bowl). Slowly add the cream in a trickle whilst continuously beating the mixture with a spatula to make a smooth, shiny, creamy mousse. Season lightly. To check the flavour and texture of the mousse, take a small teaspoonful and wrap it in a piece of cling film. Poach this in a pan of boiling water for 2 minutes, then remove, unwrap and taste. Adjust the seasoning of the remaining mousse, if necessary, then chill.

Heat a frying pan over a high heat, add a splash of olive oil, then add the mushrooms and sauté very quickly for about 2 minutes. Season lightly, drain on kitchen paper and leave to cool, then chill. Wipe the pan clean, then set it over a high heat until very hot. Drop in the diced foie gras and cook very quickly on all sides; it should take no more than a minute. Transfer to kitchen paper, leave to cool and then chill. Repeat this with the pigeon hearts and livers but cook for only a few seconds.

Make the black olive sauce. Chop the pigeon bones and carcasses into small, even pieces and place in a heavy roasting tin with the rapeseed oil. Cook over a fairly high heat for 10–12 minutes until the bones are browned, then add the garlic, reduce the heat and sweat for a few minutes. Drain off any fat, then add the salted butter and heat until it begins to foam. Add the shallot and sauté for 2 minutes, then drain in a colander, discarding the fat. Return the pigeon bones, shallot and garlic to the pan and add the chicken stock. Bring to the boil, then reduce the heat and simmer for 20 minutes. Pass through a fine sieve into a clean pan and boil until reduced to a light coating consistency. Remove from the heat, stir in the olive stones and cover with a plate. Set aside for 30 minutes.

(Continued on page 213)

(Continued from page 211)

Mix the mushrooms, foie gras, pigeon hearts and livers, and parsley through the chicken mousse. Remove the pigeons from the fridge and open out each one on a board. Season lightly inside the breast cavities, then spoon the chicken mousse into the birds. Take some fine string and a trussing needle and sew up each pigeon to resemble a whole bird. Cut off the heads, feet and wing tips and, with a blowtorch, singe off all the feathers and quills left on the birds.

Take a cocotte or casserole big enough to hold all the birds and set it over a medium heat. Add a little olive oil, then place the pigeons in the dish. Sear for 1–2 minutes on each side to colour them well, then add the butter. Let it foam up, baste the pigeons well, then transfer to an oven preheated to 160°C/Gas Mark 3. Cook for about 15 minutes or until the birds feel slightly springy when squeezed, turning them and basting with the butter every 3 minutes or so.

Pass the black olive sauce through a very fine sieve or a piece of muslin cloth into a saucepan. Bring to a simmer, then whisk in the unsalted butter to thicken the sauce slightly and make it shiny. Stir in the sliced olives.

Remove the cocotte from the oven and leave to rest for 5 minutes, then transfer the pigeons to a chopping board and remove the string. Serve immediately, with the black olive sauce on the side and vegetables of your choice. We like to serve this with fondant potatoes and maybe some spring peas and broad beans; a green salad would also work well.

SUPREME OF GUINEA FOWL WITH BROAD BEANS, FRESH MORELS AND HERB GNOCCHI

Serves 4

This is one of those delightful dishes where all the ingredients come into season at the same time. If you can't get fresh morels, use any good wild mushrooms in season.

2 guinea fowl crowns (the main body with the legs taken off)
2 teaspoons vegetable oil
1 quantity of Herb Gnocchi (see page 52)
3 tablespoons olive oil
40 small fresh morel mushrooms
160g shelled broad beans, blanched and thin outer skin removed
sea salt and freshly ground white pepper

For the herb paste
90g softened unsalted butter
80g curly parsley, chopped
100g fresh white breadcrumbs

For the sauce
1/2 garlic clove
50ml white wine
1 sprig of thyme
300ml Brown Chicken Stock (see page 44)
1/2 lemon

First, make the herb paste to go under the guinea fowl skin. Put the butter, parsley and breadcrumbs in a blender or food processor and blitz until they combine. Transfer to a piping bag.

Prepare the guinea fowl. Remove the wishbone and wings from the birds (these are used in the sauce later), then push your fingers between the skin and breasts to loosen. Pipe the herb paste into this cavity on both birds and spread it out evenly. Heat the vegetable oil in a large, ovenproof frying pan until smoking hot. Seal the guinea fowl on both breasts in the pan until golden brown. Transfer the pan to an oven preheated to 200°C/Gas Mark 6 and cook for 25 minutes, basting regularly. Remove from the oven and leave to rest for 15 minutes. Once rested, remove the breasts from the crowns and keep warm.

Meanwhile, to make the sauce, chop the wing bones into very small pieces. Heat a heavy-based saucepan, just big enough to hold the bones in a single layer, until it is very hot. Add the chopped bones to the pan with the garlic and reduce the heat slightly. There is no need to add any oil as the wings will start to release fat as they cook. Cook for 30 minutes, stirring occasionally, ensuring the pan is hot enough to roast the bones but not so hot that they burn. You are looking for the wing pieces to turn a deep golden yellow colour. Add the white wine and thyme and cook until reduced by three-quarters. Add the chicken stock and cook for

10–15 minutes or until the mixture has reduced to a light coating consistency. Season with salt, if necessary, and finish with 1 or 2 drops of lemon juice. Pass the sauce through a piece of muslin or a fine sieve.

Just before serving, heat 1 tablespoon of the olive oil in a frying pan, add the gnocchi and sauté for 2–3 minutes or until golden all over. Season with salt and pepper and keep warm.

Heat another tablespoon of the olive oil in a small saucepan, add the morels and sauté gently for 2–3 minutes or until tender. Season with a little salt. At the same time, reheat the broad beans in a pan of boiling salted water. Drain, then sauté the beans in the remaining olive oil for 30 seconds and season with salt.

To serve, slice each guinea fowl breast into 3 and place in the centre of each serving plate. Surround with the gnocchi, morels and broad beans. Finally spoon over a little sauce and serve immediately.

POT ROAST BERKSHIRE PHEASANT 'PETIT SALÉ AUX LENTILLES'

Serves 4

Pork works well with pheasant and, instead of wrapping the birds in bacon here, we have added pork in the form of a petit salé – a pork dish containing a mixture of salted cuts.

160g Puy lentils
1 litre Chicken Stock (see page 44)
60g ventreche bacon (skin removed and reserved) or pancetta
100g celeriac, peeled
2 carrots
1 small leek
12 button onions, peeled
60g Morteau sausage
60g garlic sausage
80g unsalted butter
2 cock pheasants, legs removed
2 tablespoons vegetable oil
1 sprig of thyme
4 tablespoons Madeira Jus (see page 47)
2 tablespoons chopped flat-leaf parsley
olive oil, for drizzling

Place the lentils in a saucepan and cover with cold water. Bring to the boil, then pour the lentils into a colander and hold under cold running water until the water runs clear. Drain and return the lentils to the pan, add the chicken stock and the ventreche skin if you have it, and bring to the boil. Reduce the heat and simmer for about 20 minutes or until the lentils are tender. Remove from the heat and leave to cool, then drain, discarding the liquid and ventreche skin. Set aside.

Meanwhile, place the bacon in the freezer to firm up for 1 hour.

Cut the celeriac, carrots and leek into 5mm dice and blanch in a pan of boiling salted water – first add the celeriac and carrots and cook for 1 minute, then add the leek and cook for a further 1 minute. Refresh under cold water, drain and set aside.

Cook the button onions in a small pan of boiling salted water until tender, then drain. Set aside. Put the Morteau sausage in a pan, cover with cold water and bring to the boil. Just as it comes to the boil, remove from the heat, drain and refresh under cold water. Cut the Morteau and garlic sausage into 5mm-thick slices and set aside.

Using a slicing machine, or a very sharp knife, cut 4 very thin rashers from the ventreche bacon for garnish. Using a sharp serrated knife, cut the rest into lardons about 3cm x 1cm x 1cm. Fry the lardons in 20g of the butter until golden, then drain and set aside.

To cook the pheasants, heat an ovenproof frying pan until very hot, then add the vegetable oil and pheasants and colour them for 2 minutes on each side. Add the remaining butter and the thyme to the pan and continue to cook over a high heat until the butter starts to foam. Baste the pheasants, then transfer the pan to an oven preheated to 200°C/Gas Mark 6 and cook for about 4 minutes on each breast, basting regularly. Remove from the oven and leave to rest in a warm place for 15 minutes.

To serve, warm the lentils, vegetables, sausages and Madeira jus together in a saucepan until hot, stirring occasionally, then add the parsley. Cook the rashers of ventreche under a hot grill for 1 minute, until crisp.

Remove the breasts from the pheasants and slice each one into 3. Spoon the lentil mixture into deep serving bowls. Lay the sliced pheasant breasts on top and garnish with the grilled ventreche. Finish with a little drizzle of olive oil.

ROAST GROUSE WITH GAME CHIPS, WATERCRESS AND BREAD SAUCE

Serves 2

We have our grouse hung for 2 weeks, which gives a nice gamey flavour without being too powerful. In our opinion, grouse is the king of game birds and a real luxury to be enjoyed.

For the game chips
1 large Desiree potato or similar floury potato
vegetable oil, for deep-frying
sea salt and freshly ground white pepper

For the bread sauce
1/2 onion
1 clove
10g unsalted butter
225ml milk
25g white bread, crusts removed, cut into cubes
25ml double cream
a small pinch of freshly grated nutmeg

For the grouse
1 tablespoon vegetable oil
2 oven-ready young grouse
25g unsalted butter

50g watercress, trimmed, to garnish

For the game chips, cut the potato into a cylinder shape about 3cm wide. Using a mandolin, cut the potato cylinder into wafer-thin slices. Rinse the potato slices in water, then drain and pat dry. Deep-fry in a pan of hot vegetable oil at 170°C until golden. Remove with a slotted spoon and drain on kitchen paper, then season with salt. Set aside.

To make the bread sauce, cut the onion half in 2. Very finely chop one piece of the onion and press the clove into the other piece. Melt the butter in a saucepan over a medium heat, add the chopped onion and sweat until soft. Pour in the milk, add the studded onion and bring to the boil, then reduce the heat and simmer for 15 minutes. Add the bread cubes and cook over a very low heat for a further 20 minutes. Remove the studded onion and discard, then add the cream to the bread sauce and bring back to the boil. Season with salt and pepper and the nutmeg. Remove from the heat, cover the pan with cling film and keep warm.

To cook the grouse, heat the vegetable oil in an ovenproof frying pan until very hot, then add the grouse and seal on all sides until golden brown. Add the butter, then rest each bird on one leg. Transfer the pan to an oven preheated to 230°C/Gas Mark 8 and roast the grouse for 4 minutes. Baste, then turn the birds on to the other leg and roast for a further 4 minutes. Baste again, then turn each bird on to its back and roast for a further 5 minutes. Remove from the oven and leave to rest in a warm place for 10–12 minutes.

To serve, reheat the grouse in the hot oven for 2 minutes, then remove the legs and breast from the birds and place neatly on the serving plates. Garnish each serving with a small bunch of watercress and the game chips. Serve the bread sauce separately.

GRILLED RABBIT LEGS WITH PUY LENTILS, WHITE DANDELIONS AND GIROLLES

Serves 4

Rabbit legs are very underrated. They yield lots of succulent, tender meat and are great value. If you see dandelions growing in your garden, stick a pot over them and they will come up white and tender – perfect for this recipe.

150g Puy lentils
3 tablespoons olive oil
4 rabbit legs
1 carrot
1 stick celery
¹/₂ head celeriac, peeled
25g unsalted butter
150g girolle mushrooms, trimmed and cleaned
2 tablespoons chopped mixed herbs (such as chervil, parsley and tarragon)
2 heads of white dandelion, trimmed
2 tablespoons Classic Vinaigrette (see page 50)
sea salt and freshly ground white pepper

Place the lentils in a large pan and cover with cold water. Add a good pinch of salt and bring to the boil. Reduce to a simmer and cook for about 20 minutes or until just tender. Drain well, season and keep warm.

Heat an ovenproof griddle pan over a medium heat and brush with a tablespoon of the olive oil. Season the rabbit legs and griddle until coloured on both sides, turning once. Transfer the pan to an oven preheated to 180°C/Gas Mark 4 and cook for 10 minutes, then remove from the oven and leave to rest in a warm place for 6 minutes.

Cut the vegetables into 5mm dice, then blanch in a pan of boiling salted water for 2 minutes. Drain and add to the lentils.

Heat the butter in a frying pan, add the girolles and gently sauté for about 3 minutes, until tender. Season with a pinch of salt. Add to the lentil/vegetable mixture, together with the chopped herbs, and stir together. Check the seasoning one last time. At the last minute, toss the dandelion leaves in the vinaigrette.

To serve, place a pile of lentils in the centre of each serving plate and place a rabbit leg on top. Carefully place the dressed dandelion around the outside. Drizzle with the remaining olive oil and serve.

SADDLE OF DENHAM ESTATE VENISON WITH BRAISED RED CABBAGE, CHESTNUT AND APPLE PURÉE AND BLACKCURRANT SAUCE

Serves 6

We get our venison from Denham Estate, in Suffolk, which, until his death, was run by Michael Gliksten, a former chairman of not only the Rare Breeds Survival Trust but also Charlton FC. He worked tirelessly to ensure young chefs understood the significance of provenance when it came to buying meat. Before we met him, we assumed that farmed venison was second-rate, but the meat from Denham Estate is simply the best. Wild deer have normally been stalked and so are stressed when they are killed, but Denham Estate venison is a very consistent product. Shortly before the deer are killed, they are often played classical music to soothe them!

For the cabbage
1 small red cabbage (about 1kg), finely
    shredded
60g salted butter
2 medium cooking apples, peeled and
    finely grated
200ml Riesling wine
60ml cider vinegar
45g demerara sugar
30g redcurrant jelly
1/4 cinnamon stick
sea salt and freshly ground white pepper

For the chestnut and apple purée
1/4 onion, finely diced
100g unsalted butter
100g chestnuts, peeled
175ml milk
2 Golden Delicious apples, peeled, cored
    and diced
1 tablespoon caster sugar
1 teaspoon lemon juice

For the blackcurrant sauce
10g caster sugar
20ml distilled malt vinegar
1 quantity of Venison Stock (see page 45)
50ml Brown Chicken Jus (see page 45)
75g frozen blackcurrants, defrosted

For the venison
660g venison loin
3 tablespoons black peppercorns, crushed
3 tablespoons juniper berries, toasted and
    crushed
olive oil, for cooking

To finish
20g unsalted butter
30 crosnes (Chinese artichokes)
30 Brussels sprout leaves
a little olive oil, for brushing
1 Granny Smith apple, peeled, cored and
    cut into fine strips

Put the cabbage in a casserole with the butter and cook until it becomes bright in colour and is starting to wilt. Add all the other ingredients for the cabbage and bring to the boil. Cover with a lid, then braise in an oven preheated to 140°C/Gas Mark 1 for $1^1/_2$ hours. Drain the mixture in a colander set over a bowl and leave for 15 minutes to catch the liquid. Put the liquid in a pan and boil until reduced to a thick syrup, then add to the cooked cabbage and mix well. Check and adjust the seasoning.

For the chestnut and apple purée, slowly caramelise the onion in 75g of the butter in a pan until golden brown. Add the chestnuts and cook for 10 minutes, then add a pinch of salt and the milk and simmer for 10 minutes longer, until the chestnuts are tender. Purée the mixture in a blender or food processor, then pass it through a fine sieve.

Now put the apples, sugar and remaining 25g butter in a saucepan and cook until the apples are soft. Purée the mixture in a blender or food processor, then pass it through a fine sieve. Mix both purées together and adjust the seasoning, adding the lemon juice to taste. Keep warm.

To make the blackcurrant sauce, put the sugar and vinegar in a small saucepan and boil until it has reduced by half. Add the venison stock and chicken jus and simmer until the mixture has reduced to a sauce consistency. Add half the blackcurrants and simmer for 1 minute. Pass the sauce through a fine sieve, being sure to press the blackcurrants through, then return to the pan. Add the remaining blackcurrants and simmer for 1 minute. Remove from the heat and allow to stand for 10 minutes before serving.

Season the venison with salt, then roll it in the combined crushed peppercorns and juniper berries, coating all over. Heat a little olive oil in a heavy cast-iron pan, add the venison and brown quickly on all sides. Transfer the pan to an oven preheated to 200°C/Gas Mark 6 and cook the venison for about 3 minutes on each side. The cooking time will vary according to the thickness of the loin. Remove from the oven and leave to rest in a warm place for 10 minutes.

While the venison is resting, heat the 20g butter in a small frying pan until it starts to foam. Add the crosnes, season with salt and pepper and cook over a medium heat for about 3 minutes or until tender. Blanch the sprout leaves in a pan of boiling salted water for 30 seconds. Drain, then brush the leaves with olive oil and season.

Carve the venison loin on the diagonal into 20 slices. Reheat the red cabbage and divide between 6 serving plates. Place the venison on top. Spoon the chestnut and apple purée alongside, then place alternate sprout leaves and crosnes next to the purée. Criss-cross the apple julienne over the top of the leaves, then spoon the blackcurrant sauce around and serve.

A RARE BREED

We are always looking for new ideas for ingredients and, as most chefs will tell you, an inordinate amount of time is spent in pursuit of such things. We buy our fallow deer from a wonderful supplier, Denham Estate, in Newmarket. It is run by Cecilia Gliksten, who founded the business with her late husband and our dear friend, Michael. Michael was also heavily involved in rare breeds and when we visited he took pleasure in driving us around the estate in his 4x4 to show us his prize sheep and cattle.

On one visit Michael wanted us to see his herd of Soay lamb, one of the oldest breeds in Britain, originating from a Scottish island. The Vikings even recorded their use of them and had their own name for the island after the sheep.

After we had travelled across the estate with Michael at the wheel, he suggested we take a close-up look at the lambs, which were grazing near a pond. They looked like Vikings! With their thick red fur and horns to match, there was definitely something primeval about this bunch. 'Why don't you get out and have a closer look?' said Michael to me. 'I'll take Jeff to see my White Park bull in the orchard.'

Well, I couldn't back out in front of Jeff, and so climbed out of the car against my better judgement. Off across the field roared Michael and Jeff, leaving me on the opposite side of the pond from a pack of feral-looking reprobates. No sooner had the car gone than the whole herd looked up and started running around the pond towards me. Maybe they think it's feeding time? I told myself. Then again, the rams at the front looked bloody savage, so I set off the opposite way round the pond, picking up speed all the time.

The chase went on for what seemed a very long time until the herd cleverly split and started charging both clockwise and anti-clockwise. I thought my time was up and decided that I really should visit the orchard.

At school I was the fastest boy over a hundred-metre sprint and almost forty years later I was still pretty fast. I could hear the sheep gaining but made the hedge in double-quick time. I leapt over it in one go, only to land in front of Jeff and Michael discussing the finer points of the White Park bull. 'You okay, Chris?' asked Jeff.

'Yes, thought I would have a short jog and catch you up,' I said breathlessly. I never told them what happened and when, at the end of the day, Michael asked if there was anything we would like him to send back to the restaurant to try, I told him, 'Yes, please, Michael, one of the Soay lambs – they look very tasty.'

And it was. Very dark and intense, with a hint of mutton.

DAUBE OF VENISON WITH QUINCE AND CHESTNUTS

Serves 4

This is a cracking winter dish, and a real favourite at the Bistrot. Shoulder is the perfect cut for braising, particularly if you can get the meat from a female deer, as the males can be stringy and tough. Quinces are around in October and November, so they just overlap with the fresh chestnuts.

1.5kg shoulder of venison, sinew removed
500ml red wine
250ml port
2 large carrots, cut into 6cm pieces
2 onions, each cut in half
1 stick celery, chopped
3 garlic cloves, chopped
3 juniper berries
3 white peppercorns
1/2 cinnamon stick
1 sprig of thyme
2 bay leaves
1 sprig of rosemary
75ml olive oil
100g plain flour, seasoned with salt and pepper
1 tablespoon tomato purée
2 litres Brown Chicken Stock (see page 44)
50g trompette mushrooms
10g Clarified Butter (see page 51)
12 chestnuts, roasted and skinned
sea salt and freshly ground white pepper
chopped fresh parsley, to garnish

For the quince
100g caster sugar
200ml water
1 lemon
1 quince

Put the venison, wine, port, vegetables, garlic and spices together in a non-metallic dish. Tie the thyme, bay and rosemary together with string and add to the dish. Cover and leave to marinate in the fridge for 24 hours.

Drain the meat, vegetables, spices and herbs, reserving the meat, vegetables and marinating liquor separately. Pour half the olive oil into a heavy-based ovenproof pan and heat until almost smoking, then add the reserved vegetables and cook until caramelised.

Dust the venison in the seasoned flour, add a little more olive oil to the pan and seal the meat all over. Stir in the tomato purée and allow it to cook a little with the meat. Remove the meat to a colander to drain, carefully pour the red wine and port from the marinade into the pan and cook until reduced a little, then add the chicken stock and return to the boil. Skim off any excess fat or scum that rises to the surface, add a little salt to taste and then return the venison to the pan. Cover the pan with a lid, transfer it to an oven preheated to 110°C/Gas Mark 1/4 and cook for 2 1/2–3 hours or until the venison is tender.

Meanwhile, cook the quince. Put the sugar and water in a pan and bring to the boil, stirring to dissolve the sugar. Boil for 2 minutes, then remove from the heat. Juice the lemon into a small bowl. Peel the quince and place it in the lemon juice, tossing to prevent discoloration. Cut the quince into quarters lengthwise, remove the core and seeds, then cut each quarter lengthwise into 3 to create 12 wedges. Add the quince wedges and lemon juice to the sugar syrup and bring to the boil, then cover the mixture with a cartouche (a circle of greaseproof paper) and reduce the heat to a simmer. Poach the quince for 6 minutes or until tender. Remove from the heat and set aside.

Remove the venison from the oven and leave to cool. Take the venison out of the pan and divide into 4 pieces. If the sauce is too thin, boil until slightly reduced and thickened, then pass through a fine sieve back over the meat. Just before serving, gently reheat the meat and sauce together.

Heat the clarified butter in a pan, add the trompette mushrooms and toss for 1 minute, then season and drain on kitchen paper. Keep the mushrooms warm. Reheat the quince if necessary and then remove from the syrup with a slotted spoon. Put the chestnuts in an oven preheated to 180°C/Gas Mark 4 for 1 minute to heat through.

To serve, put the venison on 4 serving plates, then scatter over the mushrooms, chestnuts and quince. Spoon over the sauce and garnish with a sprinkling of parsley. We often serve this with some buttery celeriac purée.

VENISON WITH SMOKED POTATO PURÉE, PICKLED RED CABBAGE, CHOCOLATE AND WATERCRESS

Serves 6

This is a wonderful play on sweet, sour and bitter flavours. It appears on the menu at Windows every year when the weather turns colder – the scent of the smoked potatoes is redolent of an old-fashioned night watchman's brazier on an autumn night.

For the red cabbage
1 small red cabbage
4 juniper berries
1 star anise
1 bay leaf
80g unsalted butter
30g demerara sugar
180ml red wine
180ml port
140ml Cabernet Sauvignon vinegar or
  other good quality red wine vinegar
sea salt and freshly ground white pepper

For the shoulder of venison
2 onions
2 carrots
2 sticks celery
400g venison shoulder, cut into 5cm dice
1 sprig of thyme
1 bay leaf
2 garlic cloves, chopped
10 black peppercorns
10 juniper berries
600ml red wine
olive oil, for cooking
500ml Brown Chicken Stock (see page 44)
500ml Chicken Stock (see page 44)

For the red wine and chocolate sauce
1–2 tablespoons olive oil
the trimmings from the loin of venison –
  see below
1 shallot, sliced
1 carrot, chopped
1 garlic clove, crushed
1 sprig of thyme
10 black peppercorns
5 juniper berries

1 star anise
50ml Cabernet Sauvignon vinegar or
  other good quality red wine vinegar
300ml red wine
300ml Brown Chicken Stock (see page 44)
25–30g bitter chocolate (minimum 70%
  cocoa solids), finely chopped
1 pomegranate, seeded

For the smoked potato purée
700g Charlotte potatoes or similar waxy
  new potatoes
100ml milk
100ml double cream
1 free-range egg yolk
150g chilled unsalted butter, diced

For the loin of venison
6 portions of boned and trimmed venison
  loin (about 100g each) – keep the
  trimmings
1 tablespoon olive oil
30g unsalted butter
12 sprigs of watercress, to garnish

Cut the cabbage into quarters, cut out the core, then shred the cabbage. Smash the juniper berries and tie them with the star anise and bay leaf into a muslin bag. Melt the butter in a large casserole over a medium heat until foaming, add the cabbage and cook gently for 2–3 minutes, stirring continuously. Add the muslin bag of spices and the sugar, cook for a further 2 minutes, then add the wine, port and vinegar. Bring to the boil, cover with a lid and place in an oven preheated to

140°C/Gas Mark 1. Cook for 2–3 hours, stirring every 30 minutes.

When fully cooked, the cabbage should be soft and glazed. Season with salt and leave to cool, then transfer to an airtight container, cover and refrigerate until needed. The cabbage will keep in the fridge for 3–4 days.

For the shoulder of venison, chop all the vegetables roughly into 3cm pieces, then mix in a large bowl with the venison shoulder, herbs, garlic, peppercorns and juniper berries. Pour over the wine, then cover and refrigerate overnight.

The next day, drain the venison, reserving the wine and vegetables separately. Pat the venison dry with a clean cloth. Place a large, deep casserole over a medium heat, add a little olive oil and heat thoroughly. Season the venison with salt and pepper and sear in the hot pan on all sides until browned. Remove the venison and drain on a tray lined with kitchen paper.

Wipe any excess fat from the casserole. Heat the casserole again, add a little more oil, then add the reserved vegetables and cook until browned, stirring continuously.

(Continued on page 228)

(Continued from page 227)

Add the venison and the reserved wine and bring to the boil, skimming off any scum that forms on the surface. Add the 2 stocks and bring to the boil again, then cover with a disc of greaseproof paper and the lid and place in an oven preheated to 110°C/Gas Mark ¼. Cook for 3–3½ hours or until the meat is tender when pierced with a small knife.

Remove from the oven and leave to cool for 1 hour. Drain the mixture through a fine sieve, reserving the meat mixture and cooking liquor separately. Return the cooking liquor to the casserole and boil until it has reduced to a thick and sticky sauce. Flake the meat, then add it to the reduced sauce and season. Grate the carrot pieces and stir them into the meat and sauce (discard the rest of the vegetables). Cover and set aside.

For the red wine and chocolate sauce, heat the olive oil in a large pan over a high heat, then add the venison trimmings and cook until browned all over. Add the shallot, carrot, garlic and thyme and continue to cook until softened. Crush the peppercorns, juniper berries and star anise together and sprinkle 2 pinches into the pan (keep the rest for later), then add the vinegar and cook until it has reduced to a syrup. Make sure all the meat trimmings are coated in the syrup, then add the wine and boil until reduced by half.

Add the stock, bring to the boil, then reduce the heat to low and simmer for 30 minutes, skimming off any scum that forms on the surface. Pass this sauce through a fine sieve or a piece of muslin cloth into a clean pan. If the sauce is not thick enough, boil to reduce it further until it has a light coating consistency.

Whisk in the chocolate and season to taste – if more spice is needed to balance the flavour, add another pinch or so of the crushed spice mixture, then simmer for 2–3 minutes. Strain the sauce again and set aside.

For the smoked potato purée, either wrap the potatoes in foil and bake on an outdoor barbecue over charcoal, or burn the skins with a blowtorch to give a smoky flavour, then bake them on a bed of salt in a hot oven until tender. While they are still hot (wear rubber gloves to protect your hands), peel the potatoes with a small knife, then purée them in a potato ricer or push them through a fine drum sieve to get a very smooth consistency.

Bring the milk and cream to the boil in a saucepan. Place the potato flesh in a separate pan over a low heat and pour in half the milk and cream mixture, beating until smooth. Add the rest of the milk and cream and beat until smooth, then add the egg yolk and beat well. Slowly add the diced cold butter, beating all the time to emulsify. Once all the butter has been added, season with salt and pepper, then spoon the mixture into a piping bag fitted with a medium plain nozzle.

Season the venison loin with salt and pepper. Heat a large, heavy-based frying pan over a high heat, add the olive oil, then sear the venison portions, turning every 2 minutes, until browned on all sides. Reduce the heat to low and add the butter. Cook for 2–3 minutes, turning the venison every minute in the foaming butter. Remove the venison to a warmed plate and leave to rest in a warm place for 6–8 minutes before serving.

To serve, reheat the red cabbage gently in a pan, then check the seasoning. Divide the shoulder of venison between 6 deep ovenproof bowls, about 9cm in diameter, pipe the smoked potato on top and brown under a hot grill. Put the red cabbage on 6 serving plates. Slice each portion of venison loin diagonally in half, season with a little sea salt and place on top of the cabbage.

Reheat the sauce, add a few pomegranate seeds, then spoon it over the venison loin. Garnish with the watercress. Serve the venison and smoked potato separately.

FEUILLETÉ OF ASPARAGUS WITH ARTICHOKES, PEAS AND MOUSSERON MUSHROOMS

Serves 4

This dish is redolent of spring. You could serve a smaller version as a starter. We use French or English asparagus for the best flavour.

For the feuilleté
240g Puff Pastry (see page 53)
2 free-range egg yolks, lightly beaten

For the sauce
200g chilled unsalted butter, diced
100g shallots, finely chopped
50ml white wine
2 tablespoons white wine vinegar
1 sprig of thyme
1 star anise
1 tablespoon water
100ml Chicken Stock (see page 44)
2 tablespoons double cream
a small squeeze of lemon juice
sea salt and freshly ground white pepper

For the spinach
20g unsalted butter
350g baby spinach leaves, rinsed and
    well drained

For the garnish
28 spears of green asparagus, cut into
    8cm lengths
200g shelled fresh peas
2 teaspoons olive oil
200g mousseron (St George's)
    mushrooms (girolles work well too)
6 baby artichokes, cooked and quartered
20g unsalted butter
12 sprigs of chervil

To make the feuilleté, roll the puff pastry out on a lightly floured work surface to 5mm thick. Lay the pastry sheet on a tray, brush with the egg yolks and refrigerate for 2 hours. Remove from the fridge and brush with egg yolk again. Cut out 4 rectangles, each about 8cm x 4cm, and transfer to a baking tray (discard any pastry trimmings). With the prongs of a dinner fork, score a criss-cross pattern on top of each pastry rectangle. Bake in an oven preheated to 200°C/Gas Mark 6 for 8 minutes or until golden and well risen. Reduce the oven temperature to 150°C/Gas Mark 2 and bake for a further 15 minutes (this dries out the inside of the feuilleté). Remove from the oven and transfer to a wire rack to cool. Cut each piece of pastry horizontally in half through the centre so you have a top and a bottom piece.

For the sauce, melt 10g of the butter in a saucepan, add the shallots and cook over a low heat until soft but not coloured. Add the white wine, vinegar, thyme, star anise and water. Bring to the boil, then boil until the mixture is reduced to a thick syrup. Add the chicken stock, bring to the boil again, then boil until reduced to a syrup again. Add the cream and boil for 1 minute, then gradually whisk in the remaining cold butter, piece by piece, maintaining the heat in the sauce as you go. Remove the thyme and star anise and discard, then season the sauce with salt, pepper and a small squeeze of lemon juice. Set aside and keep warm.

To cook the spinach, melt half the butter in a saucepan, then add the spinach. Cook briefly over a high heat until it starts to collapse, then remove from the heat and squeeze out any liquid. Remove the spinach to a plate. Melt the remaining butter in the pan, add the spinach and reheat. Season to taste and keep warm.

For the garnish, blanch the asparagus and peas in a large pan of boiling salted water for 3 minutes, then drain well. Return the vegetables to the pan, add the olive oil and toss the vegetables over a low heat for a few seconds, then season and keep warm. Gently sauté the mushrooms and artichokes in the butter until the mushrooms are tender, then season and drain.

To serve, spoon a tiny amount of the spinach on to the centre of each serving plate to keep the feuilleté in place. Place the bottom half of each feuilleté on top of the spinach, then fill with the rest of the spinach. Place the asparagus spears with their stalk end on top of the spinach and the spears facing out on to the plate like the hands of a clock. Next arrange the peas, mushrooms and artichokes neatly around each plate. Spoon the hot sauce over and around the vegetables. Place the feuilleté tops on the asparagus ends and garnish with the chervil sprigs.

RISOTTO OF FRESH PEAS, RICOTTA AND MINT

Serves 4

This is a great spring dish from the Café à Vin. We always offer it as a starter too, as it is so popular.

For the acidulated butter
4 tablespoons white wine
2 tablespoons white wine vinegar
30g onion, finely sliced
50g chilled unsalted butter, diced

For the mint oil
4 teaspoons virgin rapeseed oil
10 mint leaves

For the pea and mint purée
30g unsalted butter
30g onion, finely diced
120g shelled fresh peas
220ml hot Chicken Stock (see page 44)
    or vegetable stock
60g mint leaves

For the risotto
1 tablespoon extra virgin olive oil
40g onion, finely diced
400g carnaroli risotto rice
150ml white wine
350ml hot Chicken Stock (see page 44)
    or vegetable stock

To finish the risotto
2 tablespoons finely grated Parmesan
    cheese
160g ricotta cheese
100g shelled fresh peas, blanched for 3
    minutes and drained
2 tablespoons chopped mint
sea salt, to taste
juice of $1/2$ lemon
1 punnet of pea shoots

To make the acidulated butter, put the white wine, vinegar and onion into a saucepan and cook over a high heat until the liquid is reduced to about 1 tablespoon. Remove from the heat, then gradually whisk in the diced butter, piece by piece, until it is incorporated. Pass this mixture through a fine sieve and leave to cool, then place in the fridge to set for 1 hour.

To make the mint oil, mix the rapeseed oil and mint leaves together in a pestle and mortar until you have a purée, then squeeze through a piece of muslin. Set aside.

For the pea and mint purée, melt the butter in a pan over a low heat, add the onion and sweat for 3 minutes. When the onion is soft, add the peas, then the hot stock. Bring back to the boil, then reduce the heat and simmer for 2 minutes. Add the mint and simmer for a further 1 minute, then remove from the heat and purée in a blender or food processor until silky smooth. Taste and adjust the seasoning.

For the risotto, heat the olive oil in a large, heavy-based saucepan over a low heat, add the onion and sweat for 4–5 minutes, being careful not to brown it at all. Add the rice and continue to cook for 2 minutes, stirring constantly. Add the white wine and cook, stirring, until it is absorbed. Gradually add the hot stock, about 80ml at a time, stirring constantly and waiting until it has been absorbed before making the next addition.

Stir in the pea purée and bring to the boil, then reduce the heat and simmer for 3 minutes, stirring occasionally. Add the acidulated butter, Parmesan cheese, 120g of the ricotta, the blanched peas and chopped mint and cook gently, stirring occasionally, until the risotto is reheated, but do not boil it again. Finally adjust the seasoning, adding salt and lemon juice to taste.

To serve, spoon the risotto on to large serving plates, scatter the remaining ricotta on top, together with the pea shoots, and finish with a drizzle of mint oil.

BABY PUMPKIN SOUFFLÉ WITH PARMESAN GNOCCHI, CHESTNUTS AND PECORINO

Serves 4

Try to find small pumpkins for this lovely autumnal dish, no more than 20cm in diameter. You need a variety with fairly dry flesh, such as Potimarron.

1 quantity of Parmesan Gnocchi
  (see page 52)

For the soufflé
2 Potimarron or Ironbark pumpkins,
  weighing about 1.5kg each
a little olive oil, for cooking and drizzling
40g unsalted butter, diced
2 free-range egg yolks
a pinch of freshly grated nutmeg
5 free-range egg whites
sea salt and freshly ground white pepper

To finish
20g unsalted butter
100g cooked and peeled chestnuts, sliced
2 tablespoons celery leaves
50g aged Pecorino cheese, grated, plus
  extra to serve

To make the soufflé, trim the bottom of 1 pumpkin to give a secure flat base, then slice the top off and scoop out and discard the seeds. Scrape out any excess flesh and reserve, leaving a 5mm-thickness of flesh inside the pumpkin. Cut the other pumpkin in half and remove and discard the seeds. Carefully remove the skin and chop all the pumpkin flesh into large chunks.

Take the flesh of both pumpkins and place on a large sheet of foil. Season with salt, drizzle with a little olive oil and then wrap in the foil. Place in an oven preheated to 180°C/Gas Mark 4 and cook for 1 hour or until tender. Remove from the oven, strain off any cooking juices, then purée the hot flesh in a blender or food processor, gradually adding the diced butter. Finally mix in the egg yolks, nutmeg and a pinch of salt. Transfer the mixture to a bowl.

Whisk the egg whites to stiff peaks, then use a spatula to fold them into the pumpkin mixture in 2 stages. Spoon the mixture into the pumpkin shell and place in an oven preheated to 180°C/Gas Mark 4. Bake for 30–35 minutes, until well risen and golden.

Meanwhile, place a large frying pan over a high heat, add a little olive oil and fry the gnocchi for 1–2 minutes on each side, until golden. Transfer to a tray lined with kitchen paper and keep warm.

To finish, put the frying pan back over a medium heat, add the butter and when it has melted, add the chestnuts. Turn them in the butter for 3–4 minutes, until thoroughly heated through. Return the gnocchi to the pan, drop the celery leaves in and season with a pinch of salt, then add a drizzle of olive oil. Sprinkle over a little of the Pecorino, then divide the mixture between 4 serving plates.

When the soufflé is ready, sprinkle with the remaining grated Pecorino and serve immediately, placing it in the centre of the table, so everyone can help themselves. Offer some more Pecorino on the side as well.

CEP AND PARSLEY PIZZA

Serves 4

When we acquired a wood-fired oven, this was one of the first dishes we developed. Ceps are available late summer through to autumn, depending on the amount of rain.

100g unsalted butter
150g shallots, finely diced
6 small garlic cloves, crushed
750g mixed fresh wild mushrooms, finely
    chopped
4 tablespoons Madeira
4 tablespoons roughly chopped parsley
olive oil, for cooking and drizzling
3 large fresh ceps, cleaned and cut into
    5mm-thick slices
semolina flour, for rolling
a double quantity of Pizza Dough
    (see page 53)
200ml crème fraîche
200g fromage blanc
sea salt and freshly ground white pepper
Parmesan cheese shavings, to serve

Melt the butter in a large sauté pan, add the shallots and garlic and sweat for about 5 minutes, until softened. Add the wild mushrooms and cook gently for 15 minutes or until they begin to look soft and most of the moisture has evaporated from the pan. Add the Madeira and cook, stirring, until it has almost all evaporated. Spoon the mixture on to a tray and leave to cool. Season with salt and then stir in half the parsley.

Heat a frying pan, add a little olive oil, then add the ceps and cook until golden. Season to taste and set aside.

Lightly flour a work surface with semolina flour. Divide the pizza dough into 4 and roll each piece into a 30cm x 14cm rectangle about 2mm thick. Prick all over with a fork.

Put the crème fraîche, fromage blanc and some salt and pepper in a bowl and mix well. Spread this evenly over the bases, leaving a 1cm border all round. Spread the mushroom mix on top and then lay the cooked ceps over it.

We cook the pizzas in a wood-fired oven at 350°C for $2^{1}/_{2}$ minutes. At home, heat your oven to 250°C/Gas Mark 10 and cook the pizzas on the top shelf on a pizza tray or, even better, a pizza stone, for 5 minutes, until the edges are golden. Serve straight from the oven on wooden boards or plates, sprinkled with the remaining parsley and shaved Parmesan and drizzled with olive oil.

DESSERTS

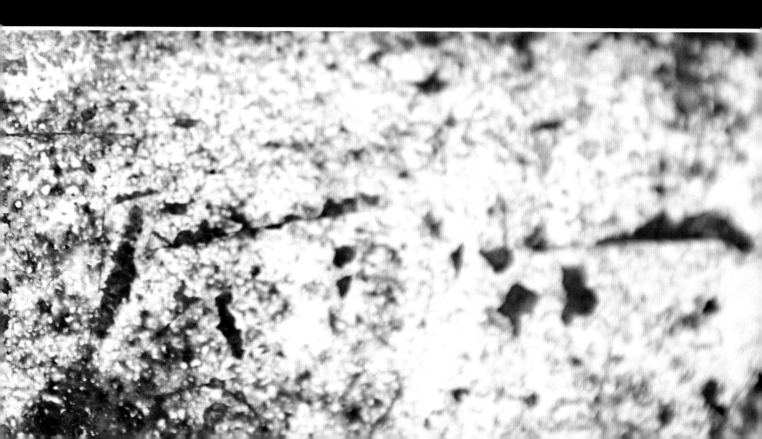

POACHED PEARS WITH PAIN D'ÉPICES ICE CREAM

Serves 6

An autumnal dessert that is very easy for home cooks to make. Most of the work can be done in advance.

200g Pain d'épices (see page 58)
225ml milk
225ml double cream
4 free-range egg yolks
75g caster sugar
20g icing sugar

For the poached pears
500g caster sugar
1 litre water
1 star anise
2 vanilla pods, split in half lengthwise and seeds scraped out
6 Williams pears (not too soft)

Cut off the outside of the pain d'épices and reserve 100g of the trimmings for the ice cream. Cut 6 rectangles from the inside of the loaf, each about 8cm x 4cm in size and about 2mm thick, and set aside. Put any leftover scraps somewhere warm to dry out. When they are dry, blitz them in a blender or food processer to make a fine powder.

For the pain d'épices ice cream, put the milk and cream in a pan with the pain d'épices trimmings and bring to the boil. Whisk the egg yolks and caster sugar together in a large bowl until pale in colour. Whilst still whisking, carefully pour the boiling milk mixture on to the yolks and sugar. Return to a clean pan and cook gently, stirring continuously, to a temperature of 82°C or until the mixture thickens enough to coat the back of the spoon. Remove from the heat, pass the mixture through a fine sieve and leave to cool. Transfer to an ice cream maker and freeze according to the manufacturer's instructions.

To make the poaching syrup for the pears, put the caster sugar, water, star anise and vanilla pods and seeds in a small, deep pan, bring to the boil and boil for 3 minutes. Meanwhile, peel the pears, leaving the stalks on. Place the pears in the syrup and cover with a cartouche (a circle of greaseproof paper). Return to the boil, then simmer for about 15 minutes – the cooking time will vary depending on the ripeness and size of the pears, but they should be cooked

through. Remove from the heat and leave the pears to cool in the syrup. Remove and discard the star anise and vanilla pods.

Using a melon baller, remove the core from each pear (by cutting through the base), leaving the stalk intact. Slice each pear lengthwise, going not quite up to the top, so they stay attached at the stalk end, then fan them out. Dust with the icing sugar and glaze with a chef's blowtorch. Soak the rectangles of pain d'épices in the poaching liquid.

To serve, sprinkle a line of pain d'épices powder across each serving plate, place a pain d'épices rectangle on the plate and then place a glazed pear on top, with a scoop of pain d'épices ice cream alongside.

PETITS POTS AU CHOCOLAT WITH SABLÉ BISCUITS

Serves 8

Don't be put off by the small portions here – it is a very rich little pot of chocolate indeed, and any more would simply be too much.

For the petits pots au chocolat
350ml double cream
1 vanilla pod, split in half lengthwise and seeds scraped out
250g dark chocolate (64% cocoa solids), chopped
150ml milk
4 free-range egg yolks
2 tablespoons icing sugar

For the sablé biscuits
100g unsalted butter, diced
50g icing sugar, plus extra for dusting
1 free-range egg yolk
125g plain flour
a small pinch of sea salt

For the petits pots au chocolat, put the cream and vanilla seeds in a pan and bring to the boil over a low heat. Whisk to disperse the vanilla seeds, then remove from the heat and leave to infuse for 30 minutes.

Put the chocolate and milk in a bowl and set it over a pan of gently simmering water, making sure the water doesn't touch the base of the bowl. Leave until the chocolate has melted, then remove from the heat and stir in the infused cream. Using an electric mixer, beat the egg yolks and icing sugar together in a bowl until pale in colour. Gradually whisk the chocolate mixture into the egg yolk mixture until well incorporated.

Pass the mixture through a fine sieve, then divide it between eight 100ml ovenproof glass or porcelain pots. Place the pots in a deep baking tray and pour enough boiling water into the tray to come halfway up the outside of the pots. Bake in an oven preheated to 110°C/ Gas Mark $\frac{1}{4}$ for 45–60 minutes or until slightly puffed up and spongy. Remove from the oven and cool to room temperature but do not refrigerate.

To make the sablé biscuits, place the butter and icing sugar in the bowl of an electric stand mixer fitted with the paddle attachment and beat until pale in colour. Add the egg yolk and when thoroughly mixed, add the flour and salt. Bring the mixture completely together to make a dough but do not over mix.

Remove from the mixing bowl, then sandwich the dough between 2 large sheets of baking parchment and roll out with a rolling pin to 3–4mm thick. Chill for 10 minutes. Carefully remove the top layer of the paper, then cut out the sablés using a 6cm plain round pastry cutter. Place on a baking tray lined with baking parchment. You can re-roll the trimmings and cut out more biscuits.

Bake in an oven preheated to 160°C/ Gas Mark 3 for 10 minutes (the biscuits should not colour at all). Remove from the oven and leave the biscuits to cool slightly on the baking tray, then carefully transfer them to a wire rack and leave to cool completely.

To serve, place the chocolate pots on serving plates. Dust the sablé biscuits with icing sugar and serve 2 on the side of each chocolate pot.

APRICOT AND CHOCOLATE SOUFFLÉ WITH DARK CHOCOLATE SORBET

Serves 6

This is one of the best marriages of ingredients imaginable. Don't be too frightened about making a soufflé – this one is based on a fruit purée thickened with cornflour to stabilise it, and is really very forgiving. You can even make up the soufflés and put them in their dishes several hours in advance, then cook them just before serving – which is what we do in the restaurant.

For the chocolate sorbet
100ml still mineral water
50g caster sugar
30g dark chocolate (70% cocoa solids), chopped
15g cocoa powder

For the soufflé base
400g apricot purée
80g caster sugar
25g cornflour
3 tablespoons water

To finish the soufflé
40g softened unsalted butter, for greasing
100g dark chocolate (70% cocoa solids), grated
7 free-range egg whites
65g caster sugar
icing sugar, for dusting

For the chocolate sorbet, put the water and caster sugar in a pan and bring to the boil, then pour on to the chocolate and cocoa powder in a bowl and whisk together to mix. Pass the mixture through a fine sieve, then transfer to an ice cream maker and freeze according to the manufacturer's instructions. Place in the freezer to set for at least 2 hours.

For the soufflé base, put the apricot purée and caster sugar in a pan, bring to the boil and boil for 10 minutes, until thick. Whisk occasionally and be careful not to let the mixture burn on the bottom. Remove from the heat and leave to cool slightly in the pan. Mix the cornflour and water together to make a paste. Whisk this into the reduced apricot purée and return to the heat. Bring back to the boil, whisking continuously to prevent the mixture going lumpy, then reduce the heat and simmer for 10 minutes, whisking occasionally. Remove from the heat, transfer the mixture to a plastic container or a bowl and place a piece of cling film on top so that it touches the surface (to prevent a skin forming). Leave to cool to room temperature.

To finish the soufflé, thoroughly grease six 200ml soufflé moulds with the softened butter. Put all of the grated chocolate into one mould, turning the mould so that the chocolate sticks to the butter and the inside is coated all over with chocolate, then tip the chocolate into the next mould and repeat this procedure until all of the moulds are lined with chocolate.

Using an electric mixer, whisk the egg whites and caster sugar together in a bowl until stiff. Transfer the soufflé base to a large bowl and, using a whisk, beat in 2 tablespoons of the stiff meringue. Gently fold in the rest of the meringue using a spatula. Transfer to a piping bag fitted with a wide plain nozzle. Pipe the soufflé mixture into the prepared moulds, filling each one just past the top so that when you then scrape a palette knife across, it forms a completely flat top. With your thumb, go around the edge of each mould to indent the mixture slightly. Place the moulds on a baking tray and cook in an oven preheated to 180°C/Gas Mark 4 for 10 minutes or until well risen and with a slight wobble in the centre.

Dust the soufflés with icing sugar and serve immediately with a scoop of the chocolate sorbet separately.

FOIE GRAS MARINATED IN CHÂTEAU D'YQUEM

In 1993 I began working as a sous chef at 90 Park Lane with Nico Ladenis, one of the true greats of cooking. It was by far the most enjoyable period of my career to date. Although Nico did not cook, he was ever present at the reception desk, where in the mornings there was relentless work on new and current dishes. It may sound unusual for a chef not to be in the kitchen but Nico managed it with great skill. He could often be seen in the small area between the pass and the restaurant inspecting each plate before it was allowed to go out to the customer. I feel extremely privileged to have spent five years helping him gain three Michelin stars and helping to write his cookery book, *Nico*.

In 1998 I was given charge of a very talented artist called Richard Bramble, who was putting together *The Star Chefs Cookbook* – a collection of recipes from the finest chefs in the UK. Interestingly, it was not going to contain a single photograph. Instead Richard was commissioned to paint the food.

At Chez Nico we had a sizeable private room that was rarely used at lunchtime and so was a perfect place for Richard to go about his business of putting brush to canvas. My role was to provide him with everything he needed foodwise. Typically, Richard would arrive at 9am, I would give him the dish he was to paint and he would be alone until late into the afternoon – quite often I did not say goodbye to him as he tended to leave at around 4.30pm and I would take my break from 3pm and then come back for dinner service at 5pm. One

morning, Richard popped his head in and asked for a bottle of the wine that would accompany the dessert he was painting that day. The sommelier was not due in for half an hour and our cellar was under firm lock and key, so I told Richard I would send the wine in as soon as the sommelier arrived. Sure enough, he duly turned up and I told him to give Richard something special that was a good marriage with the dessert.

By 10am I forgot about Richard and turned my attention to the busy lunch service we had ahead. At 3pm I popped my head in to say cheerio, then cycled back to my flat three minutes away on Weymouth Street for an afternoon rest. When I returned to the kitchen I noticed the cook on the larder had a bottle of Sauternes on his bench. This was not unusual, as we often marinated our foie gras at this time of day. What did catch my eye, however, was the fact that the foil on the top of the bottle was a different colour from the one on the Sauternes we normally used. I asked the chef to show me the label and nearly fainted when I read the words, Château d'Yquem 1929, a wine that was listed at Chez Nico for £21,000. Apparently when Richard had finished, he left the wine with a different waiter and it had somehow made its way to the kitchen, then subsequently to our rack of kitchen wines. I have always had a vivid mental picture of the look on Nico's face if we had had to tell him – and, indeed, wondered who would have told him.

RUM BABAS WITH CRÈME CHANTILLY

Serves 8

We keep rum baba on all our menus all the time – except once when we replaced it with a savarin, which is essentially the same thing but a different shape. A customer was absolutely furious with us – you know who you are!

The dough in this recipe will make 12 babas. It is very difficult to make it in smaller quantities but the extra will freeze well.

For the dough
80g sultanas
250g strong plain white flour
3g sea salt
10g caster sugar
15g fresh yeast
65ml lukewarm full-fat milk
4 small free-range eggs, beaten
120g unsalted butter, melted
40g softened unsalted butter, for greasing
50ml Dark Navy rum, for soaking

For the rum baba syrup and raisins
1 litre water
600g caster sugar
500ml Dark Navy rum
200g raisins moelleux or large golden
 raisins

For the apricot glaze
200g apricot jam
4 teaspoons water

For the crème chantilly
200ml chilled whipping cream
2 tablespoons crème fraîche
20g icing sugar
1 vanilla pod, split in half lengthwise and
 seeds scraped out

For the dough, put the sultanas into a bowl, cover with boiling water and leave to soak for 1 hour, then drain. Sift the flour into the bowl of a small electric stand mixer fitted with a dough hook attachment and turn on to the lowest speed. Add the salt and caster sugar. Dissolve the yeast in the milk and then add this to the flour mixture. Turn up the speed on the mixer a little, add the eggs and mix until the dough comes together. Slowly add the melted butter until the dough tightens and all the butter is incorporated. Finally, add the soaked sultanas and mix for 1 minute.

Transfer the dough to a clean bowl, cover with cling film and leave at room temperature until doubled in size. Return to the mixer and mix on a high speed for 2 minutes to knock the dough back. Put the dough into a piping bag fitted with a large plain nozzle.

Lightly grease 8 dariole moulds (each about 5.5cm x 5cm) with softened butter and dust each one with a little flour. Pipe some dough into each mould, filling half full (cutting the dough with a pair of scissors to finish each one). Cover with cling film and leave in a warm place again until doubled in size.

Bake in an oven preheated to 220°C/Gas Mark 7 for about 5 minutes, then reduce the temperature to 200°C/Gas Mark 6 and cook for 12–15 minutes longer, until golden brown. Remove from the oven, turn out on to a wire rack and leave to cool.

For the syrup and raisins, put the water, caster sugar and rum in a pan and bring to the boil, stirring occasionally. Remove from the heat and then pour enough syrup over the raisins just to cover them. Cover with cling film and leave to cool.

Put the baked babas in the rest of the hot syrup, leaving them to absorb it until they swell and are completely moist throughout. With a slotted spoon, carefully remove the soaked babas to a wire rack and leave to drain. Pour the remaining 50ml rum evenly over the babas.

For the glaze, put the apricot jam in a pan with the water and boil until smooth and thick. Strain through a sieve, then brush over the babas to form a shiny glaze.

For the crème chantilly, whip the cream, crème fraîche, icing sugar and vanilla seeds together in a bowl until stiff.

Put the rum babas on 8 serving plates and add a spoonful of the crème chantilly and a spoonful of raisins to each.

HOT CHOCOLATE FONDANTS WITH RASPBERRIES

Serves 6

This recipe is very easy to make but it's worth remembering that the chocolate fondants need to be prepared the day before and kept in the fridge for 24 hours. If they are not totally fridge-cold you just won't get that lovely molten centre when they come out of the oven.

For the raspberry coulis
125g icing sugar
300g raspberries
a few drops of lemon juice

To prepare the moulds
30g unsalted butter, melted
2 tablespoons plain flour

For the chocolate fondants
100g dark chocolate (66% cocoa solids),
    preferably Valrhona, chopped
100g unsalted butter, diced
2 free-range eggs
2 free-range egg yolks
55g caster sugar
10g plain flour, sifted

For the decoration
150g raspberries
6 sprigs of mint
1 tablespoon icing sugar

To make the raspberry coulis, sprinkle the icing sugar over the raspberries in a bowl and leave for 15 minutes. Transfer to a blender or food processor and blitz until puréed. Pass the purée through a fine sieve, then add the lemon juice to taste. Store in the fridge until ready to serve.

To prepare the moulds, brush six 120ml foil pudding moulds with the melted butter, then dust with the flour, tapping out any excess. Place the moulds in the fridge to chill.

For the chocolate fondants, place the chocolate and butter in a large mixing bowl set over a pan of simmering water, making sure the water doesn't touch the base of the bowl. Leave to melt, then whisk together until smooth.

Put the eggs, egg yolks and caster sugar in the bowl of an electric stand mixer and whisk together for a few minutes or until pale in colour. Whisk this mixture into the melted chocolate. Finally, fold in the flour until it is completely incorporated. Bang the bottom of the bowl with your hand to knock out any air. Pour the chocolate mixture into the prepared moulds, filling each one to about 5mm from the top, then cover with cling film and refrigerate for 24 hours.

The next day, bake the chocolate fondants in an oven preheated to 180°C/Gas Mark 4 for 10 minutes.

To serve, flood each serving plate with a generous amount of raspberry coulis, then place a small pile of raspberries to one side and decorate with a mint sprig. Turn the fondants out straight on to the plates and dust with icing sugar. The fondants should have a delicious soft centre.

VANILLA RICE PUDDING WITH CARAMELISED ALPHONSO MANGO

Serves 6

Alphonso mangoes from India are available in April. They have a very perfumed, intense flavour and we wouldn't use any other sort. It's the only time mangoes appear in our kitchens.

400ml full-fat milk
60g caster sugar
100g short-grain pudding rice
1 vanilla pod, cut in half lengthwise and
　seeds scraped out
40ml sweetened condensed milk
2 ripe Alphonso mangoes
30g icing sugar

Place the milk, caster sugar, rice and vanilla seeds and empty pod in a heavy-based saucepan and bring to the boil over a medium heat. Reduce the heat to a simmer, then cook for about 15 minutes or until the rice is soft, stirring every few minutes to ensure the mixture does not catch on the bottom of the pan (the cooking time will vary a bit with different brands of rice).

Once cooked, remove from the heat. Remove the vanilla pod and discard. Stir in the condensed milk and leave to cool, then chill in the fridge.

Peel the mangoes, cut off the flesh lengthwise and cut it into neat wedges. Cut off any mango flesh left around the stones and purée it in a blender or food processor, then pass it through a fine sieve and refrigerate.

Dust the mango wedges with the icing sugar. Heat a non-stick frying pan until it is very hot, then add the mango slices (you may need to do this in batches) and cook until they are caramelised on both sides, turning once. You need to caramelise the mango wedges quickly as ripe mango will go mushy if cooked for too long.

Spoon the cold rice pudding into small serving bowls or suitable glasses, then arrange the warm mango wedges on top. Finally, carefully pour the mango purée around the edge of the rice pudding and serve.

SAVARIN OF SUMMER BERRIES

Serves 6

With the savarin it is imperative that the berries you use taste fantastic. Don't be afraid to taste the berries before you buy them; smell is also a good indicator of ripe berries.

The quantity of dough given below will make 12 savarins but it isn't really practical to make a smaller amount. We advise freezing the surplus.

For the savarin dough
250g strong plain white flour
3g sea salt
10g caster sugar
15g fresh yeast
65ml lukewarm full-fat milk
4 small free-range eggs, beaten
120g unsalted butter, melted
30g softened unsalted butter, for greasing

For the raspberry coulis
125g icing sugar
300g raspberries
a few drops of lemon juice

For the soaking syrup
500ml water
300g caster sugar
250ml kirsch

For the glaze
100g apricot jam
4 teaspoons water

For the crème chantilly
100ml chilled whipping cream
1 tablespoon crème fraîche
10g icing sugar
½ vanilla pod, split in half lengthwise
   and seeds scraped out

For the decoration
150g raspberries
150g strawberries
50g wild strawberries (optional)
100g blueberries
6 small sprigs of mint

For the savarin dough, sift the flour into the bowl of a small electric stand mixer fitted with a dough hook attachment and turn on to the lowest speed. Add the salt and caster sugar. Dissolve the yeast in the milk, then add this to the flour mixture. Turn up the speed on the mixer a little, add the eggs and mix until the dough comes together. Slowly add the melted butter until the dough tightens and all the butter is incorporated.

Transfer the dough to a clean bowl, cover with cling film and leave at room temperature until doubled in size. Return to the mixer and mix on a high speed for 2 minutes to knock the dough back. Put the dough into a piping bag fitted with a large plain nozzle.

Lightly grease six 7cm savarin moulds with the softened butter and dust with a little flour. Pipe enough savarin dough into each mould to fill it half full (cutting the dough with a pair of scissors to finish). Cover with cling film and leave in a warm place again until doubled in size.

Bake in an oven preheated to 200°C/ Gas Mark 6 for 8 minutes or until golden brown. Turn out on to a wire rack and leave to cool.

To make the raspberry coulis, sprinkle the icing sugar over the raspberries in a bowl and leave for 15 minutes. Transfer to a blender or food processor and blitz until puréed. Pass the purée through a fine sieve, then add the lemon juice to taste. Store in the fridge until ready to serve.

For the soaking syrup, put all the ingredients in a pan and bring to the boil, stirring occasionally, then remove from the heat. Put the savarins into the hot syrup, leaving them to absorb it until they swell and are completely moist throughout. With a slotted spoon, carefully remove the soaked savarins to a wire rack and leave to drain.

For the glaze, put the apricot jam in a pan with the water and boil until smooth and thick. Brush some over each savarin to form a shiny glaze.

For the crème chantilly, whip the cream, crème fraîche, icing sugar and vanilla seeds together in a bowl until stiff.

To serve, spoon a circle of raspberry coulis on to the centre of each serving plate, spreading it out so that it is a little larger than the base of the savarins. Place a savarin on top, then place a tablespoon of crème chantilly in the centre of the savarin.

For the decoration, toss the mixed berries in the remaining coulis, then spoon the berry mixture on to the plates and over the crème chantilly. Decorate with the mint sprigs.

CARAMELISED WHITE PEACHES WITH LAVENDER ICE CREAM

Serves 8

The flavours of this dish are inspired by the southern Rhône area, where peach trees and lavender often grow side by side. If you have lavender growing in your garden, do try this ice cream.

340ml full-fat milk
340ml double cream
1 vanilla pod, split in half lengthwise and seeds scraped out
4 sprigs of fresh lavender
5 free-range egg yolks
100g caster sugar
8 ripe white peaches
100g icing sugar
lavender honey, to serve

Put the milk, cream and vanilla seeds and empty pod in a heavy-based pan and bring to the boil over a medium heat. Remove from the heat, add the lavender sprigs and leave to infuse for 10 minutes, then pass the mixture through a fine sieve and discard the vanilla pod and lavender.

Whisk the egg yolks and caster sugar together in a large bowl until pale in colour. Whilst still whisking, carefully pour the hot milk mixture on to the yolks and sugar. Return to a clean pan and cook gently, stirring continuously, to a temperature of 82°C or until the mixture thickens enough to coat the back of the spoon. Remove from the heat, pass through a fine sieve and leave to cool. Transfer to an ice cream maker and freeze according to the manufacturer's instructions.

Loosen the skin of the peaches by carefully burning the outside of each one with a chef's blowtorch, then refresh in iced water. Drain the peaches and pat dry. Peel the skin off using the point of a small sharp knife, then cut each peach into 8 wedges, discarding the stone. Arrange the peach wedges side by side on a baking tray, liberally dust them with the icing sugar and caramelise with the blowtorch. After a few seconds, you can turn the wedges over and caramelise the other side. This cannot be done more than a few minutes in advance of serving, as the sugar will draw the juice from the peaches.

Divide the caramelised peach wedges between 8 martini glasses or other glass serving dishes. Place a scoop of lavender ice cream in the middle of each glass, then drizzle with a little lavender honey.

CRÊPES SUZETTE

Serves 4

This is a classic oldie that you simply cannot tire of. It's never really been either in or out of fashion but whenever it's on our menu it's always amazingly popular. When Chris worked at the Ritz, the crêpes were always flambéed at the table by the waiter.

For the crêpes
55g unsalted butter
2 free-range eggs
25g caster sugar
100g plain flour
a pinch of sea salt
350ml milk
4 teaspoons vegetable oil

For the sauce
2 oranges
225g caster sugar
80ml water
175g unsalted butter
3 tablespoons orange liqueur, such as
　Grand Marnier
1 orange, segmented, all peel and pith
　removed

To make the crêpe batter, heat a small frying pan, then add the butter and melt over a high heat until it foams. Pour the melted butter into a mixing bowl, add the eggs, sugar, flour and salt and whisk together to combine. Slowly add the milk, whisking constantly to make a smooth batter the consistency of pouring cream. Pass the batter through a medium sieve, then leave to stand for at least 1 hour. Whisk again just before using.

To cook the crêpes, heat a small cast-iron frying pan over a medium heat. Add the vegetable oil and tilt the pan so it leaves a thin film over the base, then pour off the excess oil into a cup. Pour in just enough batter to coat the base of the pan thinly. Cook for 30–40 seconds, until golden brown underneath, then turn or toss and cook the second side for a further 30 seconds, until golden. Transfer the crêpe to a warm plate and keep hot. Repeat with the remaining batter (greasing the pan with the excess oil, if necessary), stacking the cooked crêpes on top of each other with greaseproof paper in between. You should aim for 3–4 crêpes per person.

For the sauce, pare the zest off the oranges in strips with a zester, then juice the oranges. Place the zest in a small pan of cold water and bring to the boil, then drain. Repeat this twice. Place the blanched zest back in the pan, add 80g of the sugar and the water and cook gently over a medium heat for 10–15 minutes or until the zest looks translucent and candied.

Heat a wide, shallow, heavy-based pan over a medium heat, then add the butter and allow it to foam. Add the remaining sugar and stir until it has dissolved and starts to caramelise to a straw-blond colour – this will take a minute or two. Reduce the heat and carefully add the orange juice and orange liqueur to the pan. Increase the heat to medium and allow the mixture to bubble for about 2 minutes to form a sauce, whisking occasionally.

Lay a crêpe in the gently bubbling sauce in the pan, fold in half, then fold in half again to make a triangular shape. Repeat for all the crêpes, arranging them neatly to fit in the pan.

Divide the crêpes between 4 serving plates, overlapping them on each plate. Add the orange segments to the remaining sauce in the pan and quickly warm through. Divide the segments between the plates, then spoon some sauce over each portion. To finish, scatter some strips of candied orange zest over the crêpes. Serve with vanilla ice cream (see page 58), if you like.

Tasting La Chapelle with Jacques Desvernois, winemaker at Paul Jaboulet (*opposite, top*), with the famous chapel presiding over the Rhône Valley (*opposite, bottom*).

PJA
1884

LA CHAPELLE

HERMITAGE

PAUL JABOULET AîNé

TAIN L'HERMITAGE · FRANCE

GREENGAGE CLAFOUTIS
WITH VANILLA ICE CREAM

Serves 6

Also known as Reine Claude plums, greengages are named after Sir William Gage, who brought them to England from France in the early eighteenth century. They're in season from mid-July to the end of August, and their sharp flavour works well with the soft sweetness of a clafoutis. There's also a lovely contrast between the hot dessert and the cold ice cream.

120ml milk
120ml double cream
$^{1}/_{2}$ vanilla pod, split in half lengthwise and seeds scraped out
4 free-range eggs
170g caster sugar
1 teaspoon plain flour
9 greengages
1 tablespoon icing sugar
1 quantity of Vanilla Ice Cream (see page 58), to serve

Put the milk, cream, vanilla seeds and empty pod in a pan and bring to the boil, then simmer for 1 minute. Remove from the heat. Whisk the eggs and caster sugar together in a bowl until light and fluffy, then add the flour and whisk until smooth. Pour the hot milk on to the egg mixture, whisking continuously. Pass through a fine sieve into a bowl or jug.

Cut the greengages in half and remove and discard the stones. Cut each half into 3 wedges and arrange in 6 shallow ovenproof dishes, about 11cm in diameter. Pour the batter over the greengages so it nearly comes to the top of the dishes. Bake in an oven preheated to 200°C/Gas Mark 6 for 9 minutes or until just set.

Remove the clafoutis from the oven and place each dish on a serving plate. Dust with the icing sugar and serve each portion with a scoop of vanilla ice cream.

LEMON MASCARPONE CHEESECAKE WITH WILD STRAWBERRIES

Serves 8

We serve this in our café and although wild strawberries are very expensive it is well worth treating yourself to them for this. We used to get them from France but there are some very good producers in Kent now. The cheesecake is very easy to make at home.

1 quantity of Sweet Shortcrust Pastry
(see page 56)
2 free-range egg yolks, beaten
300g wild strawberries, to serve
icing sugar, to dust

For the filling
540g mascarpone cheese
450ml double cream
240g caster sugar
3 free-range eggs
1 tablespoon cornflour
3 tablespoons lemon juice
finely grated zest of 3 unwaxed lemons

Roll the pastry out on a lightly floured work surface to a circle about 32cm in diameter, then use it to line a 25cm loose-bottomed flan tin (2.5cm deep), or a cake ring placed on a baking tray lined with greaseproof paper. Leave the excess pastry overhanging the edge of the tin as this will be trimmed after cooking. Refrigerate for 25 minutes.

Line the pastry case with greaseproof paper, then fill to the top with baking beans (if you don't have baking beans, use plain uncooked beans or rice). Bake in an oven preheated to 180°C/Gas Mark 4 for 18–20 minutes or until pale golden. Remove from the oven and lift out the paper and beans, then return the pastry case to the oven and bake for a further 4 minutes. Remove from the oven again and brush the egg yolks over the hot pastry case. Return to the oven for 2 minutes, then transfer to a wire rack. Reduce the oven temperature to 120°C/Gas Mark ¹/₂.

Whisk all the filling ingredients together in a bowl until well mixed. Pass the mixture through a fine sieve. Pour the filling into the pastry case and bake for 20–25 minutes or until set. Remove from the oven and leave to cool to room temperature, then neatly trim the edges of the pastry case with a small paring knife and refrigerate. Once chilled, carefully remove the cheesecake from the tin or ring.

To serve, place the wild strawberries neatly on top of the cheesecake, cut it into wedges with a hot knife and dust with icing sugar.

LEMON TART

Serves 8

This is one of our favourite desserts. It doesn't need any accompaniment at all, so we always resist the temptation to add to it.

1 quantity of Sweet Shortcrust Pastry
  (see page 56)
2 free-range egg yolks, beaten
icing sugar, to dust

For the lemon filling
finely grated zest and juice of 10
  unwaxed lemons (you need 450ml
  juice)
500g caster sugar
1 litre double cream
6 free-range eggs
6 free-range egg yolks

Roll the pastry out on a lightly floured work surface, then use it to line a 25cm loose-bottomed flan tin about 4.5cm deep, or a cake ring placed on a baking tray lined with baking parchment. Leave the excess pastry overhanging the edge of the tin as this will be trimmed after cooking. Refrigerate for 25 minutes.

Line the pastry case with greaseproof paper, then fill to the top with baking beans (if you don't have baking beans, use plain uncooked beans or rice). Bake in an oven preheated to 180°C/Gas Mark 4 for 18–20 minutes or until pale golden. Remove from the oven and lift out the paper and beans, then return the pastry case to the oven and bake for a further 4 minutes. Remove from the oven again and brush the egg yolks over the hot pastry case. Return to the oven for 2 minutes, then transfer to a wire rack. Reduce the oven temperature to 110°C/Gas Mark 1/4.

To make the filling, put the lemon juice and caster sugar in a pan and bring to the boil over a medium heat, stirring occasionally. Remove from the heat, stir in the lemon zest and leave to infuse for 3–4 minutes, then pass the mixture through a fine sieve.

Put the cream in a separate pan and bring to the boil, then remove from the heat and leave to cool slightly. Put the eggs and egg yolks into a large mixing bowl and whisk together, then, whilst still whisking, pour the lemon juice/sugar

mixture on to the eggs. Whisk in the cream, then pass the mixture through a fine sieve. Skim off any bubbles from the top.

Place the pastry case in the tin on a baking sheet and place this on the shelf in the oven, then gently pour in the lemon filling, taking it to the very top and being very careful to avoid any spillages. Bake for about 40 minutes or until only just set. The middle should wobble like a jelly when the tart is cooked. Remove from the oven and leave the tart to cool on the baking sheet for at least 3 hours at room temperature – do not put it in the fridge as the pastry will go soggy.

When cool, neatly trim off the excess pastry from around the edge of the tart using a small paring knife. Carefully remove the tart from the tin or ring, then cut it into wedges. Dust with icing sugar and caramelise the top with a chef's blowtorch just before serving.

PRUNE AND WALNUT TART WITH VANILLA ICE CREAM

Serves 6-8

The key to this is to use good-quality prunes. The ones from Agen in France are excellent and are available in many big supermarkets. This tart is also very good served cold with a cup of tea mid-afternoon – we can vouch for that!

1 quantity of Sweet Shortcrust Pastry
  (see page 56)
2 free-range egg yolks, beaten
100g apricot jam
4 teaspoons water
1 quantity of Vanilla Ice Cream (see page
  58), to serve

For the filling
300g stoned Agen prunes
6 tablespoons Armagnac
1 free-range egg, beaten
60g caster sugar
40g ground walnuts
200ml crème fraîche
16 walnut halves

Put the prunes in a bowl, pour over the Armagnac and leave to soak for 24 hours.

Roll the pastry out on a lightly floured work surface and use it to line a 25cm loose-bottomed flan tin (2.5cm deep) or a cake ring placed on a baking tray lined with greaseproof paper. Leave the excess pastry overhanging the edge of the tin as this will be trimmed after cooking. Refrigerate for 25 minutes.

Line the pastry case with greaseproof paper, then fill to the top with baking beans (if you don't have baking beans, use plain uncooked beans or rice). Bake in an oven preheated to 180°C/Gas Mark 4 for 18–20 minutes or until pale golden. Remove from the oven and lift out the paper and beans, then return the pastry case to the oven and bake for a further 4 minutes. Remove from the oven again and brush the egg yolks over the hot pastry case. Return to the oven for 2 minutes, then transfer to a wire rack.

Drain the Armagnac-soaked prunes into a large mixing bowl, reserving the prunes on one side. Add the egg, caster sugar, ground walnuts and crème fraîche to the Armagnac and mix until smooth. Distribute the soaked prunes evenly in the pastry case, then pour over the crème fraîche mixture and spread evenly. Sprinkle the walnut halves over the top to decorate. Bake in an oven preheated to 180°C/Gas Mark 4 for about 35 minutes, until golden brown. Remove from the

oven and leave to cool slightly on a wire rack, then carefully remove the tart from the tin or ring. Neatly trim off the excess pastry with a small paring knife.

Put the apricot jam in a small pan with the water and boil until smooth and thick. Brush over the top of the tart to form a shiny glaze.

Cut the tart into wedges and serve warm, with a scoop of vanilla ice cream.

CHILLED CHERRY SOUP WITH LEMON SORBET

Serves 6

The cherry season starts with the Spanish imports in May, moving on to French imports and then finally the English crop. The quality of the European cherries is usually excellent and this is a great way to use them up while they are plentiful. This soup is best enjoyed ice-cold, which the sorbet guarantees.

For the lemon sorbet
500ml still mineral water
330g caster sugar
finely grated zest and juice of 5 unwaxed lemons (preferably Sicilian ones)

For the soup
660ml still mineral water
330g caster sugar
750g cherries, stoned

To serve
250g cherries, stoned
10 lemon balm leaves

First, make the lemon sorbet. Put the water and sugar in a pan and bring to the boil, stirring to dissolve the sugar. Simmer for 5 minutes. Add the lemon zest and immediately remove from the heat, then leave to cool to room temperature. Add the lemon juice and pass the mixture through a fine sieve. Transfer to an ice cream maker and freeze according to the manufacturer's instructions.

For the soup, put the water and sugar in a pan and bring to the boil, stirring to dissolve the sugar. Simmer for 5 minutes, then remove from the heat and add the cherries. Purée in a blender or food processor until very smooth. Pass the mixture through a fine sieve, then chill.

To serve, make a circle of cherries in the centre of 6 chilled serving bowls. Place a scoop of lemon sorbet in the centre of these, then pour the ice-cold soup around. Finally, shred the lemon balm leaves and scatter over the top.

A stunning array of colour: the berries at Rungis Market.

MILLEFEUILLE OF YORKSHIRE RHUBARB

Serves 4

You could call this dish a take on rhubarb and custard. Make it when Yorkshire crimson, or champagne, rhubarb is available, from January to March. It is cultivated by candlelight in dark sheds, where it apparently grows so fast you can see it move.

200ml still mineral water
50ml Champagne
125g caster sugar
finely grated zest and juice of ¹/₂ lemon
250g Yorkshire crimson rhubarb, cut into 8cm lengths
1¹/₂ leaves of gelatine
240g Puff Pastry (see page 53)
50g icing sugar
28 baby red vein sorrel leaves, to decorate (optional)

For the pastry cream
75ml full-fat milk
¹/₄ vanilla pod, split in half lengthwise and seeds scraped out
1 free-range egg yolk
40g caster sugar
10g plain flour
100ml double cream, whipped to soft peaks

Put the water, Champagne, caster sugar and lemon zest and juice in a pan, bring to the boil and boil for 3 minutes. Add the rhubarb and cover with a cartouche (a circle of greaseproof paper). Bring back to the boil, then reduce the heat to a simmer and poach for 2–3 minutes or until the rhubarb is tender. Remove from the heat and leave to cool. Drain the rhubarb, reserving 200ml of the poaching liquor. Set the rhubarb aside in the fridge. Set aside 100ml of the reserved poaching liquor for the rhubarb jelly. Put the remaining 100ml reserved poaching liquor in a pan and boil until reduced to about 4 teaspoons. Remove from the heat, cool, then chill until ready to serve.

For the pastry cream, put the milk and vanilla seeds in a pan and bring to the boil. In a small mixing bowl, whisk the egg yolk and caster sugar together until pale in colour, then whisk in the flour. Pour the hot milk over the egg yolk mixture, whisking continuously. Return this mixture to a clean saucepan and cook over a low heat, stirring with a wooden spoon, until the mixture thickens and boils, then simmer gently for 2–3 minutes, stirring. Remove from the heat and cool slightly. Transfer the mixture to a plastic container and leave to cool, then refrigerate. When completely ice-cold, place the mixture in a metal mixing bowl and whisk until smooth. Fold in the softly whipped cream, then transfer the mixture to a piping bag fitted with a plain nozzle and chill until required.

To make the rhubarb jelly, soak the gelatine leaves in cold water for 5 minutes until soft. Bring the reserved 100ml of poaching liquor to the boil in a pan, then remove from the heat. Squeeze any water out of the gelatine and add to the hot poaching liquor, stirring until dissolved. Pass the mixture through a fine sieve into a plastic tray or container about 8cm square. Leave to set in the fridge. When the jelly has set, turn it out on to a chopping board and cut into 1cm squares using a hot knife. Return to the fridge.

Roll the puff pastry out on a lightly floured surface as thinly as possible and cut out a rectangle about 24cm x 20cm. Place the puff pastry on a baking tray lined with baking parchment. Place another piece of baking parchment on top of the pastry, then put a baking tray on top of that. Bake in an oven preheated to 220°C/Gas Mark 7 for about 15 minutes or until golden brown. Remove from the oven, remove the paper and baking trays and then carefully transfer the baked pastry sheet to a wire rack to cool. Cut into 12 rectangles, each about 8cm x 5cm. Take 4 of these and dust with the icing sugar, then glaze under a hot grill until caramelised. Leave the remaining pastry unglazed.

To serve, lay the 8 unglazed rectangles of pastry out on a board. Carefully pipe a thin layer of pastry cream on them to cover them completely – the cream layer should be no thicker than 3mm. Next, cover all 8 layers with the drained poached rhubarb. For each millefeuille, place one rhubarb-topped pastry rectangle on top of another and finish with a glazed pastry rectangle on top. Very gently push each millefeuille down.

To serve, place a teaspoon of pastry cream in the centre of each serving plate and place a millefeuille on top (the pastry cream will keep the millefeuille in place). Randomly drizzle the chilled reduced syrup around, then decorate each plate with 7 pieces of jelly and 7 sorrel leaves, if using.

APPLE TARTE TATIN WITH CRÈME NORMANDE

Serves 4

Usually with a tarte Tatin you arrange the apple halves flat-side down, but we prefer to stack them on their sides so you get a good depth of apple. The cooking time might look a little long but don't be tempted to take the tart out of the oven as soon as the pastry is brown; you need the full 1½ hours for the moisture to cook out of the apples, so their flavour becomes concentrated.

120g Puff Pastry (see page 53)
110g softened salted butter
130g caster sugar
7 Braeburn apples, peeled, halved and cored

For the crème Normande
120ml crème fraîche
40g icing sugar
1½ tablespoons Calvados

Roll the puff pastry out on a lightly floured surface to a 21cm round. Prick all over with a fork and rest in the fridge for 40 minutes.

Spread the butter over the bottom of a 20cm tarte Tatin mould or an ovenproof, non-stick frying pan. Sprinkle the caster sugar over in an even layer, then arrange the apple halves over the sugar, standing them on their sides, with 2 halves in the middle. Lay the pastry round over the apples, tucking the edges down the side.

Place the mould or pan over a medium heat on the hob for about 10 minutes or until the sugar starts to caramelise. Transfer it to an oven preheated to 160°C/Gas Mark 3 and bake for 1½ hours.

For the crème Normande, mix all the ingredients together in a bowl, then cover with cling film and refrigerate for 1 hour.

Remove the tart from the oven and leave to cool for at least 30 minutes. Invert the tarte Tatin on to a chopping board and cut it into 4 portions.

Serve a generous spoonful of crème Normande with each portion of the warm tarte Tatin.

PRUNE AND ARMAGNAC PARFAIT

Serves 8

It pays to use a good Armagnac here, such as a Bas. It's strange how some people think it's okay to use cheap alcohol in cooking – the flavour is just as important on the plate as it is in the glass.

For the parfait
150g stoned Agen prunes
55ml Armagnac
450ml double cream
200g caster sugar
200ml cold water
9 free-range egg yolks

For the honey biscuits
25g softened unsalted butter
50g caster sugar
25g clear honey
25g plain flour

To make the parfait, put the prunes and Armagnac in a pan and bring to the boil. Remove from the heat, then leave to soak overnight. Drain the prunes through a sieve, reserving the prunes and thick syrup separately. Cut half the prunes into 5mm dice and set aside. Cut the remaining prunes in half and set aside in the fridge for decoration. Whip the cream in a bowl to form soft peaks and then chill in the fridge.

Line a large baking tray with greaseproof paper and place 8 metal rings (each 5.5cm diameter and 4cm deep) on it. Leave in the freezer for 20 minutes.

Mix the sugar and water together in a heavy-based saucepan. Heat gently until the sugar has dissolved, then bring to the boil over a medium heat and boil until the syrup registers 114°C on a sugar thermometer.

Meanwhile, place the egg yolks in the bowl of an electric stand mixer fitted with the whisk attachment and whisk until pale in colour. With the machine running slowly, trickle in the boiling syrup. Turn the machine on full speed and whisk until the mixture is cool.

Fold the egg yolk/syrup mixture into the whipped cream, then fold in the diced prunes. Pour the parfait mixture into the metal rings and return them to the freezer for at least 6 hours.

To make the honey biscuits, beat the butter and sugar together in a bowl until pale. Beat in the honey, then the flour. Spread the mixture thinly over a non-stick baking tray or baking-parchment-lined baking tray in a rectangle about 22cm x 14cm. Bake in an oven preheated to 180°C/Gas Mark 4 for about 10 minutes or until a deep golden brown colour.

Remove from the oven and leave to cool for a minute, then cut into 8 strips, each about 20cm x 1.5cm. Place the strips on the baking tray and return to the oven to soften for a minute to make them pliable. Remove from the oven and wrap each strip around an empty parfait ring to form a round band. Leave for a minute or so to harden, then slip them off the parfait rings.

To serve, unmould the parfaits by placing your hands around the rings – this should be enough heat to release them. Place each parfait in the centre of a serving plate and arrange 3 prune halves around the outside. Place the biscuit ring on top of the parfait and then put a prune half inside the ring to hold it in place. Finish each dessert with a drizzle of the reserved prune syrup around the outside.

VALRHONA CHOCOLATE FONDANT WITH BANANA AND YOGURT ICE CREAM AND FRESH HONEYCOMB

Serves 6

Everyone does hot chocolate fondants these days – see page 244. We wanted to come up with something a little different, so we created a cold version with a soft centre as well. At the restaurant we make it in metal rings, but you could use ramekins instead.

For the soft centre
70ml double cream
40ml still mineral water
70ml full-fat milk
35g trimoline (invert sugar, available from online suppliers)
25g Valrhona dark chocolate (70% cocoa solids)
20g cocoa powder

For the banana and yogurt ice cream
250g very ripe peeled bananas
100ml whipping cream
80g caster sugar
440g Greek-style yogurt

For the honeycomb
70g glucose syrup
200g caster sugar
35g clear honey
10g bicarbonate of soda

For the fondant mixture
340g Valrhona dark chocolate (70% cocoa solids), chopped
250ml whipping cream
50g trimoline
60g chilled unsalted butter, diced

For the chocolate paint
30g Valrhona dark chocolate (70% cocoa solids)
1 teaspoon water

To make the soft centre, put the cream, water, milk and trimoline in a saucepan and whisk together over a low heat until warm. Pour the mixture on to the chocolate and cocoa powder in a bowl and stir until smooth. Pour into a 6cm x 4cm plastic container lined with cling film and freeze overnight. Turn out of the container, cut into six 2cm cubes, then return to the freezer.

For the banana and yogurt ice cream, purée the bananas in a blender or food processor, then pass the purée through a fine sieve. Gently warm the whipping cream and sugar together in a pan and as soon as the sugar has dissolved, remove from the heat. Mix the warmed cream with the banana purée and yogurt. Transfer to an ice cream maker and freeze according to the manufacturer's instructions.

For the honeycomb, put all the ingredients except the bicarbonate of soda in a large saucepan and bring to the boil, stirring to dissolve the sugar (the pan needs to be oversized because when the bicarbonate of soda is added the mixture will quadruple in volume). Continue boiling the syrup until it registers 150°C on a sugar thermometer – by this stage it should be a caramel colour. Remove from the heat and whisk in the bicarbonate of soda, then pour the mixture into a 2 litre mixing bowl lined with baking parchment. Be careful as the honeycomb will be bubbling and still gaining in volume at this point. Leave to cool completely and set, then turn out on to a board. With a serrated knife, cut the honeycomb into random-shaped pieces, each about 2cm. Set aside.

For the fondant mixture, place 6 metal rings (each 5.5cm diameter x 4.5cm deep) on a baking tray lined with baking parchment and refrigerate. Place the chocolate in a mixing bowl set over a pan of simmering water. Gently warm the cream and trimoline together in a pan, stirring until combined. When the chocolate has melted, remove the bowl from the pan of water and whisk the cream mixture in (it is crucial that the chocolate and the cream mixture are roughly the same temperature, otherwise it will split). Slowly stir in the chilled butter, a little at a time. Transfer the mixture to a jug.

Take the baking tray of chilled metal rings from the fridge and fill each ring half full with the fondant mixture. Refrigerate for 10–12 minutes. Place a cube of the frozen soft centre in the middle of each ring, then fill each ring to the top with the rest of the fondant mixture. Refrigerate for 2 hours.

To make the chocolate paint, melt the chocolate in a bowl and stir in the water.

To serve, paint a stripe of chocolate paint across 6 serving plates with a 6cm-wide pastry brush. Remove the fondants from their rings by warming them with a chef's blowtorch for a couple of seconds. Place the fondants in the centre of the plates and add 3 pieces of honeycomb and a scoop of banana and yogurt ice cream to each one.

Chef-instructor Philippe Givre, who teaches at Valrhona's Ecole du Grand Chocolat, situated in Tain l'Hermitage, working with arguably the world's finest chocolate every day.

OEUFS À LA NEIGE WITH PINK PRALINES

Serves 6

Oeufs à la neige, also called îles flottantes, or floating islands, are a classic of French cuisine. Jeff likes to make them at home with his young sons, Daniel and William, serving them up in a big oval dish.

Pink pralines are almonds covered in a bright pink sugar coating. They are a traditional delicacy from Lyons, where they are made into tarts. Look for them in delis or try an online supplier.

For the almond biscuits
30g flaked almonds, toasted
120g caster sugar

For the oeufs à la neige
10 free-range egg whites
10g cream of tartar
250g caster sugar

For the crème anglaise
330ml full-fat milk
1/2 vanilla pod, split in half lengthwise
   and seeds scraped out
4 free-range egg yolks
80g caster sugar

30 pink pralines, to decorate

First, make the almond biscuits. Arrange the flaked almonds in a single layer on a piece of baking parchment laid on a baking sheet. Place the sugar in a small, heavy-based saucepan and cook over a medium heat until it starts to turn to caramel, then stir with a wooden spoon until all of the sugar has turned into an amber-coloured liquid caramel. Carefully pour the caramel over the nuts and leave to cool and set.

Break the caramelised almond mixture into small pieces and blitz to a fine powder in a food processor. Sprinkle the powder thinly over a non-stick baking sheet or a baking tray lined with silicone paper or baking parchment. Bake in an oven preheated to 160°C/Gas Mark 3 for 10 minutes or until the powder has melted and formed a uniform sheet. Remove from the oven and leave to cool, then simply break the mixture into irregular-shaped small biscuits, about 2cm in size. Store in an airtight container.

To make the oeufs à la neige, whisk the egg whites and cream of tartar together with an electric mixer until they form soft peaks. Gradually whisk in the sugar, then continue to whisk for 3–4 minutes, until the meringue becomes very firm.

Bring the 330ml of milk from the crème anglaise ingredients to 90°C in a wide saucepan. Using 2 large metal spoons, form the meringue into quenelles (small rugby-ball shapes), releasing each one into the hot milk as you go. Poach for

2 minutes, then turn over and cook for a further 2 minutes, until firm to the touch (you may need to poach them in batches). Remove with a slotted spoon and drain on a clean tea towel. Store in the fridge. These can be made in advance.

To make the crème anglaise, pour the milk that was used for poaching into a heavy-based saucepan (it's worth checking that you still have 330ml; if not, top up with more milk). Add the vanilla seeds and empty pod and bring to the boil. Remove from the heat and leave to infuse for 10 minutes, then remove the vanilla pod and discard.

Whisk the egg yolks and sugar together in a bowl until pale in colour. Whilst still whisking, carefully pour the hot milk on to the yolks and sugar. Return to a clean pan and cook gently, stirring continuously, until the mixture thickens enough to coat the back of the spoon. Remove from the heat and immediately pass the custard through a fine sieve into a bowl. Place the bowl on ice and chill until the custard is cold. Cover with cling film and store in the fridge until ready to serve.

To serve, lift the cold 'eggs' using a palette knife or fish slice and place in small serving bowls. Spoon around the crème anglaise, then decorate with the pink pralines and almond biscuits.

MARQUISE AU CHOCOLAT WITH MINT AND CHOCOLATE CHIP ICE CREAM

Serves 12

Jeff picked up the idea for this when he worked with Marco Pierre White. The ice cream would make a great dessert on its own. We wanted to colour it green without using food colourings and eventually hit upon the idea of using crème de menthe.

We try not to use bought products but we've made an exception here with After Eight mints – possibly because we love them so much! We virtually have to keep them under lock and key to stop the chefs eating them all.

For the marquise
6 free-range egg yolks
210g caster sugar
220g unsalted butter, melted
120g cocoa powder
225g dark chocolate (66% cocoa solids),
    preferably Valrhona, melted
340ml double cream
45g icing sugar
1 box (300g) After Eight mints

For the mint and chocolate chip ice cream
550ml milk
6 free-range egg yolks
150g caster sugar
100g fresh mint leaves
2 tablespoons crème de menthe liqueur
100g dark chocolate (66% cocoa solids),
    preferably Valrhona, finely grated

For the marquise, line the inside of a 1.1 litre terrine mould with cling film, allowing it to overhang the sides. Place in the fridge.

Put the egg yolks and caster sugar in the bowl of an electric stand mixer and whisk together for 5 minutes or until fluffy and light in colour.

Pour the melted butter into a large metal bowl and whisk in the cocoa powder, then whisk in the melted chocolate.

Pour the cream into a separate bowl, add the icing sugar and whip together to form soft peaks, being careful not to over whip it.

Fold the melted chocolate mixture into the whisked egg yolk mixture, then fold in the lightly whipped cream. Transfer the marquise mixture to a large piping bag. Pipe a layer about 1cm deep in the prepared terrine mould, then place a single layer of After Eights on top. Repeat this twice so that you have 3 layers of After Eights and then finish with a layer of marquise on the top. Make sure there are no air gaps as you build the layers. Fold the overhanging cling film over the top, then refrigerate for 24 hours.

Meanwhile, for the mint and chocolate chip ice cream, put the milk in a pan and bring to the boil. Whisk the egg yolks and caster sugar together in a large bowl until pale in colour. Whilst still whisking, carefully pour the boiling milk on to the yolks and sugar. Return to a clean pan and cook gently, stirring continuously, to a temperature of 82°C or until the mixture thickens enough to coat the back of the spoon. Remove from the heat and pour over the mint leaves in a bowl. Leave to infuse for 10 minutes, then pass the mixture through a fine sieve. Stir in the crème de menthe and leave to cool. Transfer the mixture to an ice cream maker and freeze according to the manufacturer's instructions. Before placing in the freezer, fold the grated chocolate through the ice cream.

To serve, carefully unmould the marquise by inverting it on to a chopping board, then gently pull the cling film lining off. Using a hot sharp knife, cut the marquise into 1cm-thick slices. Transfer to serving plates and place a scoop of mint and chocolate chip ice cream on top of each slice.

BUTTERMILK PANNA COTTA WITH POACHED STRAWBERRIES

Serves 4

It's quite unusual to cook strawberries but here they are cooked gently then strained to make a juice, which is then poured over whole fresh strawberries to 'poach' them. The result is a beautifully intense syrup.

For the panna cotta
2 leaves of gelatine
250ml buttermilk
250ml double cream
75g caster sugar
1 vanilla pod, split in half lengthwise and
    seeds scraped out

For the poached strawberries
500g small English strawberries, hulled
25g caster sugar – or 10% of the weight
    of strawberries after the 28 have been
    selected (see method)

To make the panna cotta, soak the gelatine leaves in cold water for about 5 minutes or until softened. Place the buttermilk, cream, sugar and vanilla seeds in a heavy-based saucepan and bring to just below boiling point over a medium heat. Remove from the heat. Take the gelatine leaves from the water, squeezing out the excess, and add them to the buttermilk mixture. Stir until dissolved, then pass the mixture through a fine sieve into a metal bowl. Set this bowl on top of another, larger bowl of iced water and stir until the mixture is well chilled and starting to thicken. This is very important because if the mixture is too thin when it sets, all of the vanilla seeds will have sunk to the bottom of the moulds. Pour the mixture into four 150ml pudding moulds and refrigerate for at least 6 hours, until set.

For the poached strawberries, select 28 similar-sized strawberries, place them in a bowl and set aside. This should leave around 250g strawberries. Place these remaining strawberries in a metal bowl with the sugar and cover with cling film. Set this bowl over a pan of very gently simmering water and leave for 1 hour, until the strawberries have broken down completely. Remove from the heat and pass the strawberry mixture through a very fine sieve into a pan. Bring this juice to the boil and pour it over the reserved strawberries to 'poach' them. Leave to cool before refrigerating.

To serve, dip the panna cotta moulds into boiling water for a couple of seconds to loosen the desserts. Turn each panna cotta out on to a serving plate, place 7 poached strawberries around each one, then spoon over some of the poaching liquor.

INDEX

A

B

C

Savarin of summer berries 246
Valrhona chocolate fondant with banana and
  yoghurt ice cream and fresh honeycomb 269
Vanilla rice pudding with caramelised Alphonso
  mango 245

G

Game

Daube of venison with quince and chestnuts 224
Grilled rabbit legs with puy lentils, white
  dandelions and girolles 219
Pithivier of game with carrot purée and glazed
  onions 206
Pot-roast Berkshire pheasant 'petit salé aux
  lentilles' 217
Pot-roast squab pigeon, farci à gratin 211
Roast grouse with game chips, watercress and
  bread sauce 218
Saddle of Denham Estate venison with braised red
  cabbage, chestnut and apple purée and
  blackcurrant sauce 220
Salad of grey-leg partridge with pomegranate and
  maple sauce 123
Supreme of guinea fowl with broad beans, fresh
  Morels and herb gnocchi 214
Tagine of Bresse pigeon with cous cous and harissa
  sauce 209
Venison with smoked potato purée, pickled red
  cabbage, chocolate and watercress 227

Gnocchi

Herb gnocchi 52
Parmesan gnocchi 52
Roast sea trout with gnocchi, brown shrimps and
  new-season garlic 160
goat's cheese and basil, Salad of Heirloom
  tomatoes, 127
goat's cheese, Salad of wood-fired vegetables with
  walnuts and 128
goat's cheese ravioli, Slow-cooked Pyrenees lamb
  shoulder with pipérade and 186
Gravadlax of salmon with salad of quail's eggs and
  herbs 88
Greengage clafoutis with vanilla ice cream 254
Grilled rabbit legs with puy lentils, white dandelions
  and girolles 219
Grilled tranche of calf's liver with flat mushrooms,
  bacon and Lyonnaise onions 195
grouse with game chips, watercress and bread sauce,
  Roast 218
guinea fowl with broad beans, fresh Morels and herb
  gnocchi, Supreme of 214

H

hake with clams, mussels and tomato fondue,
  Roast 150
halibut with caramelised chicory and Italian
  artichokes, Steamed 138

Ham

Bayonne ham with celeriac remoulade 108
Bistrot deluxe cassoulet 196
Split pea and ham soup with crispy pig's ears 65
Herb gnocchi 52
herrings with a warm potato and shallot salad,
  Matjes 89
honeycomb, Valrhona chocolate fondant with banana
  and yoghurt ice cream and fresh 269
Hot chocolate fondants with raspberries 244

I

Ice cream
Caramelised white peaches with lavender ice
  cream 249
Greengage clafoutis with vanilla ice cream 254
Marquise au chocolat with mint and chocolate
  chip ice cream 274
Poached pears with pain d'epices ice cream 236
Valrhona chocolate fondant with banana and
  yoghurt ice cream and fresh honeycomb 269
Vanilla ice cream 58
Imam Bayaldi 135

J

John Dory with orange-glazed endive, cauliflower
  purée, curry oil, pine nuts and sultanas 146

Jus

Brown chicken jus 45
Madeira jus 47
Red wine jus 47
Roast côte de boeuf with truffle macaroni and
  Hermitage jus 164

L

Lamb

Assiette of Cornish lamb Provencale 190
Braised lamb shoulder with runner beans, peas,
  confit potatoes, olives and mint 189
Poached lambs' tongues with beetroot and
  mâche 120
Pressed terrine of lamb with anchoiade dressing 117
Slow-cooked Pyrenees lamb shoulder with
  pipérade and goat's cheese ravioli 186
langoustines, Vichyssoise of asparagus and 64
Lasagne of crab with beurre Nantaise 79
lavender ice cream, Caramelised white peaches
  with 249

Lemon

Chilled cherry soup with lemon sorbet 259
Lemon mascarpone cheesecake with wild
  strawberries 255
Lemon oil 57
Lemon tart 256
Preserved lemons 57

Lentils

Pot-roast Berkshire pheasant 'petit salé aux
  lentilles' 217
Grilled rabbit legs with puy lentils, white dandelions
  and girolles 219
liver with flat mushrooms, bacon and Lyonnaise
  onions, Grilled tranche of calf's 195

M

mackerel and tartare with soft-boiled quail's eggs and
  bone marrow and parsley custard, Ballotine of 98
Marquise au chocolat with mint and chocolate chip
  ice cream 274
Madeira jus 47
mango, Vanilla rice pudding with caramelised
  Alphonso 245
Marinated scallops with Noirmoutier potatoes,
  Jerusalem artichokes and mâche 82
Matjes herrings with a warm potato and shallot
  salad 89
Mayonnaise 51

Meat

Assiette of Cornish lamb Provencale 190
Bavette of beef with macaroni cheese and
  Bordelaise sauce 168
Braised lamb shoulder with runner beans, peas,
  confit potatoes, olives and mint 189
Braised veal cheeks, ham and tongue with pommes
  purées and truffle Madeira sauce 175
Poached lambs' tongues with beetroot and
  mâche 120
Pork rillettes with toasted country bread 114
Potage of broad beans with smoked duck and pea
  shoots 69

Q

R

S

Maussane-les-Alpilles in Provence.

Luigi Vespero at Galvin Bistrot de Luxe, Zac Whittle at La Chapelle, and finally David Stafford at Café à Vin. I would also like to mention our managers, Fred Sirieix at Galvin at Windows, Otto Lauterbach at Galvin Bistrot de Luxe, Alessandro Piombino, general manager, and Antonio d'Agostino, restaurant manager, at La Chapelle, and finally Tatiana Tholtova at Café à Vin.

To Clare Gorry, our assistant, who keeps our lives in order, arranges our suppliers' visits down to the last second, and helped proofread this book.

I believe in lifelong education and would like to thank the great teachers that helped me on my journey and gave me the belief that anything is possible. My biggest influence is Professor David Foskett, MBE, who is capable of making me believe I could fly! A man blessed with supreme qualities in education and one of the country's most gifted chefs.

To my family, who have supported me so much, and give me strength to do my best. My wonderful according to its heartbeat. I am always indebted to these special people who work so hard, often losing their harvest and yields to weather and other events beyond their control. It never fails to ground me, walking a mile in their shoes, and I think if you want to live a better life, look no further. The world would be a better place if we all lived by their values.

Finally to the team at Absolute and Jon Croft, our publisher, for making us believe we could actually do this whilst running the restaurants. To Matt Inwood, our art director, who somehow pieced the book together in a fashion that broke lots of rules, yet created something timeless and elegant. To Jane Middleton, our editor, who put up with our missed deadlines and still lovingly worked through each and every part of the book, encouraging us all the way, thank you. To Lara Holmes, our amazing photographer and force of nature! She works very instinctively and honestly – most importantly reflecting a chef's nirvana… simplicity.

JEFF'S ACKNOWLEDGEMENTS

First of all I have to say a special thank you to our loyal customers, whose encouragement and friendship spur us on each day. Many have followed Chris and me since we first took charge of our own kitchens, years before Galvin Restaurants was conceived.

To the many chefs who have taught, mentored and inspired me during the last twenty-five years: Anton Edelmann at the Savoy, Marco Pierre White, Robert Reid and especially Nico Ladenis, whose love of working with his family I now understand so well. And of course, my own brother, Chris, must be added to this list.

To all our staff, past and present, who got us going, continue to work so hard and are always trying to be the best – and of whom many will go on to become great chefs, managers and restaurateurs themselves.

To special friends, Dominic, Andy, Nic, Tim, Guss and Warren, the latter for introducing me to the girl who is now my wife. Thanks, guys, for wonderful friendship over the years.

To all our amazing suppliers, Dave and Lincs at Southwest Fisheries and Peter Allen, the best butcher in the country, who would also have made a great chef. To the Denham Estate owners, Cecilia Gliksten and her late husband, Michael, who we were all so fond of, for their venison. To Reg Johnson, for his amazing Goosnargh ducks and his passion. Maison Paul Jaboulet Aîné and the Frey family, for letting us name La Chapelle after their iconic wine and for giving us the pleasure of working with them. Eric Narioo, from Les Caves de Pyrène, for getting us going, for his delicious wines and for being him. And to the hundreds of suppliers, growers and producers I haven't mentioned, whose quality makes it easy for us to shine.

Our business has always been built on relationships, be it suppliers, customers, builders or staff. I believe that if there is a good relationship there, then everyone concerned will prosper in an effortless and enjoyable way. In none of our relationships could there be a better example of this than the one we have with our business partner, Ken Sanker. I feel honoured just to have spent time in his presence, let alone having conceived our company together. I feel genuinely blessed to work with you, Ken.

To the team at Absolute Press: Jon Croft, for waiting until we were ready to produce this book; Matt Inwood, for his brilliance in pulling the thing together so well; Lara Holmes, who photographed with such a free and imaginative spirit. And finally to our editor, Jane Middleton, whom it was an immense pleasure to work with after enjoying so much of her work for so many years.

Finally to my wife, Georgette, for never complaining, always loving and encouraging me, and doing such a wonderful job at home.

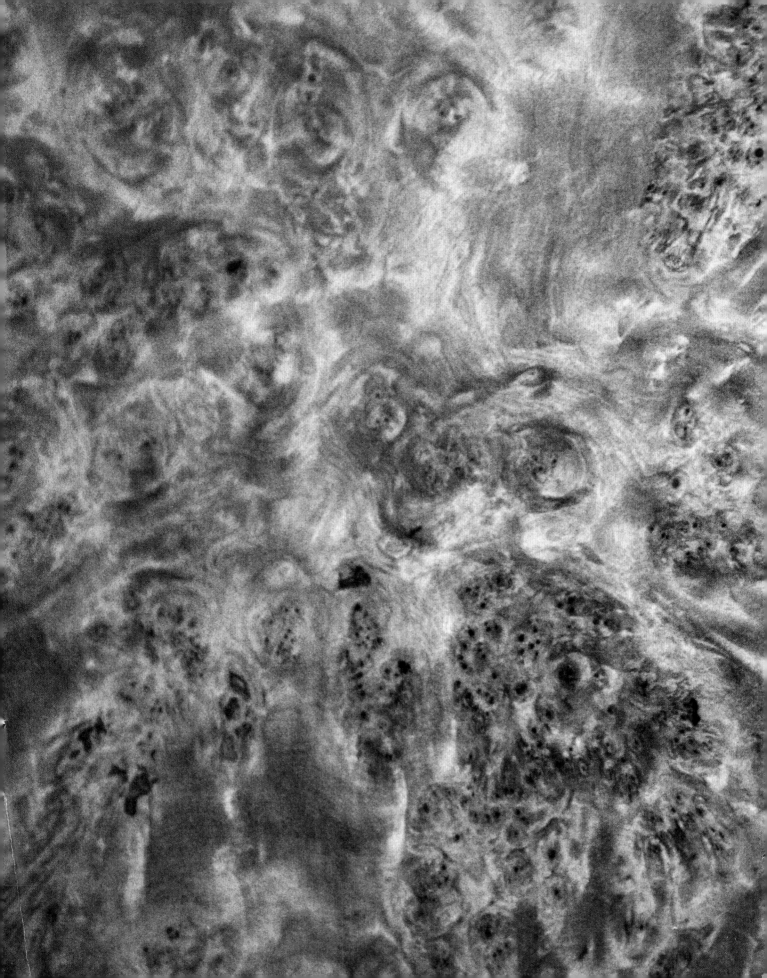